THE ELIZABETHAN
DELIVERANCE

The endpaper map depicts the track of the
Spanish Armada from an engraving by J. Pine.
(*The National Maritime Museum, London*)
Note: The number of Spanish ships shown
between Cape Clear on the southern coast of
Ireland and Ushant is greatly exaggerated.

THE ELIZABETHAN DELIVERANCE

Arthur Bryant

COLLINS
St James's Place, London
1980

William Collins Sons & Co Ltd
London · Glasgow · Sydney · Auckland
Toronto · Johannesburg

British Library CIP data

Bryant, Arthur
The Elizabethan deliverance.
1. Great Britain – History – Elizabeth,
1558–1603
I. Title
942.05'5   DA355

First published 1980
© Arthur Bryant 1980

ISBN 0 00 216207 5

Set in Monophoto Bembo by
MS Filmsetting Ltd, Frome, Somerset
Made and Printed in Great Britain by
William Collins Sons & Co Ltd, Glasgow

Humbly
dedicated
to
Her Majesty
Queen Elizabeth II
who
by her conduct
and bearing
so faithfully upholds
the honour and dignity
of the great name
immortalised
by her royal predecessor

Contents

INTRODUCTION

The *Elizabethan Deliverance* is a narrative history of the first thirty years of Elizabeth I's reign that culminated in the defeat of the Spanish Armada. During that time the creative statesmanship of a great Queen raised England little by little from a nadir of social disunity, self-doubt and economic impotence, not wholly unlike that from which we are suffering today. It is the story of how, at a time of national disintegration in the wake of a great social revolution, a leader of political genius and rare personal magnetism, reunited, inspired and restored faith in themselves to a small, temporarily depressed, but potentially virile and adventurous people, so enabling them and the future Britain to find a new destiny and role in the world.

I came to write it, because in trying to condense into a long-contemplated single-volume history of England the many books I have written about our past, there was one period in our history on which I had never written – and that the most important of all. To fill the gap, I found myself writing, not a single chapter, but a whole book on how Elizabeth put the red cross of England both into the hearts of her people and on the map of the world.

To it, with an Epilogue on Shakespeare's London, I have added a chapter on the Elizabethan harvest: the first colonial plantations in America and the foundation of the East India Company – the genesis of the United States and British Empire; and, at the very moment when England's merchants and seamen were carrying her life and influence into every ocean and continent of the globe, the emergence from a formerly rude vernacular of a literature, not only potentially, but already in achievement, as great as any known to history.

My book is in no sense a work of original research. That for the reign of Elizabeth has been superbly performed in our time by many great scholars, to the writings of two of whom, both old and dear friends, I owe more than I can express. To A. L. Rowse – one of the greatest historians our country has ever produced and whose knowl-

9

edge of the Elizabethan age is unrivalled – my debt is incalculable, as it is to that other dear friend, the late Sir John Neale, who nearly fifty years ago, when Professor of Modern History at University College London, and a frequent guest at my then home in Buckinghamshire, was writing his brilliant biography of Queen Elizabeth, at the same time as I, with his help and encouragement, was writing my earliest biography, *King Charles II*. Without the work of these two great scholars my book could never have been written at all.

There are others to whom my debt is obvious – to S. T. Bindoff for his *Tudor England* and for J. B. Black for his *Reign of Elizabeth*; to Joel Hurstfield for his *Elizabeth I and the Unity of England* and his *The Elizabethan Nation*; to G. R. Elton for *England under the Tudors* and E. M. W. Tillyard for *The Elizabethan World Picture*; A. G. Dickens for his great book, *The English Reformation*; J. A. Williamson for *Hawkins of Plymouth* and *The Age of Drake*; Edward Grierson for *The Fatal Inheritance*, and Lady Antonia Fraser for *Mary Queen of Scots*; Michael Lewis for his brilliant *The Spanish Armada* and *Armada Guns*, and A. M. Hadfield for *Time to Finish the Game*, Canon Ian Dunlop for *Palaces and Progresses of Elizabeth I*; Christopher Lloyd for *The British Seaman*; Pieter Geyl's *Revolt of the Netherlands*; Gareth Mattingly's *The Defeat of the Spanish Armada*; Wallace Notestein – another old friend – for *The English People on the Eve of Colonisation*; Walter Oakeshott, *The Queen and the Poet*; Martin Holmes's *Shakespeare's Public*, A. H. Dodd's *Life in Elizabethan England* and C. Walter Hodges's *The Battlemented Garden*. There are many more.

ARTHUR BRYANT

The Close
Salisbury

Prologue
ACCESSION TO A THRONE
OF THORNS

'For Harry our King
Is gone hunting
To bring his deer to bay.'
Old Song

In the three centuries between the Norman Conquest and the Black Death England enjoyed a succession of great French-speaking kings – Norman, Angevin and Plantagenet – who made the emergent and formerly tribal Anglo-Saxon and Danish land of Alfred of Wessex and Canute the best-governed, most unified and powerful feudal kingdom in western Christendom. The stark Conqueror, his son Henry I – 'the Lion of Justice' – and his great-grandson Henry II who established the rule of law and the supremacy of the royal courts; Edward I, conqueror of Wales and creator of Parliament and the English law of entail; his grandson Edward III, the victor of Crecy and founder of the Order of the Garter; and the warrior heroes, Coeur de Lion and the Black Prince; all left behind them institutions or traditions which helped to shape England's future.

Yet in the second half of the fourteenth century – with her population all but halved by three catastrophic waves of bubonic plague; the loss, through lack of manpower, of most of her French possessions; the Peasants' Revolt of 1381; and the arbitrary tyranny and dethronement of Richard II – there set in a rapid decline in the nation's strength and cohesion, only arrested by Henry V's brilliant victory of Agincourt and his marriage to the heiress of a temporarily defeated and divided France. Within three decades of his death, with the final liquidation of all the Kingdom's overseas conquests except Calais, and the outbreak of the dynastic civil Wars of the Roses, the England 'that was wont to conquer others had made a shameful conquest of herself', sinking to a nadir of lawless violence unparalleled since the 'nineteen long winters' of Stephen's reign and the pre-Conquest anarchy under Ethelred the Redeless. During the greater part of the fifteenth century the succession remained in dispute, and no one could feel sure who the next wearer of the crown would be. No fewer than five times in thirty years it was forcibly seized, twice by a Yorkist from a Lancastrian, twice by a Lancastrian from a Yorkist, and once by a Yorkist from a Yorkist. Of four successive kings, all but one died from violence.

This state of affairs ended – though no one realized it at the time – when in 1485 a young Welsh exile, Henry Tudor, last survivor of the Lancastrian royal line, landing with a handful of followers in Pembrokeshire, defeated the ruthless but able Yorkist, Richard III, who expiated by his death on Bosworth Field his usurpation and, as was generally believed, murder of his royal nephew and ward, Edward V. No King of England had a weaker hereditary claim to the throne than Henry VII; few exercised its power with more wisdom, patience and success. He remained on it for nearly a quarter of a century, defeating with little bloodshed every attempt to dethrone him, without the help of a standing army or police force other than his household Yeomen of the Guard and Chamber.

Henry VII was perhaps the cleverest and certainly the hardest-working monarch ever to wear the English crown. He started his reign heavily in debt and ended it, long after he had repaid all his creditors, richer than any king before him. He used his wealth, so industriously accumulated and carefully husbanded – for he audited and signed almost every page of his accounts himself – to increase the royal power and free it from incumbrances and restraints. To end the tyranny of 'the overmighty subject', especially the over-mighty subject with royal blood in his veins, Henry invested the Crown with a new mystique, setting it in lonely majesty as a thing apart from every subject, even the highest. With only one duke and one marquis left after the holocausts and attainders of the Wars of the Roses, he chose his councillors mostly from new men who depended solely on himself, and used his Council, Court of Star Chamber and the regional Councils of the Marches and the North, to discipline the rich and powerful who employed their wealth and power to pervert the course of justice. Under these courts he governed an England, long used to aristocratic turbulence, through the unpaid local magistracy drawn from the landed gentry, which Edward I had created two centuries earlier and on which, by successive commissions of the peace, Henry laid ever-increasing burdens.

Where Henry VII was circumspect, secretive, parsimonious and unceasingly industrious, his son, Henry VIII, was an extrovert, bursting with self-confidence, extravagant and avid for pleasure. Succeeding in 1509 to the throne at eighteen, he was a superlatively handsome, accomplished and, at first, immensely popular Renaissance prince. Longing to shine, he at once started to get through his father's accumulated treasure by costly foreign adventures, including war with his kingdom's old rival of Plantagenet days, France. Against the latter's ally, Scotland, whose James IV invaded Northumberland in keeping with his wild country's traditional policy, the English under Thomas Howard, Earl of Surrey, won in 1513 an annihilating – and, for Scotland, shattering – victory at Flodden, in which the Scottish king and the flower of his nobility fell, so avenging Robert Bruce's defeat of Edward II at Bannockburn two centuries before, and bringing to an end the harassing raids on England's northern counties which had continued, on and off, ever since.

But, in France, unlike the earlier King 'Hal' of the previous century, young Henry VIII sought the palm without the dust. The highlight of his campaigning was the Field of the Cloth of Gold in 1519 in which he vied with the French King, Francis I, in extravagant magnificence, but for whom his amateur military forces were no match. For since 1429, when a French peasant girl, Joan of Arc, had breathed a new spirit into her defeated countrymen, rallying them round their ancient throne, France, under her shrewd and grasping Valois kings, had gone from strength to strength and, acquiring province after province, had grown to three times England's size and population. And, through a series of dynastic marriages, a new and even greater power had arisen in Western Europe, that of imperial and Hapsburg Spain. The marriage of King Ferdinand of Aragon to Queen Isabella of Castile, and their joint conquest of the Moorish kingdom of Granada in 1492 – the year in which the Genoese navigator, Christopher Columbus, sailing under their auspices, discovered the West Indies – gave a newly united Spain a seaboard on both the Mediterranean and Atlantic. During the next forty years, by their conquest of the vast Aztec and Inca empires of Mexico and Peru with their prodigious mineral riches, a handful of Spanish conquistadors brought to Spain a wealth which made her mercenary armies the arbiters of Europe. And the marriage of the daughter of the 'Catholic kings', Ferdinand and Isabella, to the son of the Hapsburg Archduke of Austria and his wife, the heiress of Charles the Bold of

Burgundy, added the rich industrial plain of the Netherlands to a vast matrimonial amalgam of sovereignty, stretching across the Atlantic from the new-discovered Pacific to the Danube and North Sea.

Born in 1500 in the Flemish and Burgundian city of Ghent and succeeding at the age of sixteen to the throne of Spain, Charlies V, the Hapsburg heir to these vast dominions, was also elected in 1519 Emperor of the Germans and, as such, titular head of the Holy Roman Empire. Neither Charlemagne nor the Roman Constantine had been the ruler of so vast a share of Christendom. Yet, by a strange irony of circumstance, at the very moment when western Christendom seemed nearer becoming united politically than at any time in its thousand years of anarchic history, its spiritual unity, long achieved under the bishops or Popes of Rome, was about to be fatally shattered. For in the year after the new Charlemagne entered upon his far-flung Spanish inheritance, and two years before he became Emperor of the Germans, a Saxon monk and university teacher, Martin Luther, nailed his thesis against Papal Indulgences to the door of Wittenberg church.

Luther's challenge to the Church's monopoly of instructing and directing the human conscience, and its priesthood's claim to be the sole interpreter and medium between God and man, was fiercely denounced by the Roman hierarchy as heresy. Earlier challenges to its power by the Lollards in England and the Hussites in Bohemia had been suppressed by the ferocious sentences and punishments of the Church's Holy Inquisition and their enforcement by the secular arm of Europe's Christian kingdoms. This time, however, so widespread was popular sympathy for Luther's appeal to the validity and freedom of individual conscience and his denunciation of the abuses of a corrupt priesthood, that the Church failed to receive the automatic support of the secular arm, particularly in Germany with its hundreds of fragmented independent states and principalities. Protected by the Electoral ruler of his native Saxony, Luther was thus able to defy his would-be persecutors. His revolutionary message, preached from a thousand pulpits by his disciples and by rival theologians and reformers, aided by the invention of printing and the inflammatory pamphleteering spawned by it, spread with alarming rapidity, not only throughout Germany but to the neighbouring kingdoms of France and England, the Netherlands, the Swiss cantons, and even far-away Scotland.

Luther's heresy, however, received no support from the young King of England, who, like most crowned heads, resented the challenge to established authority. He even engaged personally in the warfare of the pamphleteers, writing a book against Luther and winning from a grateful Pope the vaunted title of 'Defender of the Faith'.* Intent on his pleasures and his cultural and intellectual pursuits, for the first twenty years of his reign he left the management of his kingdom's affairs to a brilliant and immensely ambitious churchman of humble birth. Son of an Ipswich butcher, Thomas Wolsey rose between 1509 and 1527 to be the richest, most magnificent and powerful man in the country – Lord Chancellor, Archbishop of York, a Cardinal and Papal Legate.

Yet there was one problem to which, even in those years of pleasure and display, the King was forced to give his mind – that of the succession. For his Spanish wife, Catherine of Aragon – to whom his father had affianced him after the death of her boy husband, Henry's elder brother – gave him only one surviving child, a daughter named Mary born in 1515. When it became clear that she could never bear another, Henry VIII, who had to provide for the country's future security, sought a papal annulment of his marriage. Accustomed to having his way in all things, he was also deeply in love – 'stricken' as he put it, 'with the dart of love' – with a *femme fatale*, Anne Boleyn, granddaughter of a rich London merchant, whose price was marriage.

For several years Henry and his minister, Wolsey, importuned the Vatican for a divorce. He would have had little difficulty in obtaining one had not his queen been aunt to the most powerful Catholic monarch of the time, the Emperor Charles V, on whose goodwill the Pope was dependent against the French invaders of Italy. Thwarted, Henry finally got his way by breaking with the Papacy, dismissing Wolsey, and appointing as Archbishop of Canterbury a married churchman of reforming sympathies named Thomas Cranmer. Under his aegis an ecclesiastical court pronounced Catherine divorced, so enabling the King to make Anne his queen.

During the fifteen-thirties, Henry and his new minister, Thomas Cromwell – a lawyer and brilliant administrator completely dependent on him – carried through, with the help of a strongly anti-clerical Parliament, the most drastic revolution in English history. A century and a half after Wycliffe had denounced the corruptions of the medieval Church and sixteen years after Luther had nailed his thesis

* Still retained on England's coinage.

against Papal Indulgences to the door of Wittenberg church, Henry VIII and his Parliament repudiated the authority of the Pope. Declaring, in an Act against Appeals to Rome, that the realm of England was 'an empire . . . governed by one supreme Head and King', they ended all links with the Papacy, constituted the King Supreme Head of the Church of England, and later dissolved the monasteries, confiscating their enormous wealth, most of which passed, in that corrupt and chaotic age, into private hands. Yet, though Henry broke with Rome and ruthlessly suppressed in 1538 the Pilgrimage of Grace – a North Country rising in support of the Cistercian monasteries – he never himself accepted the doctrinal and theological tenets of the more drastic Continental reformers. He executed both Anne Boleyn, who failed to give him a son, and his Protestant minister Cromwell, as he did also another of his six successive wives, Catherine Howard, a Catholic, and persecuted as heretics all who deviated from orthodox belief.

During his last years Henry was sole and absolute master of his kingdom. Though striking terror into all who dared oppose him, he remained, despite his personal despotism – which only affected the rich and powerful – immensely popular with his subjects. He was a great patron of seamen like his father, Henry VII, who had sent out the Genoese-born Bristol merchant, John Cabot and his son, to explore the barren shores of Labrador and Newfoundland in the closing years of the fifteenth century, when Columbus was discovering the West Indies for Spain and Bartholomew Diaz and Vasco da Gama rounding the Cape of Good Hope for Portugal. In this the Cabots were as much the first discoverers of North America for England as the Portuguese were of Brazil and the sea-route round Africa to the Orient, and the Spaniards of the Caribbean, Florida, Mexico, the Isthmus of Panama, Peru and Chile. Yet though, unlike the sunlit crusading kingdoms of the Iberian peninsula, England – still a backward half-island in the Atlantic mists – established no transoceanic settlements for more than another century, Henry VIII prepared the way for her oceanic future by founding the nucleus of a regular Royal Navy. Its ships, built or bought, instead of hired, for employment by the Crown, carried the best guns in Europe. Firing no longer from high boarding towers in the bows and stern but discharging broadsides from rows of portholes in their hulls, they constituted a revolutionary innovation in warship design for fighting in ocean, as distinct from Mediterranean and inshore, waters.

Yet the immediate legacy of this able but terrifying monarch's thirty-eight years' reign was a social revolution in whose throes he left his country struggling. Like all revolutions it created a trail of destruction, sweeping away much that had become sterile and unproductive, but much also that was beneficial in social cohesion, time-honoured charity, and artistic achievement, including the products of a school of native ecclesiastical painting and sculpture which were all but totally destroyed in an orgy of brutal and ignorant iconoclasm. Its immediate beneficiaries were a breed of grasping opportunists, as hard-hearted as they were hard-headed, whose grim, unpleasing faces look down from the portraits of Holbein, the brilliant young German painter first introduced into England by the great Catholic humanist and Lord Chancellor, Sir Thomas More, who was later executed by Henry for denying the royal supremacy.

★ ★ ★

When the King died in 1547 the chickens hatched under his despotic and wilful rule came home to roost on the throne of his nine-year-old son, Edward VI. These were an empty Treasury, rising inflation engendered by reckless expenditure on foreign wars and an unscrupulous debasement of the currency, with all its attendant injustice to individuals; widespread popular unrest, vagrancy and pauperism, no longer relieved by religious and monastic charity. Bishop Ridley of London told the Lord Protector's secretary, William Cecil, that Christ was lying in the streets of his diocese, 'hungry, naked and cold'. A generation of enclosures by get-rich-quick land-grabbers and money-lenders, acting without regard to social justice, followed an over-rapid and unbalanced transition from England's former principal export of native wool to the far more lucrative export of manufactured cloth through the great international commercial and financial emporium of Antwerp. This, absorbing more and more of the country's energies and capital, reduced the acres employed in subsistence farming, causing ploughlands to be converted into pasture and uprooting ancient villages and communities. It was accompanied by growing inflation brought about by successive deliberate debasements of the currency by the tyrant King and his son's ministers to pay for his wars against France and Scotland. Within two years of Henry VIII's death, prices of essential commodities had more than doubled. In 1550 there was a temporary collapse of the Antwerp market for English cloth, followed by a prolonged slump.

Above all, there remained from Henry's reign the growing religious differences unloosed by an as yet purely royal and parliamentary Reformation which in England had destroyed the links and disciplines of long Catholic habitude while retaining an enforced conformity to outworn and increasingly questioned religious assumptions and beliefs. The only outstanding problem Henry had settled was that of the succession, caused by his matrimonial adventures, and that only precariously. For though by one of his wives, Jane Seymour, who had died in childbirth in 1537, he had at last achieved a son, he bequeathed him but a feeble constitution. Of his two daughters, the elder, Mary, was a devoted Catholic, eager to undo what her father had done, while the younger, Elizabeth – child of Anne Boleyn – inclined to the reformed beliefs. And though their succession, in the event of Edward predeceasing them without heirs, was provided for by Henry's Act of Settlement, both were women, and therefore, considered by most people incapable of ruling a turbulent and divided realm.

Though the old King, seeking to rule from the grave, had hoped to preserve the religious *status quo* he had established, the councillors he appointed to act during his son's minority allowed the reforming elements in the Church and laity a divisive freedom hitherto denied. Chief among them was the boy King's uncle, Edward Seymour, Duke of Somerset – a hero of Henry's Scottish and French Wars – who constituted himself Lord Protector. Under his tolerant aegis English Protestants in exile were allowed to return from the Continent and the clergy to marry, while Communion in both kinds took the place of the Mass, Henry's anti-heresy laws being repealed by Parliament. In the hope of checking the clandestine circulation of unauthorized translations of the scriptures, in the last years of his reign Henry had licensed the publication of an English Bible – translated by a former Austin friar, Miles Coverdale, and based largely on an earlier and forbidden translation by the exiled and martyred William Tyndale, whose beautiful English and fine scholarship were to become a main inspiration for the Authorized Version of the next century. The latter's controversy with his Catholic opponent and fellow scholar, and later martyr, Sir Thomas More, crystallized the issues between the English reformers and the defenders of the old Faith, the former appealing to scripture and individual judgement and conscience, and the latter to the authority and transmitted ritual and cumulative wisdom of the Church and its apostolically descended episcopacy. 'If they shall burn me,' Tyndale wrote before his heretic's death at the hands of the Imperial authorities, 'they shall do none other than I looked for . . . There is none other way into the Kingdom of Life than through persecution and suffering of pain and of very death after the ensample of Christ.' 'If God spare my life,' he had told a priest at the outset of his great work of translating the New Testament, 'ere many years I will cause a boy that driveth the plough shall know more of the scripture than thou dost.'* It was this direct introduction in the vernacular to the Hebrew, Greek and Latin scriptures – 'the Word of God', the reformers called it – which was eventually to make the English a Protestant people and turn what until then had been a political Reformation into a popular one. Thirteen years after Tyndale's martyrdom at the stake, in the first year of Edward VI's reign, Henry VIII's Archbishop of Canterbury, Thomas Cranmer, put the seal on the translators' work of the past thirty years by issuing in 1549 his Book of Common Prayer, which endowed the Church of England and the English people with the lovely cadences and consoling wisdom of its incomparable liturgy.

Though, like everyone else in power, the Protector Somerset, a kindly man, feathered his own nest, he was genuinely anxious to redress the social wrongs from which the poor were suffering through enclosure, inflation and the dissolution of the monasteries. Unfortunately by attempting to do so too quickly he aroused such unruly hopes in the rough uneducated common people that they rose in rebellion, so provoking a violent reaction which led to his supersession, and ultimate execution, by a more ruthless and ambitious dictator, John Dudley, new-made Duke of Northumberland – a son of Henry VII's hated financial agent, Edmund Dudley. During the last three years of young Edward VI's reign this able, unscrupulous careerist, so typical of the new lords thrown up by the Henrician revolution, enjoyed complete control of the Council and young King – a brilliantly precocious but, as his diary showed, cold and reserved prig. But his plans for excluding the Catholic Princess Mary from the succession in favour of Lady Jane Grey, a sixteen-year-old Protestant great-granddaughter of Henry VII affianced to his own

---

* 'Translator of the Holy scriptures in the language of the English people,' runs the inscription on Tyndale's memorial in Westminster Abbey. 'A martyr and exile in the cause of liberty and pure religion, he fulfilled the precept which he had taught.'

son, were thwarted by Edward's death of consumption in 1553 at the age of fifteen.

★   ★   ★

Mary Tudor's brief reign was almost the saddest in English history, both for herself and her people. The daughter of Henry VIII by his divorced Spanish wife, she had suffered deeply from her father's treatment of her mother and his schismatical breach with the Church of her forebears. Child of a princess of Spain, she was aunt to the Emperor Charles V of Spain, ruler of the Netherlands, and of half Germany and Italy, and master of the immense mineral wealth of the New World. When, after years of insults and humiliations Mary's youthful half-brother's failing health made her accession to the English throne imminent, she, who had once been bastardized by her own father, suddenly became at thirty-seven a match even for Charles V's heir, Philip of Spain. For one who had suffered so many years of loneliness and whose dearest wish was to restore her erring country to its former Faith, marriage to the young crusading champion of the Catholic Counter-Reformation, and earth's richest monarch to be, seemed a dazzling prospect.

Mary was kindly, charitable, affectionate, scrupulously honest – an un-Tudor like trait – and excessively devout. She was also, like all her family, brave and stubborn, most of all in defence of her religion. When, in the days of the Protestant triumph after her brother's accession, the Bishop of London – whom afterwards she burnt at the stake – had called on her to adopt the new Prayer Book and expressed the hope that she would not 'refuse God's word,' she replied, 'I cannot tell what ye call God's word; that is not God's word now that was God's word in my father's days . . . You durst not for your ears have avouched that for God's word in my father's days.'

At the time of her accession, because of the loyalty to the Crown instilled by her Tudor father and grandfather, Mary enjoyed the loyalty of her people, even of those who had embraced the new religion – still then only a minority. When the Duke of Northumberland raised a rebellion and proclaimed his daughter-in-law, Lady Jane Grey, in her place, the country rallied instantaneously to its legitimate and Catholic Queen, despatching the ambitious Northumberland and his innocent protege to the scaffold.

The enthusiasm soon evaporated. Mary's marriage in 1554 to

ACCESSION TO A THRONE OF THORNS

Philip of Spain, against the advice of her counsellors and Parliament, proved intensely unpopular with an insular people. For Mary it was a barren and cruel disappointment. Having performed his matrimonial duty to enlarge his dynastic empire, her youthful king and husband stayed little more than a year in England with her. At thirty-seven, with failing health, she was prematurely old, and the cold correct Philip and his arrogant Spanish hidalgos made no bones about it. 'What,' asked one of them, 'shall the king do with such an old bitch?' Her hopes of a child, desperately sustained until time and her husband's prolonged absence made it impossible, proved a chimera. His one and only brief return for a few months in 1557 was solely to involve her and England in a disastrous war with France, in which, unlike Philip, she had nothing to gain and everything to lose.

All the Queen had left was her religion and her fierce Tudor resolve to re-impose it on her heretic subjects. Innocent of the world out of which she had so long lived, and ill advised, she went about it in the worst possible way. As well as having the leading Protestant churchmen, Archbishop Cranmer and Bishops Ridley of London and Latimer of Worcester*, burnt at the stake, she authorized, during her last three years, the burning of some three hundred humble Protestants, more than fifty of them women. This atrocious business, carried out in public, had an effect on the English very different from that which their Queen intended. For if – the only tangible result of the Spanish marriage and alliance – the capture in 1558 by France of Calais, England's last Plantagenet conquest, was engraved on Mary's heart, when, in that year, she died, the memory of the Smithfield martyrs, more than any single factor, was to make the English people for the next three centuries undeviating enemies of Rome.

---

* 'We shall this day,' said Latimer to Ridley, 'light such a candle by God's grace in England as, I trust, shall never be put out.'

21

Chapter One

THE VIRGIN QUEEN

'She shall be, to the happiness of England,
An aged princess; many days shall see her,
And yet no day without a deed to crown it.'

Shakespeare

On November 17th 1558 at the age of twenty-five, Elizabeth
succeeded to the vacant throne of her father, brother and sister. Born
on September 7th 1533, at the riverside palace of Greenwich – the
first heir to the English revolution against the rule of the international
Church – she had been christened, with Archbishop Cranmer as
godfather, in the arms of Henry VIII while, to the sound of trumpets,
Garter King-of-Arms proclaimed, 'God in his infinite goodness,
send prosperous life and long to the high and mighty princess of
England, Elizabeth!'

Yet within three years of her birth she had been disowned and dis-
graced. Before she was out of her cradle, her terrifying father had had
her mother, Anne Boleyn, executed for alleged infidelity and herself –
her child – bastardized. Banished the court, Elizabeth had been brought
up in the country with her half-sister Mary, nineteen years her senior,
whose mother's marriage had also been annulled. Much of her youth
was spent at Ashridge, the old monastery of the Bonhommes in the
Chiltern beechwoods, which after the Dissolution the King used as a
retiring place for the children of his successive queens. Restored in
1544 to the junior place in the succession by Act of Parliament, she
had lived after her father's death with the Queen Dowager, Catherine
Parr, in Chelsea. 'Schooled in danger and discretion,' when she was
only fifteen the latter's husband, the Lord Admiral, an ambitious,
thrustful man of forty and brother to the Lord Protector Somerset,
had been executed for treason for courting her – a lesson which taught
her how dangerous it was for a woman in her position to indulge her
affections. In an age of treachery and violence, when an occupant of,
or aspirant to, the throne had every incentive to eliminate rivals, her
life during the reign of her Catholic sister had been in constant

danger. Soon after Mary's accession, when hardly out of her teens, the young princess had been thrown into the Tower and subjected to almost daily cross-examination. Only her cool head and stout heart saved her. But for her Spanish brother-in-law's hope of marrying her after her childless sister's demise and so bringing England into his Atlantic empire, with her known Protestant sympathies she would never have been allowed by England's Catholic rulers to live to inherit the Crown.

Superbly educated – she was widely read and mistress of six languages, including Latin and Greek★ – her accession came as a providential deliverance to her Protestant subjects and herself. For both they and she faced tremendous risks. Her kingdom was near bankrupt and defenceless, divided by bitter religious differences in an age of increasingly embattled faiths, with unscrupulous profiteers battening on the spoils of the monasteries and the ruins of the feudal state and medieval Church. She inherited an exhausted Treasury, a depreciated currency and a society vitiated by lawlessness and vagabondage, and a countryside impoverished by a run of bad harvests. Abroad the prospect was still darker. Dominating half Europe, imperial Spain, with its invincible infantry, its dazzling conquests in central and south America and its world-wide oceanic power, had all but absorbed England through Philip's short-lived, but childless, marriage with Mary Tudor. Nearer home the traditional alliance between a giant France and Scotland, the upper and lower millstones, threatened to crush Protestant England and substitute for Elizabeth her half-French Catholic cousin and heir presumptive, Mary Stuart, now Queen both of France and the Scots. There were many in a still divided country who would have welcomed such an event. 'The Queen poor,' a contemporary wrote, 'the realm exhausted; the nobles poor and decayed; good captains and soldiers wanting; the people out of order; justice not executed; the justices unmeet for their offices; all things dear; division among ourselves; war with France and Scotland; the French king bestriding the realm, having one foot in Calais and the other in Scotland; steadfast enmity

★ 'She has just passed her sixteenth birthday,' her tutor, the great Greek scholar, Roger Ascham, reported of her, 'and shows such dignity and gentleness as are wonderful at her age and in her rank. Her study of true religion and learning is most eager. Her mind has no womanly weakness, her perseverance is equal to that of a man, and her memory long keeps what it quickly picks up. She talks French and Italian as well as she does English . . . When she writes Greek and Latin nothing is more beautiful than her handwriting. She delights as much in music as she is skilful in it.' J. E. Neale, *Queen Elizabeth* 26.

but no steadfast friendship abroad.' England was a weak unimportant half-island on the fringe of a Continent dominated by two great Catholic powers, shut out from the trade and wealth of the trans-atlantic New World and the golden East by papal decrees and the might of Spain and Portugal, to whom, as their discoverers and colonizers, the Pope had granted an eternal monopoly. To most Englishmen the great days of their country and its one-time military glory seemed altogether things of the past. The vast continental possessions of the Plantagenet and Lancastrian kings had gone like a dream, and, with the loss of Calais, the last of the old landmarks had vanished.

It was such a realm and such a situation that Elizabeth was called upon to master. To her subjects, Protestant and Catholic alike, she seemed a weak, inexperienced woman; they would naturally have much preferred a man to rule them. Yet, unlike her predecessor with her Spanish ancestry and sympathies, she was, in her own words, 'mere English'. With her flaming hair, commanding will and gift of telling oratory, she was King Harry's daughter, while, through her beheaded mother – a great granddaughter of a London mercer – there was bourgeois blood enough in her veins to enable her to share her people's feelings. Everything turned on her ability to win their confidence and love, and so unite them behind her.

From the start she seized every opportunity of courting them. Her entry into London three weeks after her proclamation was the first act of a drama which was to continue to her dying day. 'To all that wished her well,' wrote one who witnessed it, 'she gave thanks. To such as bade "God save her Grace", she said in return, "God save you all", and added that she thanked them with all her heart. Wonder-fully transported were the people with the loving answers and gestures of their Queen . . . How many nosegays did her Grace receive at poor women's hands. How often she stayed her chariot when she saw any simple body approach to speak to her. A branch of rosemary given to her Majesty, with a supplication, by a poor woman about Fleet Bridge was seen in her chariot when her Grace came to Westminster.'

'If ever any person had the gift or style to win the hearts of people,' another recalled, 'it was this Queen, and if ever she did express the same it was at that present, in coupling mildness with majesty as she did, and in stately stooping to the meanest sort. All her faculties were in motion, and every motion seemed a well-guided action: her eye was set upon one, her ear listened to another, her judgment ran upon a third, to a fourth she addressed her speech. Her spirit seemed to be everywhere, and yet so entire in herself as it seemed to be nowhere else. Some she pitied, some she commended, some she thanked, at others she pleasantly and wittily jested; contemning no person, neglecting no office, and distributing her smiles, looks and graces so artificially that thereupon the people again redoubled the testimony of their joys, and afterwards, raising everything to the highest strain, filled the ears of all men with immoderate extolling their prince.'*

A magnificent actress who knew well how to hide her thoughts and feelings there was no doubt of the sincerity with which she identified herself with her people. 'Have a care over them,' she told her judges in her first address to them; 'do you that which I ought to do. They are my people. Every man oppresseth and spoileth them without mercy. See unto them, see unto them, for they are my charge. I charge you even as God hath charged me.' 'Far above all earthly treasures,' she was to declare many years later, 'I esteem my people's love.' 'You may well have a greater prince,' she told them; 'you shall never have a more loving one.'

Elizabeth and her ministers, whom she chose with great shrewdness, had to play for time: time for the nation to resolve its religious discords, to reform the currency, to solve the problems of poverty and vagabondage, to recover national unity, above all to grow strong enough to meet the challenge of the immense foreign forces threatening it. She played it with cunning, equivocation, parsimony, constant delays and every womanly and queenly art with which she was endowed, and, when the crunch could no longer be avoided, with magnificent courage. 'I thank God,' she told one of her Parliaments, 'that I am imbued with such qualities that if I were turned out of the realm in my petticoat, I were able to live in any place in Christendom.'

★   ★   ★

Her first task after her accession was to resolve the bitter ideological divisions wrought by the religious changes of the past quarter of a century. Under her father they had cut the country's links with Rome and secularized the wealth of the monasteries and chantries, under her brother had carried England into the revolutionary camp of the Continental reformers, and under her sister back again to Catholicism, and a reformed, intolerant, persecuting Catholicism at that. Before

* Cited by Sir John Neale, *Queen Elizabeth* 65.

26

THE VIRGIN QUEEN

the Marian persecutions, a hard conservative core, sustained by the
rule of a Catholic Queen, had clung to the old Catholic Faith and
acknowledged the supremacy and disciplines of Rome. A smaller,
but vehement, minority of 'Puritan' extremists had passionately
denounced as idolatrous superstitions all the leading tenets and practices of the medieval Church – transubstantiation, the confessional,
the efficacy of indulgences and papal remission of sin, pilgrimages,
relics, and the intercession of saints. The majority of ordinary English
men and women, including the heir presumptive, the Princess
Elizabeth, while repudiating the authority of Rome, were instinctively
traditionalist and, like her father, felt no great enthusiasm for doctrinal and theological abstractions. For though the sale of monastic
and chantry lands had given English landowners of all classes an
irreversable vested interest in the secular results of the Henrician
Reformation, there had been as yet no clear border-line in most men's
hearts between the priest-led ritualistic, candlelit worship of the past
and the congregational and private scripture-reading and impromptu
prayers and sermons of Protestant piety.

But the Smithfield fires and the inhumanity of Mary's reactionary
advisers had decided the issue. With a young Protestant princess on
the throne, and with as her principal adviser and minister, William
Cecil – once the reforming Protector Somerset's secretary – England
was irrevocably set again on a Protestant course.

In breaking with Rome, however, Elizabeth moved with characteristic caution. For in the near bankrupt and ill-armed state of her
small, vulnerable and still divided kingdom, she dared not do anything
that could precipitate an attack by either of her giant Catholic
neighbours, France and Spain. Her first, and decisive, step, though
accompanied by every expression of friendship and affection, was to
delay – until he grew impatient of waiting and betrothed himself to a
French Catholic princess instead – acceptance of a proposal of
marriage from her lately bereft brother-in-law, Philip, the 'most
Catholic King' of Spain and arch-champion of the Counter Reformation. But at the opening of her first Parliament on January 25th,
when the abbot and monks of Westminster met her with tapers
burning in broad daylight, she waved them aside and all that they
stood for with a firm, 'Away with those torches! We can see well
enough!' Then, having made sure of her ground, she absented
herself from Mass and, at Easter 1559, publicly received Communion
in both kinds. Using Parliament as her father had done to secure

27

national assent for her policies, but deliberately declining the title of 'Head' of the Church assumed by him and her brother, and acting instead, in the words of her new Act of Supremacy, merely as 'supreme Governor of all persons and causes, ecclesiastical as well as civil', this wise, temporizing and clement young ruler firmly opted for a moderate Protestant episcopacy with an English Liturgy and a seemly ritual, not too novel or difficult for those who had been brought up under the old Catholicism.

For in her church reforms, Elizabeth's purpose was not primarily doctrinal but political. It was to reunite her people behind a religious belief and prayer to which their character, temperament and experience inclined them to conform. She made her choice for a clear, simple, middle way, easy for moderate men to follow and, therefore, typically English. Idolatrous practices on the one hand and private preaching on the other were discouraged, as were 'contumelious and opprobrious words such as heretic, schismatic and Papist'. 'To unite the people of the realm in one uniform order' all were to attend their parish church on Sunday, while non-attendance was to be punished by a modest fine, though, only if ostentatiously persisted in, by imprisonment. At the same time a curb was placed on the verbal extravagances of Puritan extremists, intoxicated by the polemics of continental theologians and the new wine of the translated and printed scriptures. In Elizabeth's Act of Uniformity and in the Thirty-nine Articles which laid down guidelines for the Anglican Church, there was no abuse of Pope or Rome, while the words of the gentle, martyred Cranmer's restored Communion Service left communicants free, in their own minds, to accept or reject as they pleased the old Catholic dogma of the transubstantiation of the bread and wine of the Eucharist into the Real Presence of Christ's body and blood. Elizabeth's pragmatic attitude towards the furious controversies which raged round this beautiful but unprovable conception – ideological controversies which, with others like them, were about to plunge Europe into a century of persecution, massacre and civil and international war – was neatly expressed in some lines often attributed to her:

> 'Twas Christ the word that spake it,
> He took the bread and brake it;
> And what the word did make it
> That I believe and take it.'

THE VIRGIN QUEEN

Or, as she was to put it many years later, when only England was free from the welter of religious strife dividing almost every other Christian land: 'If there were two Princes in Christendom who had good will and courage, it would be easy to reconcile the differences in religion, for there was only one Jesus Christ and one faith, and all the rest they dispute about but trifles.'

Within the Anglican Church, Catholic and Apostolic but not Roman – reaching back, in the view of its apologists, to the pristine traditions of early Christianity – there was room for all who accepted the outward forms of unity laid down by its royal Governor. And, at first, within the country at large, for those, too, who, worshipping in the privacy of their own homes, did not try to propagate or impose divisive views on others. 'The law touches no man's conscience so as public order be not violated by external act or teaching,' Elizabeth told the Holy Roman Emperor, whose Catholic son, the Archduke Charles, was a suitor for her hand. In a universally intolerant age this broad-minded, merciful young Queen set a rare example of moderation and good sense, insisting only – though that in no uncertain terms – on total loyalty to the Crown and the ideal of national unity which all her life she strove to foster. That the settlement reached was, broadly, acceptable is shown by the fact that of 9,400 English clergy only a few hundred refused the new Oath of Supremacy, compared with a sixth who had resigned or been ejected from their livings when Mary had restored the Roman supremacy. Thanks to the hard work and administrative zeal of Elizabeth's three Archbishops of Canterbury – the scholarly Matthew Parker, son of a Norwich weaver, his less successful successor, Edmund Grindal, and John Whitgift, whom, honouring for his celibacy, she used to call her 'little black husband' – parochial order was restored and the educational standards of the clergy raised out of all recognition during her forty-five years' reign. But it was from the Queen's humanity, breadth of vision and good sense and the noble and inspiring Book of Common Prayer, with its glorious collects, supervized and bequeathed to England by her godfather, the martyred Archbishop Cranmer, that the reformed Anglican Church derived its continuing spirit and soul. 'It is impossible,' the great Elizabethan historian, A. L. Rowse, has written, 'to over-estimate the influence of the Church's routine of prayer and good works upon society: the effect upon imagination and conduct of the Liturgy with its piercing and affecting phrases, repeated Sunday by Sunday . . . They provided a system of belief, making a whole

29

world of experience within which to live, giving satisfaction to the inmost impulses of the heart while not disturbing the critical standards of the mind, setting a guide to conduct in all the concerns of life, instructing in duty to God, one's neighbour and oneself, offering such consolation as nothing else in grief, in sickness and in the hour of death.'* Nearly three hundred years later the Duke of Wellington was to declare that it was the Church of England which had made England what she was, a nation of honest men.

The speed and magnanimity of Elizabeth's comprehensive religious settlement gave the country the unity essential to preserve it from the external perils threatening it. By the Treaty of Cateau-Cambresis signed in the spring after her accession, the rival dominating powers of Europe, France and Spain, made peace, leaving the latter's satellite, England, to whistle in vain for her lost Calais. That they might now combine against her at the instance of a fanatic Pope, eager to redeem a little lapsed island kingdom from heresy, was a possibility the Queen and her ministers could not safely ignore. For, with the rapid growth of Catholic strength and conviction following the reforms of the Roman Church set in train by the Council of Trent and the foundation in 1540 of the great international crusading Society of Jesus to combat heresy and win back souls – and nations – to the Faith, the position of the heretic ruler of a little state of barely five millions was becoming increasingly precarious. Facing England across the Channel and Biscay Bay, with their orthodox sovereigns both committed by their religion to root out heresy in their dominions, and with only the sea separating their powerful armies from her shores, lay the immense global empire of Spain, with its oceanic discoveries and conquests, and a France with more than three times England's size and population, now joined with Scotland under a single Crown.

For the 'auld alliance' between England's ancient enemy beyond the Channel and her restless, marauding northern neighbour had recently taken a new and menacing form. Eleven years earlier, following the death in 1542 of James V of Scotland after a shattering defeat by the English at Pinkie, the former's widow, Mary of Guise – a French princess – had joined in 1547 with the Scottish Estates in sending her five-year old child, Queen Mary Stuart, out of Scotland to be educated at the French royal court, out of reach of English invaders and her own feuding and kidnapping nobles. Here, a few months before Elizabeth's accession, the young Scottish Queen had

* *The England of Elizabeth*, 433–4.

been married at the age of fifteen to the even younger Dauphin of France, with a secret agreement, unknown to her distant subjects, that, in the event of her dying before him without issue, he and his successors should inherit the Scottish Crown. Meanwhile French troops had been sent to Scotland to garrison the capital and royal castles. They both helped its French-born Dowager Queen and Regent – Mary's mother – to keep the English at bay and suppress the growing outbreaks of heresy which, as in every northern land, including France itself, were seeping into the country from the reformed Lutheran and Calvinist strongholds in Germany and Switzerland.

Less than a year after the marriage of Mary Queen of Scots, her young husband succeeded to the French throne. Originally intended by Scotland's then would-be conquerer, Henry VIII, for his son, Edward, and Queen now of both France and Scotland, the sixteen-year-old Mary Stuart – a great-granddaughter of Henry VII – now also claimed the English Crown, to which she was heir-presumptive. For under Catholic law, its heretic new wearer, Elizabeth, was illegitimate and, therefore, a usurper.

Yet in the very summer in which the young Queen of Scots – who, on Mary Tudor's death had assumed the royal arms and titles of England – found herself Queen of France, and, while her Protestant cousin was laying with her Parliament the foundations of the Anglican Church, dramatic events were taking place in Scotland. For in the Easter which saw Elizabeth avowing her Protestant sympathies by publicly receiving Communion in both kinds, the French Regent, Mary of Guise, now a very sick woman, alarmed by the spread of heresy among her daughter's subjects, ordained a compulsory enforcement of the religion of their fathers. Her edict was openly defied by a strong group of dissident nobles, who, calling themselves the Lords of the Congregation of Jesus Christ in Scotland, had recently subscribed to a Covenant renouncing the idolatry of the Roman faith – that of the established Church of their country. They now assembled at Perth with a number of defiant Protestant preachers whom the Scottish bishops had summoned to answer for their heresy. Here they were joined by John Knox, a fanatic and highly eloquent veteran reformer, who had just returned from self-imposed exile in the stronghold of Calvinist Protestantism, Geneva. Knox, who had suffered for his heretical preachings in the galleys of his country's French invaders and whose austere and uncompromising beliefs were well attuned to the dour, unrelenting humours of Scottish character had played a leading part in fomenting opposition to Scotland's corrupt, effete and over-endowed ecclesiastical establishment. He now, on May 11th 1559, preached a sermon in Perth so inflammatory and 'vehement against the idolatry' of 'dumb dogs' and 'idle bellies', as he called the endowed priests and monks of the Roman Church, that the mob rose in enthusiastic response and sacked every monastic and religious house in the town.

Up till now the pent-up Protestant heresy, which had been raging for two generations on the Continent, had so far only simmered in Scotland. It now exploded with the force of a tornado. A substantial part of its greedy and lawless nobles and lairds – like their fellow land-owners in England, 'lusting for kirklands' – joined with the more vocal elements of its poverty-stricken people in repudiating the ancient faith of their country in favour of a congregational or presbyterian system of church government, ruled by parish ministers and lay elders, and based on the ecclesiastical and civil discipline of Knox's friend and master, the great French-born scholar and prophet of Predestination, Grace and Election, John Calvin of Geneva. Everywhere Scottish Protestants took up arms in defiance of the dying Regent's attempts to repress the rebellion of her daughter's heretical subjects.

But they proved no match for the trained, disciplined troops of the French garrisons of Edinburgh castle and Scotland's key port, Leith. As the indecisive campaign of that summer and autumn wore on, knowing that reinforcements from France would soon be arriving to crush them, Knox and the Lords of the Congregation appealed to Scotland's ancient enemy, England, and its young Protestant Queen to save the nascent Scottish Reformation and free their country 'from the bondage and tyranny of strangers'. Elizabeth had no love for rebels and none whatever for John Knox, who shortly before her accession had published from Geneva a highly scurrilous and offensive attack on the then female Catholic rulers of Scotland, France and England entitled *A Blast of the Trumpet against the Monstrous Regiment of Women*. Yet, though the risks for her, both political and military, of armed intervention were daunting, the consequences of letting Scotland be forced back into the French and Catholic fold seemed even graver. Acting as secretly and unprovocatively as possible, and using every expedient to conceal her plans, she and her Secretary of State, William Cecil, sent first money, and then, greatly daring, in the winter of 1559/60, a fleet to blockade Leith and the Firth of Forth. Finally in

April 1560, they scraped together an army to enter Scotland and help compel the blockaded French garrisons to leave it. And when she had done so, by subsequently withdrawing her own forces from Scotland without asking any recompense, Elizabeth not only, in that crucial summer, won the gratitude of the Scots – something no English ruler had ever done before – but closed a vital gap in her country's defences against potential Catholic enemies in Europe. Henceforward they would have to reckon, not, as until now, with a small Protestant half-island, outflanked by another and hostile Catholic half-island tradi-tionally allied to France and offering a foothold from which to attack England in the rear, but with a single island bound together by a common Protestantism.

What had happened had changed the course of history. It was a first and, as it proved, decisive step in the creation of a new political entity in the world – Great Britain. It had been brought about by three factors – the cool courage and patient statesmanship of a young Queen and her wise counsellor, Cecil; the realization of far-sighted Scots, like William Maitland of Lethington, that what he called 'the earnest embracing of religion' would inevitably cause the old heredi-tary enemies of Scotland and England to 'join straitly together'; and the fine seamanship and hereditary skill of English sailors. For it had been young Admiral William Winter's midwinter voyage to Scotland and his blockade of the stormy Firth of Forth, at a time when ships of war were not built, or expected, to remain at sea at such a season in northern waters, which had broken the French stranglehold on Scotland. Two attempts by French fleets and transports, first to fore-stall and then to raise Winter's blockade, had ended in disaster for them with the loss of half a dozen ships and several thousand soldiers in tempests. Cecil's and the Queen's subsequent refusal to relax their naval grip had decided the issue. For so long as the French garrisons of the Scottish royal castles could be supplied and reinforced by sea, they could never have been taken by storm or reduced by the un-trained and undisciplined ragged Scots levies and their allies, the equally ineffective English militia men. As it was, they were forced to accept, in the summer of 1561, the terms of the Treaty of Edinburgh, as the only means of getting their besieged and starving troops back to France in English bottoms. In return for that concession – the only alternative to starvation – the French troops were to leave at once, their fortress at Leith was to be dismantled, the government of Scot-land to be transferred to the Council of Protestant nobles, and the

French King and Queen were to abstain from any further challenge to Elizabeth's right to her throne. For her and Cecil it was a tremendous triumph.

Yet it had been a near-run thing, and right up to the end it had not been clear whether the French would give in and leave Scotland free and Protestant. At one moment during the campaign it had even looked as though Philip of Spain might intervene to suppress the Scottish heretics while protecting his English sister-in-law – whose kingdom he still hoped to redeem from heresy – against any attack across the Channel by his rival France. As it was, England's slender financial resources had been strained to the utmost to supply her own and the Scottish insurgents' fighting forces.

Nor had her rustic militia – for she had no other army – shown any sign that it could compete with the professional armies of the Continent, armed as it still was with bills and bows, and raised from the rag, tag and bobtail of the countryside. Since the days, less than a century and a half before, when England's archers had been the arbiters of every battlefield, the nature of land warfare had changed out of all recognition. The masters of the field were now the huge regiments of highly paid Spanish, German, French and Italian mercenaries, with a discipline and esprit de corps based on professional pride and comradeship and the lively hope of gain, rape and plunder. Advancing in huge phalanxes of massed pikes, under the supporting fire of arquebusiers, musketeers and artillery, they dominated and broke the ranks of any opponent. They had sprung originally out of the little indentured 'retinues' or companies of English archers, who, armed with a devastating weapon which they alone could yield – the long bow of Gwent – under Edward III, the Black Prince and Henry V, had laid low the armoured and mounted feudal chivalry of France and western Christendom. Thereafter, taking service under elected captains as so-called 'free companies', they had sold themselves to any petty tyrant or walled corporate Italian or German city able to afford their services. Gradually, absorbed in their own civil wars, the English had dropped out of the European battle league and receded into their remote and misty island. Meanwhile mercenary soldiering had become a highly lucrative profession for the toughest and most aggressive members of society, for whose services the great dynastic monarchies of Spain, France and Austria, who alone could afford to pay them, competed. From them they drew their unchallengeable military strength, supporting them with the powerful and costly new weapons which European Renaissance technology had evolved. The most famous of all were the huge Spanish three-thousand-strong regiments or 'tercios' recruited from the hardy peasants of the Castilian plains. Once landed on England's shores, the invincible veterans of St Quentin and Muhlberg would be certain to overwhelm, 'with push of pike', her little ill-trained and ill-armed companies of balotted county militiamen. Under her archaic local military system these were recruited by corrupt muster-masters who, falsifying their returns, let off the able-bodied and well-to-do for bribes, and filled the ranks with criminals, cripples and beggars. 'Tattered prodigals, ragged as Lazarus,' Shakespeare was to describe them in the latter years of Elizabeth's reign, 'such as were never soldiers, but discarded unjust serving men, younger sons to younger brothers, revolted tapsters and ostlers trade-fallen, the cankers of a calm world and a long peace.'* Nor could England, with her Treasury drained dry by the extravagance of Henry VIII and the financial bankruptcy of his two successors, afford to hire armies of disciplined mercenaries like wealthy France and Spain.

For the moment her only defence lay in playing off these powerful rivals against one another and taking advantage of their internal difficulties. Eighteen months after the expulsion of the French from Scotland, roused by a massacre of their co-religionists by a Catholic mob who had surrounded a church filled with worshippers and set it alight, the Huguenots – as the French Protestants were called – took up arms and, like the Scots, appealed to Elizabeth to help them. Promised by their leaders the return of their lost Calais and offered in the meantime the port of Havre as a pledge for it, in September 1562, by the Treaty of Hampton Court the Queen, under strong pressure from the more Protestant members of her Council, undertook to do in France what she had done in Scotland two summers before.

---

* Born six years after Elizabeth's accession, Shakespeare, writing six years before the end of her reign, drew in his *Henry IV* a picture of the time-honoured recruitment for war of England's county militia. 'I have misused the King's press damnably,' he made his fraudulent captain, Sir John Falstaff, confess. 'I have got, in exchange of a hundred and fifty soldiers, three hundred and odd pounds . . . A mad fellow met me on the way and told me I had unloaded all the gibbets and pressed the dead bodies. No eye hath seen such scarecrows. I'll not march through Coventry with them, that's flat; – nay, and the villains march wide betwixt the legs, as if they had gyves on; for, indeed, I had the most of them out of prison. There's but a shirt and a half in all my company.' Not till 1595, seven years after the defeat of the Armada and two years before Shakespeare's play did the Privy Council decide that musketeers, instead of archers, should be enrolled in the country's Trained Bands. A. L. Rowse. *Expansion of Elizabethan England* 329.

Yet, though the West Country seamen joined with the Huguenot deep-sea fishermen of La Rochelle and Brittany to sweep that Catholic kingdom's commerce from the Channel, the war on land went ill for the French Protestants. Unlike the Scottish reformers outnumbered by their orthodox countrymen, they were driven that winter out of their strongholds in Normandy. While the English were still assembling at Havre, the Prince of Condé, the Huguenot leader, surrendered to his royalist and Catholic countrymen. Thereafter abandoned and attacked by both Catholics and Protestants, the English defenders of Havre, after a three months' siege in the summer of 1563, were forced to lay down their arms after a third of the garrison had perished in an outbreak of bubonic plague. Brought back to England by them, it swept the country, carrying off in 1564, the year of Shakespeare's birth, one in six of the population of Stratford-upon-Avon.

★　　★　　★

This costly and humiliating experience cured the young English Queen of what little taste she ever had for war. Henceforward, she did everything she could to avoid it, and, by doing so, gave her people twenty-two years of much-needed peace, during which time they grew rich and strong, while her own slender financial resources, like those of her frugal grandfather, Henry VII, increased. Yet if, to protect her country, Elizabeth shunned man's costly expedient of war, she relied instead on her instinct and art as a woman to achieve the same ends. The weapon she used was marriage, and, by denying rather than giving it, held out herself and the dowry of her kingdom as a bait for the ambition, greed and vanity of her fellow princes.

In the sixteenth century international diplomacy moved in two main channels, war and dynastic marriage. For the first Elizabeth had nothing but dislike, not so much because it was cruel – though she hated cruelty – but because it was wasteful, uncertain and, in the universally corrupt state of public administration, disastrously expensive, and her frugal mind revolted at it. But for the diplomacy of courtship she was perfectly fitted by temperament. Hers was a genius for intrigue, a taste for coquetry and a passion for flattery. As the heiress of England, open to offers from the highest bidder, and free to carry into international politics all the bewildering ways of a maid with a man, she was in her element. With as her dowry a kingdom, which, though as yet of little account by itself, could bring a major accession of strength to any European power allied to it, she had a diplomatic and matrimonial card to play of the highest consequence, so long as it remained unplayed.

During the early years of the reign, she received at least fifteen proposals of marriage from Spanish, French, Swedish, Austrian, German and Danish, as well as Scottish and English, suitors. Two were from kings, two from hereditary princes, seven from dukes, two from earls, and two from her own subjects, a courtesy lord and a knight. After her rejection, by deliberate procrastinating, of her brother-in-law, Philip of Spain, the most powerful monarch on earth, in order to retain his friendship during the crisis with France over Scotland, Elizabeth had continued to keep a foot in the Spanish camp by favouring the suit of his cousin, the young Archduke Charles of Austria. For several years he seemed the most likely foreign aspirant for her hand. Later, at different times, she invited and encouraged proposals of marriage from a succession of young French princes. For, so long as she remained unmarried, France and Spain each nursed hopes, heretic though she was, of bringing her country into its dynastic orbit and herself and her people back to the Roman fold. It was the essence of her policy to keep alive the hopes of both rivals and use her virgin state and her woman's art of procrastination to play one against the other until such time as England was strong enough to stand on her own feet without the friendship of either.

At first it seemed inevitable – to everyone, that is, except herself – that she would marry, both to secure for her throne the guidance, strength and wisdom of a man, and to provide her kingdom with a male heir, so averting the dangers of a disputed succession. 'It is inconceivable that she should wish to remain single and never marry,' wrote the Austrian ambassador to his royal master, the Holy Roman Emperor. Nor could her counsellors understand her repeated changes of heart. The multiplicity of her suitors and the encouragement she gave them all puzzled and scandalized them. 'God send our mistress a husband, and in time a son, that we may hope our posterity shall have a masculine succession,' was Cecil's repeated prayer. 'Here is great company of wooers,' the poor man complained; 'would to God the Queen had one and the rest honourably settled . . . This song hath many parts, and I am skilled only in plainsong.'

The Queen suffered from no such inhibitions. She encouraged them all. Her reluctance to marry – however carefully concealed, at first, possibly even from herself – may have been due to many reasons: to her desire for liberty, to inability to make up her mind, to a womanly preference for delay, to the embitterment in which her first girlish love affair had closed, above all, and always, to a sense of the true interests of her country and her supreme means of serving it – her hold on her subjects' hearts.

Only one suitor at this time seems to have touched her heart. Lord Robert Dudley was a younger son of the upstart Duke of Northumberland who had supplanted the Lord Protector Somerset in Edward VI's reign and – like his own father before him, Henry VII's hated financial agent, Edmund Dudley – had been beheaded for treason. This tall, dark, handsome, distinguished looking and forceful young man of Elizabeth's own age – 'the gipsy' to the contemptuous older nobility – had shared her captivity in the Tower during Mary's reign. Robin, she called him, keeping him never far from her presence* while he, with an eye on the throne, courted her assiduously. But he was married, and during the second year of the reign ugly rumours began to circulate that he meant to do away with the lonely wife, Amy Robsart, whom he kept languishing in the country while he attended the Queen and Court. Then in September 1560, the horrifying news reached Windsor that she had been found dead with a broken neck at the bottom of a flight of stone stairs at Cumnor Hall in Oxfordshire.

Faced by a scandal that could have shaken the throne, Elizabeth placed the trust and love of her subjects above her passion as a woman and the dictates of her heart. Though she never doubted his innocence, her Robin was banished from the Court until an Inquest and a legal inquiry had shown that the cause of his wife's death must have been either accident or suicide. And though he resumed his affectionate intimacy with the Queen, his hopes of a royal marriage were never realized. For, while she continued to reward his devotion and her love for him with gifts, including the great castle of Kenilworth and, later, the earldom of Leicester, she kept him, like all her suitors, firmly in his place. 'God's death,' she is reported to have rebuked him for his jealousy of a rival, 'I have wished you well, but my favour is not so locked up in you that others shall not participate thereof... I will have

* 'She was no angel,' Elizabeth confided to the Austrian ambassador; 'she did not deny that she had some affection for Lord Robert.' In October 1562 when she was thought to be dying of smallpox, she protested that, 'though she loved, and had always loved Lord Robert dearly, as God was her witness, nothing improper had ever passed between them.'

here but one mistress and no master.' 'Which so quailed my Lord Leicester,' her earliest biographer, Sir Robert Naunton, added, 'that his feigned humility was long after one of his best virtues.'

Subjects who tried to dictate to their imperious royal mistress suffered the same fate. Throughout the first decade of her reign, conscious that her life alone stood between them and the perils of a disputed succession – civil war, anarchy and invasion – successive Parliaments kept petitioning her either to marry and provide the kingdom with a male and, as they hoped, Protestant heir, or, in default, name a successor. To her intense indignation they once went so far as to refuse to vote her urgently-needed financial supply until she married. At this she turned on them with fury. 'It did not become,' she said, 'a subject to compel the Sovereign.' 'Was not I born in this country?' she asked. 'Were my parents born in any foreign country? Is there any cause that should alienate myself from being careful over this country? Is not my kingdom here?' 'I marvel,' she rated the Commons on another occasion, showing the Coronation ring on her finger, 'that ye have forgotten the pledge of this my wedlock and marriage with my kingdom . . . And do not upbraid me with a miserable lack of children; for every one of you, and as many as are Englishmen, are children and kinsmen to me.' It was for her, their anointed Queen, she told them, not for some unknown and unpredictable heir to provide for the succession and safeguard the country's future. 'For though I be never so careful of your well-being and mind ever so to be, yet may my issue grow out of kind and become, perhaps, ungracious. And in the end this shall be for me sufficient that a marble stone shall declare that a Queen, having reigned such a time, lived and died a virgin.'*

Yet though – to use her dynamic phrase – she would 'never be by violence constrained to do anything' and left the Commons in no doubt that, in this as in other matters, she would abate no jot of her royal prerogative and England's immemorial constitutional practice – under which the wearer of the Crown initiated policy, like her father she regarded the 'counsel and consent' of the nation's representatives in their parliamentary Estates of Lords and Commons as an essential part of that constitutional practice. For it preserved and ensured that unity of the realm which was the supreme purpose of her reign. When, womanwise, outraged by the insolent language of a more than usually outspoken member of the Commons, she clapped him into

* A. L. Rowse, *The England of Elizabeth*, 296.

the Fleet prison, she bowed at once to the House's outraged protest at this infringement of its right of free speech, and apologized handsomely, ordering his immediate release and declaring that nothing had been further from her intention than to impugn the rights of parliamentary debate. In the reconciliation between her and Parliament which followed, the Commons voted supply without any further attempt to make it dependent on her promise to marry, while she, in her turn, her prerogative admitted, graciously waived a third of the subsidy voted her. 'Do not think,' she told them in the speech from the throne which closed the session, 'that I am unmindful of your surety by succession, wherein is all my care, considering I know myself to be mortal. No, I warrant you. Or that I went about to break your liberties. No, it was never in my meaning, but to stay you before you fell into the ditch.' That declaration of January 2nd 1567, marked a decisive moment in the relations between the Queen and her Parliaments. Henceforward, whatever rifts arose between them, there was never any question but that it was she who directed the ship of state, while Lords and Commons, the hereditary and elected representatives of her people, meeting periodically at her summons to authorize and grant fiscal supply, gave her, through proved and custom-hallowed channels of consultation and debate, their counsel, advice and consent.

★ ★ ★

During her late twenties, while Elizabeth was keeping both foreign suitors and her own people guessing her intentions, she ceased to be the only marriageable queen in the European matrimonial stakes. For in December 1560, three days before her eighteenth birthday, Mary Stuart, Queen of France and Scotland and Catholic heir presumptive to England's childless throne, found herself a widow. With her sickly boy husband died her hopes of presiding over the brilliant sophisticated French royal court – the most cultivated in Europe – in which she had grown up. Instead, it became her fate to reign over a barren, divided, half barbaric, northern kingdom of barely a million people, half of whom, including a majority of its nobles, had passionately repudiated their, and her, ancient faith, which they now reviled as an idolatrous superstition. Apart from her claim to the English succession, which her Protestant cousin would not allow herself or her subjects to acknowledge, all she had to rely on when, a lonely girl of eighteen, she landed at Leith in August 1561, was her appealing beauty, her fascination to men, and an unshakeable belief in her right to sovereignty. In the course of the next four years, with her courage, gaiety and vivacity, she contrived to win for herself a following among Scotland's feuding and fickle nobility and to preserve intact her Catholic faith and worship. Warily watched by Elizabeth – who, in the hope of binding her and Scotland to England, offered her her own favourite, Leicester, as a consort – she made several attempts to negotiate a match with one of Europe's leading Catholic princes, including Don Carlos, the epileptic and repulsive son and heir of the all-powerful Philip of Spain. In the end, before Don Carlos's mysterious death – murdered, it was widely believed, by his own despairing father – she followed her fancy by marrying, in July 1565, according to Catholic rites, her nineteen year old cousin, Lord Darnley, with whom she had fallen in love. Heir to the earldom of Lennox, and, like Mary herself, a descendant of Henry VII with a reversionary claim to the English throne, he was a handsome, but as it soon turned out, spoilt and dissolute weakling.

Though the marriage broke down almost at once through his vices, it brought her, in the summer of 1566, a son and heir. Less than eight months after the wedding, refused the crown matrimonial which he coveted and bitterly resentful of the influence of a low-born Italian musician, a former boon companion and favourite of his own named David Riccio, whom, to the general scandal, Mary, with her love of music and gaiety, had made her private secretary, the jealous husband allied himself in return for their political support with a gang of disgruntled Protestant nobles. Together they broke into the palace of Holyroodhouse, where the pregnant Queen was supping with Riccio, her lady-in-waiting and friends, and, dragging the terrified Italian from the room as he clung to her skirts, hacked him to pieces in the doorway.

Held prisoner by the murderers, with splendid courage Mary planned her revenge. Wheedling her weak cowardly husband into deserting his fellow conspirators, she escaped, heavy with child, from her captured palace in a wild midnight ride to Dunbar. Here, rallying her supporters, she resumed her reign. Nine months later, at midnight on February 9th 1567, despite an apparent reconciliation, her unwanted husband, the titular King, was murdered under horrific circumstances which brought her under grave suspicion of being party to the crime. For the man universally regarded as its instigator, the

Earl of Bothwell – a reckless Border baron with a fatal facility with women – was widely believed to be the Queen's lover and was known to be divorcing his wife, apparently with a view to marrying her. Suspicion turned to near certainty when, a few weeks after the murder of her husband, he abducted Mary, and, immediately afterwards, pardoned by her for the rape, married her.

In the ensuing popular outcry and fury Bothwell had to fly the country, while Mary, with mobs crying 'Burn the whore', was forced to abdicate in favour of her infant son, James VI, and accept a regency under her bastard Protestant half-brother, the Earl of Moray. Imprisoned in the lake castle of Loch Leven for nearly a year, she escaped at the beginning of May 1568, only to be at once defeated by the Regent's forces at Langside. After a desperate flight through the heather, she crossed the Solway in a fishing boat and, almost penniless, sought refuge in England. 'I am now forced out of my kingdom,' she wrote to Elizabeth, 'and driven to such straits that, next to God, I have no hope but in your goodness.'

These terrible events in Scotland – saved only eight years earlier by Elizabeth's intervention from French domination and an enforced return to Rome – placed the English Queen in a grave dilemma. On the one hand she wished to succour her unfortunate cousin and restore her to her throne, for she regarded the rights and duties of anointed sovereigns, and their responsibility to God for the governance of their realms as sacrosanct and not to be impugned or abrogated by subjects. On the other hand – for, unlike Mary, she was ruled by her head and not her emotions – she needed for her people's safety to preserve the Scottish Reformation and maintain friendly relations with the Regent Moray and Scotland's new Protestant rulers. These were now all the more important to England's future as the guardians of Mary's infant son James VI – Elizabeth's own godchild and the next legitimate successor after Mary to the childless English throne. For these reasons, and, in view of the dangers threatening both countries from the religious-riven Continent, she dared not let her fugitive and unwelcome guest out of her keeping. There had long been a love-hate relationship between the royal cousins, the one – so much a Tudor, resenting the other's early attempt to impugn her legitimacy and claim her throne, the other – so much a Stuart, equally resenting the other's understandable reluctance to acknowledge her claim to the succession. But Elizabeth was profoundly shocked by the Scots' dethronement and imprisonment of their hereditary sovereign. 'They had no warrant nor authority by the law of God or man,' she wrote, 'to be as superiors, judges or vindicators over their prince and sovereign, howsoever they do gather or conceive matter of disorder against her.' And when Mary indignantly declared herself guiltless of the crimes her rebellious subjects charged against her, she replied, 'O Madam! there is no creature living who wishes to hear such a declaration more than I, or will more readily lend her ears to any answer that will acquit your honour.'*

Ignoring, therefore, the protests of her Ministers and Council, who regarded Mary's presence as a threat to the realm's peace and safety, Elizabeth, though keeping her captive, treated her as an honoured royal guest, offering her the hospitality of her northern castles and hunting forests but declining to receive her at Court until she had been cleared of the charge of murdering her husband. Mary, however, indignantly demurred at the idea of her cousin adjudicating between her and her rebel subjects. But, assured by Elizabeth's promise to restore her to her kingdom, by force if necessary, should their charges against her be disproved, she acceded, reluctantly, to an English Commission of Enquiry being set up in York in October 1568. Almost at the same time, she began to make secret overtures through the Spanish ambassador to King Philip and the Pope, offering, with the help of a foreign invasion, to raise the English North in favour of a restoration of the Catholic Faith. For, ignoring her cousin's warning at her first coming that 'those who have two strings to their bow may shoot stronger but rarely shoot straight,' and indignant at her captivity, Mary could not refrain from intriguing to regain her freedom and lost power, using her fatal charm to win men's hearts to her ends. And as northern England – remote, underpopulated and backward-looking – was still by far the most Catholic part of the country, she soon became, as Elizabeth's ministers had feared, a romantic rallying point for all who longed to restore the old Faith under a Catholic, instead of a Protestant, Crown. Nor, with her sanguine, emotional nature, did she find it difficult to persuade those of her English neighbours of a like way of thinking to share her hopes.

---

* Sir John Neale, *Queen Elizabeth*, 163, 168.

Chapter Two

O PEACEFUL ENGLAND

'In her days every man shall eat in safety
Under his own vine what he plants; and sing
The merry songs of peace to all his neighbours.'

Shakespeare

It so happened that in the fall of the year in which Mary sought refuge in England the relations between that country and Spain – in the past traditional allies against their common enemy, France – were coming under growing strain. For a clash of interest had lately arisen in two quarters gravely affecting both England's trade and her people's feeling. One was in the Netherlands – the rich industrial and commercial community of cloth towns in the continental alluvial plain facing the Thames estuary which from time immemorial had provided the country's, and London's, principal trading outlet to Europe. Formerly part of the powerful independent Burgundian dukedom – 'waterish Burgundy' as the greatest of Elizabethan poets was to call it – it had passed by marriage into the Spanish-Hapsburg dynastic empire of Charles V and, on his abdication in 1555, to his son, Philip II of Spain. Indeed, it had been the Emperor's hope when he married Philip to his niece, Queen Mary Tudor, that England and the Netherlands – the favourite province of his vast empire – would henceforward be joined politically, as well as commercially, in an oceanic dominion presided over by the Spanish crown.

Instead, however, of becoming more closely linked to another outward-looking trading community like itself, after Mary Tudor's death the seventeen loosely joined provinces and three hundred thriving walled cities and towns of the Netherlands – stretching for more than two hundred miles along the shores of the German Ocean from Friesland in the north to the French frontier and inland Luxembourg in the south – passed with its three million industrious peoples to the exclusive control of a remote Spanish sovereign. King Philip's character and outlook, unlike that of his internationally minded father, had been formed by the stark, uncompromising Iberian land

45

in which he had grown up and to which, after his father's death, he withdrew, never again to leave it. And as, like his country, he was intensely and devotedly pious and, by temperament and occupation, a dedicated bureaucrat with a passion for uniformity, he and his distant easy-going Netherlander subjects soon found themselves at loggerheads. More particularly in their northern, trading seaboard a growing number of them disagreed with their distant Iberian King over the matter dearest to his devout and perfectionist heart, Catholic religious orthodoxy.

For the opening years of Philip's reign had coincided with a rapid escalation of heretic preaching in the Netherlands, as in the adjoining territories of the Holy Roman Emperor, Germany and France. They also witnessed, with the final conclusion in 1564 of the Council of Trent, the full force of the new Catholic Counter Reformation against the subversionist and divisive doctrines of Luther, Zwingli and Calvin. In no country was that great campaign for the Faith welcomed more whole-heartedly than in Spain. Her whole history for five centuries had been a continuing crusade to win back by the sword formerly Christian lands from Moors and infidels. For, to a Spaniard, a heretic and an infidel were one.

Though still predominantly Catholic, particularly in its richer southern provinces, the peoples of the Netherlands, who were of several races, cultures and languages, did not feel in this way. When a Flemish heretic, who had trampled on a consecrated wafer, had his offending hand and foot wrenched off by red-hot irons and his tongue torn out before being publicly roasted to death in chains over a slow fire, the citizens of Bruges and the Estates of the Catholic province of Flanders petitioned their Spanish sovereign against the Inquisitor who had inflicted such a punishment. And the country's leading princes and nobles, many of whom had served and fought under Philip's father, and even his own Regent, his illegitimate half-sister the Duchess Margaret of Parma, pleaded for less drastic methods of securing religious orthodoxy and uniformity in such a comparatively sophisticated and civilized society as Renaissance Burgundy – the land of Memling and Van Eyck.

But to the autocrat Philip, in his remote and austere Castilian hinterland, such appeals smacked of treasonable weakness, putting those who made them in the category, if not of heretics, of rebels. And when such criminal, as he viewed it, leniency on the part of the provincial authorities resulted in a fanatic minority of Protestant zealots breaking into Antwerp Cathedral and other churches to smash sacred statutes, pictures and ornaments as idolatrous and superstitious baubles, the 'Most Catholic' Majesty, as Philip's proud title was, resolved to teach the Netherlanders, leaders and people alike, a much-needed lesson they would never forget.

During the summer of 1567, when the marriage of Mary Queen of Scots with her husband's murderer was being expiated by her dethronement and imprisonment, armed with King Philip's commission as Captain General of the Netherlands a man as stern and inflexible as himself and far more ruthless and cruel – the Castilian grandee and veteran military commander, the Duke of Alva – was marching north through the Mount Cenis pass at the head of an army of 10,000 crack mercenaries from Spain's Italian provinces to discipline the Low Countries. Reaching Brussels on August 22nd, he wasted no time. Within a fortnight he had arrested the country's two leading Catholic princes – one of them, Count Egmont, the Stadtholder of Flanders and hero of the great Spanish victories against the French of St Quentin and Gravelines. At the same time he instituted a court of summary justice, with overriding powers of life and death, entitled the Court of Tumults, but soon to be known popularly as the Court of Blood. Through it he inaugurated a reign of terror, under which hundreds of Netherlands nobles perished on the scaffold or were sentenced to imprisonment. Meanwhile Spanish garrisons were installed in every provincial capital to enable the Inquisition to carry out its work of detecting and eradicating heresy in its torture chambers and dungeons and at the public stake fires of its *autos da fe* and *braseros*, unimpeded by any manifestations of public opinion. The sole expression of feeling permitted the public was fear.

Stunned at first by the magnitude of the calamity which had befallen them, the unwarlike peoples of the Low Countries watched in horror the extinction of their provincial liberties as the iron Spanish military autocrat sent to rule them abrogated, in the name of royal and religious uniformity, every time-honoured and customary right. But in May 1568, the month in which the Queen of Scots fled to England from the wrath of her subjects, a rising, impelled by desperation, broke out against the alien tyrant under the leadership of William Prince of Orange – the one magnate who, by leaving the country, had escaped Alva's initial arrest. Though joined by his brother, Count Louis of Nassau, it was short lived and mercilessly crushed by the Spanish army of occupation. Meanwhile thousands of

47

helpless Protestants – for the most part humble artisans and craftsmen – fled by sea to the only refuge open to them, England, their old commercial customer and supplier. Their coming, and the pity aroused by their plight, caused a wave of popular feeling against Spain and Catholicism. So did the dislocation brought about by the persecution to England's long-established trade-links with the Netherlands. Of particular concern to the Queen and her Ministers was the disastrous effect it had on the highly sensitive money-market of Antwerp – then Europe's chief banking centre – on which the English Government, like most other governments at the time, depended for credit and supplies of specie.

That December a convoy carrying bullion from Genoese bankers, urgently needed for the payment of Alva's army in the Low Countries, was scattered by storms and took refuge in Plymouth and other south coast ports from the pirates and privateers swarming in the English Channel as a result of a new outbreak of religious civil war in France. Itself short of bullion through the collapse of the Antwerp money-market, the English government refused to allow the gold to proceed while they entered into negotiations with the Genoese bankers, whose property it legally was until delivered to its Spanish borrowers, with a view to borrowing it for themselves. This high-handed action had the dual effect of precipitating a furious complaint from Spain and ultimately, of causing a mutiny among Alva's mercenary troops. But it so happened that at that moment Elizabeth was able to counter it by complaining of a far more high-handed action against her subjects and property by Philip's officers on the other side of the Atlantic.

For another cause of difference between the two countries had arisen four thousand miles away, where Spain and her Castilian king's and people's intolerance in matters of faith was matched by their equal rigidity in matters of commerce. Their claim to a monopoly of all trade with America and the Indies, beyond the arbitrary ocean line drawn by the papal grant of 1493 to Spain and Portugal, had always been contested by England even before she repudiated the papal authority. For it constituted a threat to interests even more vital to her than the trade and markets of the Netherlands. And that Christmas news reached England of a shocking outrage committed by a Spanish Viceroy and his troops against English seamen and traders in the harbour of San Juan de Ulloa, the chief port of colonial Mexico.

Earlier that year John Hawkins, a thriving shipowner and merchant of Plymouth, had sailed for the West Indies with ten small ships, two of them owned by the Queen, bearing a consignment of negro slaves from the Guinea coast for sale to the Spanish colonists in the Caribbean, who, needing labour for their plantations, offered a ready and remunerative market for them. It was the third of such voyages made by him since 1562, when, learning, while trading with the Spanish Canaries, of the colonists' demand for slave labour, he had followed up his father's, William Hawkins's, pioneer voyages of twenty years earlier to the Guinea coast of Africa, in search of gold and ivories. Breaking into this far more lucrative trade and purchasing from local chieftains and slave-raiders a consignment of negroes – the cheapest and easiest-come-by commodity of that barbarous continent, where slave-owning, slave-trading and slave-raiding had flourished from time immemorial – he shipped them across the Atlantic to the Caribbean and Spanish Main. No one at the time could see anything wrong in this inhuman traffic, least of all the Spanish settlers, whose demand for merchandise from the Old World was constantly being frustrated by a dilatory imperial bureaucracy's rigid and jealous regulation and control of all traffic across the Atlantic. It was the Spanish Crown's greedy and pious enforcement of its papal monopoly of all seas and lands beyond the invisible 'Line', drawn by Pope Alexander VI three-quarters of a century earlier, which clashed with the rights and needs of a seafaring nation whose livelihood depended not, like Spain and Portugal, on the gold and silver, jewels and spices of America and Indies, but on the speculative and perilous profits of exchanging and transporting by sea surplus goods between those who made them and those who needed them.

In September 1568, having disposed of his cargo of slaves and made a highly profitable mutual exchange of goods with the Spanish colonists – whose easy-going local officials turned a blind eye to this forbidden but providential commerce with interlopers and heretics – Hawkins, his ships battered by a storm in the Gulf of Mexico, put into San Juan de Ulloa to refit and re-victual before returning to his native Devon. It so happened that he had hardly anchored in the harbour, when the annual Plate Fleet arrived from Spain with the new Viceroy of Mexico aboard, Don Martin Enriquez. Unlike the colonial authorities, this stately functionary could not be expected to overlook any open breach of his royal master's orders. Though much inferior in tonnage and numbers, the superior gunnery of the English traders could have enabled Hawkins to keep the newcomers out of the port until he was ready to leave it. But, deeply conscious that he claimed to hold a commission from his Queen and even to be acting in the interests of King Philip himself – who only ten years earlier had been England's titular king and closest ally – and that any act of violence, even in self-defence, could involve war for his royal mistress who had strictly enjoined him not to harm any Spanish subject, he made a pact with the Viceroy. In return for allowing his fleet to enter the harbour, he secured from him an undertaking that the English ships should be allowed to complete their revictualling in peace before proceeding on their way home.

Having gained admission to the port, instead of honouring his word the Viceroy secretly summoned by night a thousand soldiers from the nearby garrison of Vera Cruz and used them to surprise and board the English trading vessels, whose crews they imprisoned and sent to the galleys or dungeons of the Inquisition. Only two ships managed to escape, the little *Judith* of 50 tons, whose commander, a twenty-five year old salt named Francis Drake, by fine seamanship cleared the harbour in time and returned home with her crew intact, and the scarcely larger *Minion*, a Queen's ship, which evacuated two hundred men, including Hawkins himself, from his doomed flagship. But, bereft of food and water on the long voyage home, after indescribable sufferings only fifteen survivors reached England in January 1569.

That act of black treachery – and the subsequent torture and martyrdom of helpless Protestant seamen – aroused feelings among their fellow west countrymen against Spain and the Roman Church even more bitter than those of the Londoners who had witnessed the Smithfield fires. Coming on top of the pitiful flood of fugitives from Alva's persecutions and Elizabeth's retention of the bullion intended to pay his mercenaries, its immediate impact was to exacerbate relations between England and Spain. The latter placed an embargo on English trade with the Netherlands and arrested English traders and travellers, while the islanders retaliated in kind. It was an exchange in which the latter were much the gainers, since, with their strategic position athwart Spain's sea communications with the Netherlands, they were able to play havoc with all Spanish merchandise and shipping using the English Channel. And the seamen and privateers of the southern and western ports reaped a rich harvest for themselves from doing so.

★   ★   ★

It was under these circumstances that the captive Queen of Scots was able to repay the shelter Elizabeth offered her from her rebellious Protestant subjects by fomenting a rebellion of her English hostess's Catholic ones. 'Tell the Ambassador,' she informed an emissary from that diplomat, 'that if his master will help me, I shall be Queen of England in three months, and Mass shall be said all over the country.' And as the warlike Catholics of the North flocked to pay court to this romantic and beautiful exile of their own Faith, herself the heir presumptive to the English throne, rumours of coming change began to circulate from mouth to mouth throughout the fells and dales of Westmorland, Yorkshire, Durham and Northumberland. Among those who succumbed to her charm was the chairman of the Court of Enquiry set up to investigate the criminal charges brought by the Scots against her – the Duke of Norfolk. To him – England's sole remaining duke and a member of the Queen's Council – Mary secretly addressed affectionate letters implying that, if her marriage with Bothwell could be set aside, he might aspire to her hand. Warned by her ministers' intelligence agents of the purport of this clandestine correspondence, Elizabeth summoned Norfolk to Court. When he failed to take the chance offered him of making a full disclosure, she clapped him into the Tower.

That autumn it became known that, anticipating an English rising in Mary's favour, the Pope was preparing to pronounce Elizabeth excommunicate, releasing her Catholic subjects from the duty of obeying her. Before he could do so, the feudal North was already in arms. The church bells were rung backwards – the ancient summons to war of the Marches – and the Catholic farmers and shepherds of the dales turned out in their thousands with their fathers' arms. Too late to draw back from the treasonable brink into which Mary's tragid beguilements had led them, the earls of Northumberland and Westmorland, with their armed Percy and Neville retainers, marched into Durham on November 14th. At their head was the aged Catholic Sheriff of Yorkshire, Richard Norton, bearing the banner of the Five Wounds. It was the Pilgrimage of Grace of thirty years earlier over again. And, while already removed in haste from Bolton Castle in Wensleydale to Tutbury Castle in Staffordshire, Mary was hurried away still further south to Coventry, the rebels heard Mass in Durham Cathedral, burnt the English prayer book, and, seizing the port of Hartlepool for Alva's hoped-for landing, marched on York.

Yet though rumours circulated in London that Alva had sworn to pay his soldiers their arrears in Cheapside and make England's heretic Queen hear Mass in St Paul's at Candlemas, the rising collapsed as quickly as it had begun. Throughout the entire south and midlands the forces of the Crown and countryside, both Catholic and Protestant, remained solid in loyalty. Within a month of taking up arms the northern rebels, hopelessly outnumbered, dispersed without giving battle, their leaders flying across the Border to join Mary's sympathizers in southern Scotland. It was the last tragic chapter in the long feudal saga of Neville and Percy. The Earl of Northumberland, captured by the Scottish Protestants, was handed over to justice in England and beheaded, while his fellow earl of Westmorland, finding no shelter in Scotland, fled abroad and lived out his life in exile as a pensioner of Spain. There was a brief recrudescence of fighting early in 1570, when another great northern magnate, Leonard Dacre, having failed to come out with his tenants in November owing to a personal quarrel with Norfolk, belatedly rose in the New Year. But he received his quietus at the battle of the Gelt on February 19th, when the Queen's cousin, Henry Carey, Lord Hunsdon, encountered him with only half his numbers and totally routed him. 'I much doubt, my Harry,' Elizabeth wrote to the gratified victor, 'whether that the victory were given me more joyed me, or that you were by God appointed the instrument of my glory; and I assure you that for my country's good the first might suffice, but for my heart's contentation the second more pleased me.'

Nor did any invasion from Spain follow the rising. For neither Alva in the Netherlands nor his distant master in Madrid were prepared to entrust an army to the mercy of the elements and of English seamen so long as England herself stood four square in loyalty to her Queen. And, as the rising had failed and there was no invasion, the Pope's excommunication of Elizabeth, when it came in February 1570, proved a damp squib. And though that January Elizabeth and the Scottish Protestants suffered a setback when the Regent Moray was assassinated, the Queen, striking swiftly back, put new heart into the adherents of the boy king, James VI and the Calvinist reformers. Using the flight of the rebels across the Border as a pretext, she sent a force after them under the President of the North, the Earl of Sussex. It struck such terror throughout the Marches that, from the great English border fortress at Berwick to the Solway Firth, a peace, such as that restless region had scarcely ever known, reigned there for months. As a historian of the raid put it, it was 'the honourablest journey that ever was made into Scotland, with so few men, with so safe a return'.

The romantic Scottish Queen's attempt to plunge England into the murderous internecine religious strife sweeping the Continent had ended in failure and tragedy for her adherents. For, under the martial law which accompanied the pacification of the wild dales and moors of the North, hundreds perished on the gallows or suffered forfeiture and exile.* But it did not end either the Queen of Scots' intrigues to win her freedom and, with it, the English crown, nor the persistent refusal of her royal cousin to accede to the now almost universal demand of her ministers and people for her death.

'Among those operating on Mary's behalf that summer was a Florentine banker named Roberto Ridolfi. Well known socially in City, and even government circles, as an undercover papal intermediary, he had been a principal party in secretly smuggling the Pope's bull of excommunication into England. An ardent Catholic, he entered that summer into a clandestine correspondence with Norfolk, whom, giving him the benefit of the doubt as to the degree of his involvement in the late rising, the Queen had just released from the Tower. Persuading that nobleman, to whom Mary was still writing love-letters, to resume his hopes of marrying her, he unfolded a wild plan of his own devising, blessed by the Pope and favoured, so he assured him, by King Philip, his ambassador in England, and Alva. Under this a Spanish invasion force of 10,000 men from the Netherlands was to land at either Portsmouth or Harwich, and, overturning the government, place Mary on the throne with Norfolk as her consort and king.

Armed with the names of forty supposedly dissatisfied peers who, in his sanguine belief, would take up arms for Mary, this self-important financier set off in the spring of 1571 for the continent to prime Alva, the Pope and the King of Spain. With his hands fully employed eradicating rebellion and heresy in the Netherlands, Alva, a military realist, had no intention of risking his army in an invasion of England until either Elizabeth was dead or a successful rising of Mary's followers had first secured, and held for forty days, a bridgehead for his troops. With his plotter's list of names of potential rebels, Ridolfi struck him as a dangerous babbler. But the Pope and Philip proved of

* Two centuries later, drawing on local memories of the Northern Rebellion, Wordsworth enshrined the tragic fate of the ancient Norton family in his poem, *The White Doe of Rylestone*.

more credulous stuff, and at Madrid Ridolfi proposed that, as a prelude to the rising and invasion, Elizabeth should first be assassinated. All this he reported at length in elaborately concealed cypher letters to his fellow conspirators in England, including Mary and Norfolk, who, dazzled by the hope of exchanging a ducal coronet for a matrimonial crown, weakly lent himself to Ridolfi's temptingly ambitious but perilous dream. But the watchful and omnipresent spies of Cecil's intelligence network and that of its unresting organizer, Francis Walsingham, intercepted Ridolfi's messengers and eventually broke his cyphers, the keys to which were found hidden under the tiles of Norfolk's London house. The duke's arrest and return to the Tower followed immediately, and in January 1572 he was tried by his peers in Westminster Hall, found guilty and sentenced to death for treason.

A popular figure at Court and in the country, and, as England's solitary duke and, though himself only lately a convert to Rome, head of the nation's leading Catholic family, Norfolk survived for a further five months before the merciful and temporizing Queen could finally bring herself to sign his death warrant. 'The Queen's Majesty,' wrote Cecil – now promoted to the peerage as Lord Burghley – 'hath always been a merciful lady, and by mercy she hath taken more harm than by justice, and yet she thinks that she is more beloved in doing herself harm – God save her to his honour long among us.' It took the combined pressure of her anxious Council and of a new Parliament, which met in May 1572 to make special provision for her safety, to bring her to the sticking point and let Norfolk die, the first noble of the reign to perish on the scaffold.

Yet, though horrified by the Ridolfi plot, the entire country clamoured for Mary's death – 'the bosom serpent,' as Walsingham called her – nothing could bring Elizabeth to sacrifice her to public clamour. She agreed to her closer surveillance and restraint in the northern castles where, under the watchful eye of one nobleman or other, she kept her phantom court, and for the moment – though not permanently – the English Queen abandoned the hope of restoring her, either alone or in conjunction with the boy King James, to the Scottish throne. But when, in the summer of 1572, a joint committee of both Houses of Parliament, specially summoned to make provision for Elizabeth's safety, petitioned for Mary's immediate death, describing their request as 'a call and cry to God of all good subjects against the merciful nature of the Queen,' they were met by a firm royal refusal. It was couched in terms of such loving gratitude for their care and loyalty that one member even proposed voting her thanks for the good opinion she had of them. Frustrated in its attempt to bring in an Act of Attainder against Mary, Parliament passed a bill, depriving her of all claim to the English throne and making it a treasonable offence for anyone to advocate it, even legalizing lynch law against her if she should ever again plot against Elizabeth's life or throne. But the compassionate Queen again refused to give it the royal assent.

★   ★   ★

The country's rage against Mary was the measure of Elizabeth's popularity. This now seemed boundless. To Protestants abroad, struggling against the terrifying force of the persecuting Counter-Reformation or flying in their thousands to England for shelter, the Queen appeared as a Deborah raised by God to save his faithful.★ To her own people her frail, irreplaceable, indomitable life alone stood between them and a repetition of the horrors which had overwhelmed the continent – the massacres, rapes, tortures and burnings of a brutal soldiery and a merciless Inquisition. After the defeat of the Northern Rebellion the anniversary of Elizabeth's accession – November 17th – was kept as a day of national thanksgiving and rejoicing, with pealing church bells, feasts and bonfires – the answer of a free people to the Pope's excommunication and anathemas and the Smithfield fires of the divisive Marian past. 'We have cause daily to praise God,' the Speaker of the House of Commons addressed her, 'that ever you were given us!'

For in fourteen years of ruling, in the face of all perils and problems, Elizabeth had made a united nation. And, as it grew in wealth and strength, it was becoming a confident one. To make it so had from the start been her aim and that of her ministers. Chosen by her from the new, non-feudal middle class, their strength, like hers, lay in their understanding of England and of its people's needs and feelings. High and resplendent office the Queen conferred on her favourites and on the figureheads of the old aristocracy, but real power she reserved for a little group of men who made statecraft and her service the business

★ The great Protestant reformer, Zwingli's successor at Zurich, Henry Bullinger, described her as a virgin-queen, beloved of God, whose wisdom and clemency, felicity and dexterity were a marvel and a model for all Christian princes. *Cambridge Modern History II*, 598.

of their lives. Their fidelity she ensured by seeing that they were committed up to the hilt to the success of her policies, and by rewarding them enough – but no more – to raise in them the expectation of further favours to come.

At their head was the great Secretary of State, William Cecil, who for forty of the forty-five years of the reign, until his death in 1598, was the Queen's *fidus Achates*. On the death of the old Marquis of Winchester in 1572, she made him Lord Treasurer. In him, though she gave him many anxious moments, she reposed a noble trust; her 'spirit', she called him. No prince in Europe, she once said, had such a counsellor as she had of him.* 'This judgment I have of you,' she had told him on his appointment to her Council, 'that you will not be corrupted with any manner of gift, and that you will be faithful to the State, and that without respect of my private wish you will give me that counsel that you think best, and that, if you know anything necessary to be declared unto me of secrecy, you shall show it to myself only, and assure yourself I will not fail to keep taciturnity therein.' Never was mutual trust better justified.

At the start of the reign, faced by the bankruptcy of the Treasury and the country's almost total defencelessness, the Queen's and Cecil's first care had been to buy from abroad the arms and munitions it so desperately needed, and to restore the purity of the currency, debased by the dishonourable clippings of the last three reigns. To restore public confidence in the medium of exchange, they called down the value of all the base money minted in the past fifteen years and issued in its place a completely new silver currency. In both operations they were aided by the genius and immense experience of the Crown's financial agent at Antwerp, Sir Thomas Gresham – a man of infinite resource after Elizabeth's own heart. 'As the exchange,' he wrote to her, 'is the thing that eats out all princes to the whole destruction of their common weal if it be not substantially looked into, so likewise the exchange is the chiefest and richest thing only, above all others, to restore your Majesty and your Realm to fine gold and silver, and is the means that makes all foreign commodities and your own commodities with all kinds of victuals good cheap, and likewise keeps your fine gold and silver within your Realm.'†

Operating from Antwerp – before Alva's persecutions the financial centre of Europe – by foresight, meticulous attention to detail and

* *Hist. Mss. Com. Salisbury Mss. II*, 145.
† cit. A. L. Rowse, *The England of Elizabeth*, 121.

unfailing punctuality in meeting the Crown's obligations, Gresham, with the Queen's backing, brought down the rates of interest, at which English governments had been forced to borrow, from thirteen and fourteen per cent to half and less than half that rate. Other European rulers with far larger resources, as a result of their procrastination in repaying, were forced to go on borrowing at ruinously high rates. 'It will not be a little spoken of through all the world,' Gresham noted proudly, 'that Her Majesty in her wars doth make payment of her debts, when neither King Philip, the French king nor the King of Portugal in peacetime payeth nothing, who oweth no small sums of money.'* It was his contention that the Queen should borrow, not from foreigners, but from her own subjects, 'whereby,' he claimed, 'all other princes may see what a Prince of power she is.' It was a situation which he did much in his lifetime to bring about. Before Alva's arbitrary taxes and the sack of Antwerp by his unpaid soldiery had driven its bankers and capitalists to seek in Protestant London a new and more secure international money and credit market, Gresham had built at his own expense an English Bourse or Exchange in Lombard Street, crowning it with his crest of the frugal and industrious grasshopper. Here, in the year after the Northern Rising, the Queen, after dining with him in his magnificent Bishopsgate mansion, caused her heralds to proclaim the new institution he had created – the Royal Exchange – to the sound of trumpets, so setting her seal on a process which in the fullness of time was to make the City of London the financial capital of the world.

With the economy operating now on a sound monetary basis the royal and Cecilian policy was to encourage every activity which could strengthen a small nation dependent, in a world of vast Powers, on quality rather than quantity. It rested on a recognition that England's real wealth lay in the character – the virtue, integrity, industry and enterprise – of her people. Building on its natural resources of corn, wool, timber, coal and iron and its strategic position athwart northern Europe's ocean trade-routes, Cecil sought to make England self-sufficient, first in the means of defending itself and then of creating enduring riches.

Serving both these ends was his encouragement of fishing, the trade which bred and trained seamen to carry the nation's merchandise, both coastwise and across the broad seas, and, in war, to man the Royal Navy. With her long, deeply indented coastline, something

* J. W. Burgon, *Life and Times of Sir Thomas Gresham I*, 344–5.

like half her four or five million people depended for their livelihood, directly or indirectly, on the sea.★ To encourage fishing, after agriculture England's chief source of wealth, Cecil in 1563 increased from two to three the number of compulsory weekly fish days – originally established by his former chief, the Lord Protector Somerset, to replace the medieval Church's enforcement of Lent, Fridays and fast-days. 'Let the old course of fishing,' he wrote in a memorandum for Parliament, 'be maintained by the straightest observation of fish days for policy's sake, so the sea coast should be strong with men and habitations, and the fleet flourish.' With Ember days and Lent this policy ensured a protected market for fish for half the year, so providing, with the help of bounties on shipbuilding, a livelihood and training for the country's hardiest, most daring and adaptable sons, giving point and purpose to the old fishermen's song:

> 'The husbandman has rent to pay,
> Blow, winds, blow!
> And seed to purchase every day
> Row, boys, row!
> But he who farms the rolling deeps,
> Though never sowing, always reaps,
> The ocean's fields are fair and free,
> There are no rent days on the sea.'

In other directions Elizabeth and her ministers pursued the same protective, fostering and socially cohesive policy. The crying problems of unemployment and vagrancy – so menacing since the dissolution of the monasteries† – were met by a succession of Poor Laws. These, in the course of the reign, made the parish the unit of relief, dividing those in need of assistance into two classes. For those willing and able to work, but unable to obtain it, work and the necessary tools and working materials were to be found by the parish. The aged and impotent who were unable to work were to be supported by outdoor relief in their own homes. Those who could, but would not, work were, as in the past, to be branded as 'idle rogues and vagabonds', whipped and sent back to the parish of their origin or 'settlement', or, in larger units of population, to Houses of Correction, there to be made to work 'as a true man should do'. But the great principle of a

★ See C. V. Wedgwood, *The King's Peace*, 25.

† Before the Northern Rising of 1569 a national search for 'vagabonds' ordered by an alarmed Privy Council, resulted in the temporary apprehension by justices and constables all over the country of no fewer than 13,000 'masterless men'. H. D. Traill, *Social England Vol. III*, 550.

statutory provision for the poor – to be defined by Dr Johnson as the test of a civilized society – was by the end of the reign part of the permanent law of England. A compulsory poor rate, enforced by the Privy Council, levied by Justices of the Peace and payable, in proportion to their means, by all rate-payers, was the ultimate Elizabethan administrative legacy to England, comparable in importance to the supremacy of the King's courts and Common Law bequeathed to it by Henry II, and to the legislative power of the Crown in Parliament established by Edward I. No other country in Europe as yet possessed such a socially stabilizing institution. To operate it annually appointed Overseers of the Poor were added to the existing constables and churchwardens of the parish, whose responsibility to the Justices of the Peace appointing them was to provide work or relief for all who, through no fault of their own, were in need. Evolved, as was the English way, out of pragmatic experiment and proved experience, it was based, like the country's ancient jury system, on the knowledge, judgment and responsibility of the neighbourhood.

All this, like the Statutes of Labourers, Artificers and Apprentices, was part of Cecil's triple strategy of fostering and safeguarding employment by protective monopolies and tariffs; of ensuring quality of workmanship by a compulsory seven years' apprenticeship for all skilled crafts; and – in search of the ancient Christian ideal of the 'just price' – of regulating wages to meet the inflationary rise caused by the fortuitous influx of precious metals from the Spanish mines in America. Yet, such were the moderation and careful nature of the man and his royal mistress, that this paternalistic policy was combined with a far greater freedom from internal tolls and interference with trade than existed anywhere else in Europe, whose great rivers – Rhine, Rhone, Loire and Elbe – were studded with princely and feudal fiscal obstructions to the flow of commerce. Nor was any country so lightly taxed as Elizabeth's and Cecil's England. Like Gladstone long after them, they believed in letting the subjects wealth fructify in his own hands, realizing, in an age of corrupt and inevitably inefficient administration, that the individual was far more capable of augmenting his income and wealth for his own and the general good than any Government, however well-meaning.

Frugality in administrative costs and public expenditure – 'parsimony', as Elizabeth's critics called it, but, in effect, the only realistic way of combatting and checking corruption at a time when cheating the Crown was a universal practice – served the ends both of Cecil's patient, far-sighted, conservative and conserving policy and the Queen's natural bent and conviction. In this she so much resembled her frugal grandfather, Henry VII, and so little her extravagant father, Henry VIII. It was under the fostering care and with the encouragement of such a government – careful, prudent yet cautiously experimental – that, during the long Elizabethan peace of close on a quarter of a century, Englishmen of all classes, shaking off the lethargy, inertia and fears of the past, set themselves to make their island home a more comfortable one, and to win, by hard work and venturing, a higher standard of living for themselves and their children. Freed by their sovereign's tolerant and unifying ecclesiastical settlement from the ideological and religious frenzies which had formerly divided their country and which were now devastating the Continent, and sustained by a strong personal faith in God and the revealed and translated Scriptures, an insular Protestant people embarked, individually and collectively, on a prolonged period of growing prosperity and accumulation of wealth.

It was during Elizabeth's reign that the villages of southern England began to assume the appearance which was to characterize them for the next three centuries. Beautifully built farmhouses and cottages of half timber and brick or half-cast, and, in the limestone belt, of stone, began to take the place of the rude mud and wattle shacks of the medieval peasantry, while stone manor houses, with lattice-windows, porches, and panelled rooms, set among formal gardens, rose to partner the stone church towers of the older Catholic England. And, before the reign ended, much grander houses, many on the site of dissolved abbeys, took their place in the English landscape, built in the new classical style of the Italian Renaissance but with homely English differences, vast oriel windows and long galleries and gateways.

All the three main sources of English wealth – agriculture, seafaring and the cloth trade – flourished under the stimulus of individual ownership, freed from the shackles of the medieval clerical past, and within the framework of a stable and united kingdom whose ruler's objective was to make her people self-sufficient, confident and prosperous. In little more than sixty years after her accession, shipments of sea-coal to London from the Northumbrian mines multiplied roughly tenfold, the size of the country's merchant fleet five-fold, while, in the course of the reign, receipts from Customs on overseas trade doubled. 'If I should say the sweetest speech with the eloquentest tongue that ever was in man,' the Queen told Parliament, 'I were not able to express that restless and care which I have ever bent to govern for the greatest wealth.'*

Confident of being able to transmit their lands to their posterity, the owners of the monastic acres which had passed into private hands in the reign of Elizabeth's father and brother now embarked on long term improvements of the soil – liming, marling, composting, draining, hedging and enclosing. 'Their hearts, hands, eyes and all their powers,' John Norden, the map-maker, wrote of the improving squires and yeomen of the West Country, 'concur in one, to force the earth to yield her utmost fruit.' Nothing was wasted, everything used to enrich themselves and their families. Works like John Fitzherbert's *Book of Husbandry* and Thomas Tusser's rhyming *Five Hundred Points of good Husbandry* enjoyed a popularity second only to the translated Bible and Foxe's *Book of Martyrs*.

Nor was it only in agriculture that Englishmen sought to improve their environment and turn it to private and public enrichment. Released from the stultifying tyranny over thought and imagination of the medieval Church in decay – in its youth and prime the teacher and civilizer of Christendom – English minds in search of material betterment began to explore the possibilities of exploiting the physical phenomena of the land they inhabited. Elizabeth's reign saw the dawn – a first faint flush across the virginal rustic landscape – of an industrial revolution which in coming centuries was to transform England, and, following her lead, Europe and America. Interrupted after Elizabeth's death by the tragic struggle between Crown and Parliament, its course was resumed after the Restoration and the Revolution of 1688.

During her reign, aided by the credit facilities afforded by Gresham and his fellow financiers of London's new money-market, England began to take the lead in industrial technology, hitherto enjoyed by Germany – split and fragmented now by the terrible internecine strife of the Reformation and Counter-Reformation. Mining and processing not only iron and tin, as in the past, but also for the first time copper and brass, by the end of the century the output from the great monastic coalfields of Northumberland and Durham, stimulated since the Henrician dissolution by the enterprise and inventiveness of their new private owners, far exceeded that of the rest of the continent put together. Much of the advance in mineral technology

* J. E. Neale, *Queen Elizabeth*, 177.

and production was due to Elizabeth's and Cecil's determination to make the country, in view of the perils facing it, independent of foreign arms and armaments. Under their encouragement and that of the Navy Board, the foundries of Sussex and Kent made long-range guns whose quality gave England's armed trading ships and privateers an ascendency, ship for ship, over those of every other nation, while John Evelyn, the diarist's grandfather, given a monopoly for manufacturing gunpowder, supplied from his mills in the wooded Surrey valleys the force and flame which enabled them to survive and prevail in every sea of the widening ocean world.

The very intolerance and inhumanity with which, in the years while Elizabeth was cultivating her peaceful English garden, the rulers of Spain, France, Portugal and Austria suppressed heresy in their dominions helped, too, to enrich England, as thousands of skilled Protestant workers fled across the Channel and North Sea to seek refuge under the Protestant Deborah's protecting wing. They brought with them the jealously guarded secrets and mysteries of their lucrative crafts. To the hereditary skill of the native smiths, nailors, scythe and harness-makers of the Black Country and the tin-miners of Cornwall – 'as hard and diligent labourers in that kind of trade as are to be found in Europe,' as one of their countrymen put it – there was added, in the second decade of the reign, an ever-growing stream of Flemish, Dutch and French craftsmen flying from the persecuting bigots and zealots of the Counter Reformation. German steel workers were settled in Sussex and paper-makers at Dartford in Kent, Huguenot glass-makers in Sussex, Dutch sugar-refiners from Antwerp in London, and Dutch engineers, brought into Cambridgeshire to drain the vast watery, half-tidal Fens. Most beneficial of all to the country's economy were the thousands of Flemish weavers with their specialist skills who poured into the country to escape Alva's holocausts. They added a new impetus to England's thriving cloth trade, now widespread across the country from Yorkshire to East Anglia, and westwards into Gloucestershire, Wiltshire and Devonshire.

Much of the credit for the restored and flourishing state of the English economy belonged to Elizabeth's great minister, now Lord Burghley, who had so carefully nursed and nourished it. Yet it was the Queen who had appointed and sustained him, and without whose support he could have done little or nothing. And it was she who, by her dazzling and magnetic personality, and her love for her people, had infected the whole nation with her confidence, sense of purpose and awareness of its unity and destiny. Throughout her reign she continued the wooing of them begun at her accession and coronation and which, together with her diplomatic and political achievements, evoked such an astonishing response. For she did not govern only from cabinet, council and presence chamber, but from her people's hearts, and in this lay her strength and magic. Moving from palace to palace – from riverside Greenwich to Whitehall, Richmond to Hampton Court, and Windsor – she was continuously on display, seeing and being seen by her subjects and communicating to them 'the affability', as well as splendour and majesty, 'of their prince'. Every summer she went on progress, travelling with her enormous Court on horseback or raised high in an open litter. At the border of every county she was met by the sheriff and a train of local notables, and, wherever the common people thronged to see her, she would order her coach or litter to be taken to where the crowd was densest, there to address and talk familiarly with them. It was a dialogue between Queen and people, more informal but no less meaningful than between Queen and Parliament. And it was conducted in the language of love. At Coventry where the Mayor presented her with a purse of £100, she observed gratefully, 'It is a good gift, I have but few such, for it is £100 in gold.' 'If it please your grace,' replied the Mayor, 'it is a great deal more.' 'What is that?' asked the Queen. 'It is the faithful hearts of all your loving subjects,' was the answer. 'We thank you, Mr Mayor,' she replied, 'that is a great deal more indeed.'

At other times she would honour one of her richer subjects by staying in his house or castle – a costly favour, though one for which many vied. It was probably in the summer of 1575, at one of these elaborate sojourns, held at her favourite, Lord Leicester's newly rebuilt Kenilworth Castle – a visit which lasted three weeks and, attended by an entire countryside, was marked by the most splendid entertainments, masques and pageants, 'princely pleasures,' as they were called – that the young William Shakespeare, then a grammar schoolboy of eleven and son of an alderman and cornfactor of the neighbouring town of Stratford-upon-Avon, first set eyes on the Queen, before whom in her old age he was to act in his own plays in one or other of her royal palaces. And at the end of the autumn's progress, when she and her glittering Court returned to keep their wonted Christmas feast at Whitehall, they would be met by the Lord Mayor, aldermen and liverymen in their ceremonial finery, with the customary exchange of greetings, 'God save your Grace!' and 'God save my people!' amid jubilant shouting and the roll of drums and blare of trumpets.

'It is difficult,' Sir John Neale wrote in his great biography of Elizabeth, 'to convey a proper appreciation of this amazing Queen, so keenly intelligent, so effervescing, so intimate, so imperious and regal. She intoxicated Court and country, keyed her realm to the intensity of her own spirit. No one but a woman could have done it – and no woman without her superlative gifts.' 'Her mind,' recalled her godson, Sir John Harington, 'was oftime like the gentle air that cometh from the westerly point in a summer's morn; 'twas sweet and refreshing to all around. Her speech did win all affections, and her subjects did try to show all love to her commands. . . . Again she could put forth such alterations when obedience was lacking as left no doubtings whose daughter she was.' Sir Christopher Hatton was wont to say, 'The Queen did fish for men's souls, and had so sweet a bait that no one could escape her network.'

Such was this great woman. Her character was a series of amazing contradictions; indeed, there were few attributes, good or bad, which she did not in some measure possess. She could make supreme decisions at moments, and in the long run nearly always arrived at the right conclusion, and yet it often seemed to her ministers that she was incapable of making up her mind or of pursuing a consistent course. 'For in truth,' wrote Cecil, 'she was more than a man, and sometimes less than a woman.' 'Now I see,' said the carter whom she had kept waiting while the royal plans for a journey were changed and rechanged a dozen times, 'she is a woman as well as my wife!'

Her vitality was amazing. She would do business with her ministers for hours before breakfast, walk in garden and gallery with the learned, showing off her wide knowledge and remarkable linguistic attainments, hunt all day and feast with music and dancing till long into the night. Like all persons of outstanding personality, she had the power of imparting her vitality to others, and her Court was a very lively place. Poor old Sir Francis Knollys complained he could not sleep because of the Maids of Honour, 'that they used, when retired for the night, to frisk and hey about so'. Behind her fierce, energetic nature was a strong sense of humour, and good humour at that. 'Keep your arithmetic to yourself,' she bade the tactless divine who preached to her in her old age on the text, 'Teach us so to number our days.'

Though she could be queenly beyond dreams, she could at other times unbend and, without losing her majesty, abandon all formality. When, creating her favourite Earl of Leicester so that he could woo the proud Queen of Scots, she could not refrain at the height of the investiture from slipping her hand down his neck to tickle him. Once, in the midst of her court, a noble lord, bowing low before her, inadvertently let out a most uncourtly report and, ashamed beyond measure, fled the country in self-disgrace. Returning some years later after being assured that all was forgiven, he was received most graciously by the Queen, who held him long in conversation. As he was withdrawing, she called him back and whispered in his ear, 'My Lord, the fart's forgot!'

★   ★   ★

Greatest of all the Queen's services to England was the peace she gave her. When a divided Christendom was wracked by cruel ideological passions, within their watery bounds the English were at peace and unity. It was of this Elizabeth was most proud, and deservedly, for it was she who had saved them from the maelstrom by her diplomacy, her womanly dissimulation and cunning and, after her brief initial intervention in the religious wars of Scotland and France, her determination to spare both her people and purse from the waste, folly and destruction of war. She loved to receive, in the presence of foreigners, testimonies of the regard in which she and her Catholic subjects held one another, and when the outbreak of the Northern rebellion in 1569 for a moment shook her faith in her people's loyalty – before their overwhelming response, Catholic and Protestant alike, showed how little reason she had to doubt it – the French ambassador found her in tears.

Yet events in Europe were now moving fast, threatening the continued peace of her realm. In 1572, shortly after the exposure of the Ridolfi Plot, the people of the Netherlands once more rose in arms against Alva's intolerable tyranny and taxation. Powerless in the open field against the Spaniards' new weapon, the musket, but letting in the dykes to flood their land and taking to their boats, the sailors and fishermen of Holland and Friesland, calling themselves the Sea Beggars, made common cause with the Huguenot seamen of La Rochelle and the French western ports to wage merciless war against Spanish shipping in the North Sea and Channel. During the summer of that year they surprised and captured the outlying ports of Brill and Flushing – key to the Netherlanders' sea links with England and their best future hope of freeing themselves from an intolerable tyranny. For once again a wave of passionate sympathy for their co-religionists swept the English people, and hundreds of volunteers crossed the sea to serve under the Prince of Orange who had placed himself at the head of the rebellion.

That August, on St Bartholomew's Day, the menace of the Counter Reformation in arms took a new and unexpected turn in a massacre of Huguenot leaders and followers, gathered in Paris for the wedding of the young Protestant King of Navarre to the French Queen Mother's daughter, Margaret de Valois – a union which it had been hoped would end the ideological civil wars which had been tearing France apart and lead to a live-and-let-live religious settlement, not dissimilar to that which Elizabeth had achieved for England. Thousands perished in the holocaust, caused by a sudden hysteria and fanaticism, which, magnified by rumour, appalled English Protestants, whose own Queen, as part of her deliberate balancing act against Spain, had earlier that year negotiated a treaty of alliance with the French Queen Mother, Catherine de Medici, and her young son, Charles IX – a former aspirant to her hand.

Still more horrifying news for Protestant ears followed from the Netherlands where Alva and his soldiers now embarked on a campaign of deliberate terror and massacre. The town of Zutphen, which refused to admit his troops, was sacked and its inhabitants put to the sword. In his *Rise of the Dutch Republic* the historian, Motley, graphically described the fate which befell the people of Naarden when, hoping to escape the fate of Zutphen, its terrified burghers opened their gates to the Spaniards, only to be shot down without mercy.

'The town was then fired in every direction, that the skulking citizens might be forced from their hiding places. As fast as they came forth they were put to death by their impatient foes. Some were pierced with rapiers, some were chopped to pieces with axes, some were surrounded in the blazing streets by troops of laughing soldiers, intoxicated, not with wine but with blood, who tossed them to and fro with their lances . . . Those who attempted resistance were crimped alive like fishes and left to gasp themselves to death in lingering torture. The soldiers, becoming more and more insane as the foul work went on, opened the veins of some of their victims and drank their blood as if it were wine. Some of the burghers were for a time spared, that they might witness the violation of their wives and daughters, and were then butchered in company with those still more unfortunate victims.'

O PEACEFUL ENGLAND

It was small wonder that an English member of Parliament – contrasting the fate of his co-religionists in Europe with what he called the 'peaceable government of Her Majesty' who 'doth make us to enjoy all that is ours in more freedom than any nation under the sun at this day,' – spoke of 'depopulations and devastations of whole provinces and countries, overthrowing, spoiling and sacking of cities and towns, imprisoning, ransoming and murdering of all kind of people.'

The feelings aroused by these happenings made it more difficult for Elizabeth both to keep England out of war and preserve the balance of her own tolerant and unifying church settlement. As religious persecution abroad intensified, she was subjected to increasing pressure from the growing body of Puritan activists in the country, and their demands for extreme measures against what they regarded as 'papist' ceremonies and idolatry – vestments, crucifixes, candles, the wearing of surplices, caps and gowns, and even kneeling at Communion. But though she was unable to control the wave of iconoclastic vandalism which, at the instigation of fanatics, was robbing the country's parish churches, like the abbeys before them, of England's rich inheritance of medieval statuary, painting and art, she persisted in retaining in her chapel royal the outward forms of worship and ritual music with which she had been familiar since childhood. Nor would she suffer gladly what she described as 'domine doctors with their long orations' or their dogmatic insistence on the theological tenets of Calvinist Geneva and of the new Protestant 'popes' who had succeeded the former Roman ones. And though she put no obstacles in the way of those who volunteered for service under the rebel patriot leader, William of Orange, and so won experience in the military art – of which her realm had been so perilously lacking at the time of her accession – she did her best to mediate between her old admirer, King Philip, and his rebellious Dutch and Flemish subjects. While trying to persuade him to grant them the same religious tolerance that she allowed her own – a freedom of conscience nothing would induce that most devout of princes to allow – she would have no truck with proposals to deprive him of their allegiance, and rejected out of hand William's offer to her in 1575 of a protectorate or sovereignty of the revolted provinces. For what she sought for herself and her people was not dominion over the territories and subjects of a fellow sovereign, but merely peace and freedom to trade where trade had been before.

Instead, she fell back on the matrimonial diplomacy by which she

67

had sought to save her realm from the rival Catholic giants of France and Spain in the early years of her reign, setting the hopes and fears of one against the other. Now, as then, she had to keep a balance between two conflicting perils, doing what she could to help the struggling Netherland provinces recover their ancient liberties without goading her brother-in-law, King Philip, into war, while simultaneously discouraging their expansionist southern neighbour, France, from taking advantage of their revolt to free them from its old enemy, Spain, and absorb them itself. In pursuit of this aim, the preservation of the independence of the Low Countries – which was to remain a major principle of English foreign policy for the next three centuries – as soon as Elizabeth and her government had recovered from the shock of the Massacre of St Bartholomew's Day, which her more extreme Protestant subjects never did, she resumed her devious negotiations for a possible future marriage with a French prince. It was her way of insuring against both the risks that faced her and what to her was the biggest risk of all, the destructive and costly evil of war. And this in spite of the fact that she was now well into her forties and past the age when child-bearing was considered safe for a woman who had never borne a child. So that while in her twenties, when she had dangled the crown matrimonial before the fascinated eyes of Europe, her ministers and people, passionate to ensure their future safety by the birth of a suitable male heir to the throne, had viewed what Cecil called her 'prolonging and mincing' with ill-concealed impatience, they were now far from enthusiastic over the prospect of her marriage, especially as the foreign suitor favoured by her was a Catholic – though not a particularly devout one – with a bulbous nose and more than twenty years her junior. Her 'frog' she affectionately called him, and for nearly a decade until his death in 1584, the little Duke of Alençon – a younger brother of the French king and later, as Duke of Anjou, his heir – was, on and off, her official wooer, visiting England, first by proxy and then in person, and, with the dazzling prospect of its crown matrimonial before him, proving an eager and even, to her apparent delight, ardent one.

But by the time of his passing the great Queen had transformed her virginity, long used by her as an instrument of state, into a national patriotic emblem. Attended by every concomitant of romantic courtship and flowery bejewelled phrase, in which all her leading courtiers engaged, using the language of lovers to express their loyalty and adoration, the ageing royal vestal had become the inspiration of a resurgent nation. All her lovers, including her old and now elderly flame, Lord Leicester, were treated, and expected to behave, as devoted aspirants to her unattainable hand. In their exploits, her sailors, soldiers and explorers thought of themselves as her knights, serving an adored lady and mistress, and, when her favourites bestowed their attentions on – or married – anyone else, it was as suppliant lovers that they had to seek her forgiveness. 'How can I live alone in prison, when she is afar off,' wrote the bold adventurer, Sir Walter Ralegh, Captain of her Guard, after she had clapped him into the Tower for getting one of her Maids of Honour with child and, even worse offence in her eyes, marrying her; 'I that was wont to behold her riding like Alexander, hunting like Diana, walking like Venus, the gentle wind blowing her fair hair about her pure cheeks like a nymph, sometimes sitting in the shade like a Goddess, sometime playing like Orpheus.' In Edmund Spenser's romantic allegorical poem, *The Faerie Queene*, published in the fourth decade of the reign, she figured as Britomart, Queen of Chastity. To foreign Catholic onlookers, it almost seemed as though a nation of heretic iconoclasts had unconsciously reverted to the Mariolatry of their devout medieval forebears, who had been famed throughout Christendom for the honour they paid to the Virgin Queen of Heaven.

Chapter Three
CAPTAINS COURAGEOUS

While Elizabeth was still pursuing her aim of keeping her subjects out of the continental wars of religion, so enabling them to grow rich and strong, some of them were beginning – not wholly unbeknown to her – to enrich themselves by waging private war at sea on their own account, thousands of miles away on the other side of the Atlantic. Before Hawkins's three trading voyages to the West Indies, the English had made no attempt to enter the forbidden Caribbean through which the fabulous Spanish wealth of Central and South America poured into Europe. Though, even before Henry VIII's breach with Rome, they had refused to recognize the Spanish and Portuguese monopoly of the newly-discovered lands and oceans allocated by Pope Alexander VI, they had taken little advantage of the global opportunities offered to the countries of Europe's Atlantic seaboard. Apart from the hardy West Country fishermen who, in the wake of Cabot's discoveries, annually followed their Breton and Norman counterparts to the misty cod-haunted Banks of Newfoundland, English ventures outside European waters before the fifteen sixties had been mainly confined to the efforts of a few enterprising Bristol and Plymouth merchants. One of the latter, John Hawkins's father, William, had broken into the fringe trade of the Guinea coast, first opened up by the Portuguese navigators of the fifteenth century on their exploratory way round Africa and the Cape of Good Hope to the far golden treasures of Indian Goa and the spice islands. Some abortive attempts by London and Bristol merchants to find a way round the frozen northern shores of Russia to the fabled riches of Cathay, had led, following a shipwreck, to an overland journey to Moscow and the Kremlin by Hugh Willoughby, who had sailed with the ill-fated Richard Chancellor from the Thames five years before Elizabeth's accession. Still more remarkable were the adventures at the court of Ivan the Terrible of a humble agent of the Muscovy Trading Company – founded in 1555 to promote the sale of English cloth in Russia – one Anthony Jenkinson, an ancestor of the future Prime Minister, Lord Liverpool. His friendship with the terrifying Czar and his travels across the camel routes of central Asia to the Oxus, Caspian and Persia, peddling English wares in the markets of Astrakhan, Bokhara and Kasbin, was a saga of fairy-tale romance and successful sales promotion. Another Elizabethan bagman, John Newbery, travelling at risk of his life for his country's trade, crossed the Syrian desert in a camel caravan, went down the Euphrates to Babylon, reached Goa in India, where he was imprisoned by the Portuguese, escaped and, by way of Golconda, arrived at the court of the Great Mogul at Agra. His fellow traveller, Ralph Fitch, even got as far as Burma, Siam and Malacca.*

What English merchants in search of trade could do by land they could do far more effectively by sea. Following the loss to the French of their staple port of Calais, it was Spanish tyranny in the Netherlands impeding, and ultimately closing, their export of cloth through Antwerp, which forced them to seek new markets in the wider world opened up by ocean discovery. And their experience of navigating and building ships for the stormy Atlantic and North Sea waters round their shores fitted them even better for this than the brave Portuguese, Spanish and French mariners who had preceded them. For France, too, though its ambitious rulers' eyes were focused on European rather than American conquests, had also entered the ocean field before England, exploring the St Lawrence estuary and annexing its vast empty Canadian hinterland. Further south Huguenot dissidents had founded a colony in Florida – later destroyed by the jealous Spaniards – while French pirates of the same persuasion, carrying their warfare against Catholic shipping in the English Channel to the other side of the Atlantic, had taken to preying on Spanish coastal vessels in the Caribbean and Gulf of Mexico.

As the ports of Europe became increasingly closed to their trade, more and more English merchants and seafarers set out to break the

* A. L. Rowse, *The Expansion of Elizabethan England*, 169–70, 197–200.

economic blockade around them by seeking a passage to Cathay and the Indies through the frozen polar seas round northern Europe and America. And when the inexorable ice continued to bar them, during the second decade of Elizabeth's reign, 'like salmon leaping at a fall too high for them,' as one historian put it, they ultimately turned westwards and, flinging down the gauntlet, drove their cockle boats into the heart of the Spanish Caribbean and Main.

It was a young sea-captain of genius who first pointed the way. Son of a poor Protestant bible-reader who had left his native Devon for Kent to escape Catholic persecution, Francis Drake had learnt his seamanship as a boy in small coasting vessels in the stormy tidal waters of the Thames estuary, Dover Strait and North Sea. In his middle twenties, having taken service with his kinsman, John Hawkins – Plymouth's leading merchant and shipmaster – he had sailed under him on the ill-fated trading expedition to the West Indies which had ended in the disaster of San Juan de Ulloa, and from which, thanks to his quick wits and presence of mind, he had escaped unscathed, bringing his fifty-ton bark *Judith* and its crew safely back to Plymouth.

The experience left him with a burning hatred of Spanish treachery and cruelty and a resolve to avenge the fate of his companions in the dungeons of the Inquisition and recoup Hawkins's and his own losses by attacking King Philip's apparently impregnable but, as he was quick to see, strategically vulnerable transatlantic empire. After two exploratory voyages to the Caribbean, he sailed from Plymouth in the early summer of 1572 with two small ships of seventy and twenty-five tons, manned by seventy-three picked young seamen, including two of his own brothers. His destination was the Darien Isthmus, the narrow mountainous land-link across which – in mule-trains from Panama on their closed Pacific Ocean to the Atlantic port of Nombre de Dios – the Spanish conquerors and exploiters of South America carried the fabulous Peruvian treasures of silver, gold and jewels from the mines of Peru, and which subsequently a huge, heavily-armed plate-fleet from Spain bore back every year to Europe in order to finance King Philip's armies.

The sling with which this obscure English David armed himself for his duel with the Spanish Goliath was of minute size. Yet it was of the highest human quality. And in embarking on his one-man crusade against Spain, Drake took precautions against every foreseeable contingency. For it was one of his characteristics that, while ready to

73

challenge almost inconceivable odds, like England's other supreme sailor after him he never took risks until he had done everything possible to ensure success. It was this which gave him, and communicated to those under him, such immense confidence.

Drake was the first Englishman of England's great age of enterprise. Beginning in Elizabeth's reign and continuing until that of Queen Victoria, its hallmark was the belief that there was nothing which a man of courage and resolution, sustained by individual Christian conscience, might not accomplish if he were convinced it was his duty. There is no more amazing story than that of Drake and his seventy young seamen setting out in four small pinnaces, brought from England in sections and assembled by his ships' carpenters in a secret harbour on the Spanish Main which he had prepared as a base during an earlier visit. Landing before dawn, with drums beating and trumpets blaring, he and his handful stormed the fortified Spanish city of Nombre de Dios and all but succeeded in taking it. Then, when all hell broke loose as the sleeping town awoke, they advanced in two converging columns, amid volleys of musketry and the ringing of church bells, to the market place. Thence, though severely wounded, Drake led the way, first to the Governor's residence and then to the King's Treasure House where the silver and gold from the Pacific were stored. 'I have brought you to the Treasure House of the world,' he told his men; 'blame nobody but yourselves if you go away empty.'

But when they tried to break open the door, a sudden storm of tropical intensity descended, quenching the priming matches without which their muskets could not fire. While Drake was trying to rally them, he fainted from loss of blood. Attacked by growing numbers of Spanish soldiers – now recovering from their initial panic – the little band of Devonshire seamen, deprived of Drake's leadership and fearful of being cut off from their boats, carried their unconscious captain back to the waiting pinnaces and put off, defeated, for their hidden base.

Yet it was not in Drake's nature to admit defeat. As soon as he had recovered from his wound, having failed in his attempt to seize the treasure from under the noses of the garrison set to guard it, he resolved to obtain it another way. Living in the forest interior of the Isthmus were the half-caste descendants of the negro slaves whom the sugar planters of the Spanish Main had imported from Africa earlier in the century but whom they had treated so badly that they had escaped and, taking refuge in the jungle, intermarried with the Indian aborigines. Both, having suffered so much from the Spaniards, were relentless enemies of them and all their works.

It had been an attack on Nombre de Dios by the Cimaroons, as they were called, shortly before Drake's arrival that had caused its hitherto inadequate garrison to be reinforced and so brought about the failure of the English assault. Because of the reputation for friendliness and generosity he had won in his exploratory visits to the Isthmus and his habit of releasing, instead of killing, his prisoners, Drake was already known to the Cimaroons, and had no difficulty in forming an alliance with them against their hated foes and oppressors. Making a show of force, two hundred miles to the east, against the capital of the Spanish Main, Cartagena – from whose harbour he ostentatiously carried off two merchant ships, so leaving the enemy under the impression that he was on his way back to England – he completely vanished. Having found a new harbour and hiding place in the Bight of Darien, he spent the next five months there, keeping up the morale of his men by hunting and playing games, while living off the fat of the land from captured Spanish coasters. Meanwhile he perfected his plans for a joint operation with the Cimaroons, as soon as the winter rains should end, against the hundred-mile track from Panama to Nombre de Dios, along which the mule-trains bore the Peruvian treasure across the Isthmus to await the arrival from Europe of the annual Plate Fleet.

This time Drake planned his attack where he would be least expected, on the far side of the Isthmus, somewhere between the Pacific port of Panama and the little Spanish mountain garrison station of Venta Cruces, half way along the forest track to Nombre de Dios. Before laying his ambush he was taken by his allies to the highest point of the forest, where from a bower built in a giant tree he and his lieutenant and fellow Devonian, John Oxenham – 'silent upon a peak in Darien' – set eyes on the far Pacific Ocean, the first Englishman ever to do so. Then, having ascertained when the first treasure train was expected to leave Panama, with eighteen Englishmen and thirty Cimaroons he carefully laid his ambush.

Once more his plans, so meticulously prepared, miscarried. The shout of a drunken sailor, who had been fortifying his courage from a flask, aroused the suspicions of a passing horseman. Suspecting an ambush and keeping back the treasure, the captain of the convoy sent his baggage train ahead to spring the trap. Disappointed of his prey, in order to escape being caught between the troops coming up from Panama behind him and the Spanish garrison of Venta Cruces on the track ahead, Drake, with instant presence of mind and quick decision, 'plucking the flower, safety, from the nettle, danger,' led his men and the Cimaroons in a sudden surprise attack on the little hill town. Yet, having driven its defenders into the jungle, before making good his escape to the coast and his waiting pinnaces he restrained his half-savage allies from avenging themselves on the Spanish civilians, and chivalrously found time to visit and calm the fears of some Spanish ladies convalescing there.

By now the seventy-three men with whom he had left Plymouth ten months before had been reduced by wounds and jungle-fever to thirty-one. Yet he remained, as always, cheerful and determined to accomplish what he had come to do. 'Before I depart,' he had told a Spanish prisoner after the failure of his initial assault on Nombre de Dios, 'if God give me life and leave, I mean to reap some of your harvest which you get out of the earth and send into Spain to trouble all the earth.' And on the last night of March 1573, as yet another mule-train laden with gold and silver jingled through the forest, he achieved it almost at the gates of Nombre de Dios where he had begun. A chance encounter with the captain and crew of a Huguenot privateer, from whom he learnt of the Massacre of St Bartholomew, brought a timely addition of force, and together the English and their French fellow Protestants surprised and routed in open fight a strong escort of Spanish troops. The spoil they shared between them, it is now known from Spanish sources, amounted to £40,000 in the money of that day, or, at least two millions in ours.*

Drake had done what he had intended. For more than a year he had lived at the expense of the Spanish in the waters and forests of the Caribbean and had treated the authority of their government with contempt and, with his tiny handful of seamen, made their supposedly invincible military forces dance to his tune, eluding, like the legendary Robin Hood, all attempts to capture him. And, in the end, he had made Spain's rulers pay in full for their treachery at San Juan de Ulloa, seizing under their very noses the treasure he had come to take. Yet, though he knew he could expect no mercy if captured, he had waged his private war on the enemies of his country and religion by

* Writing in 1951, before the inflation of the past three decades, J. A. Williamson the historian of Elizabethan maritime expansion, reckoned it then as equivalent to a million. J. A. Williamson, *Francis Drake*, 46.

his own humane and chivalrous standards, taking no life save in open fight and showing courtesy and generosity to his captives, all of whom he subsequently released.

It was characteristic of Drake that, before he returned to England, he paid a final visit to Cartagena, where the Spanish plate fleet lay at anchor, and, with St George's Cross at his maintop and streamers flying, made a ceremonial cock of the snoot at the Goliath he had flouted and plundered. His subsequent arrival home at Plymouth, after a fifteen months' absence, on Sunday 9th August 1573, was a red-letter day in West Country history. As his ship, laden with treasure, anchored in the Cattewater, and the rumour ran round the town that Drake was home, everyone hurried to the waterside to greet the young hero, the congregation pouring out of St Andrew's church during sermon time, 'so filled with desire and delight to see him, that very few or none remained with the preacher!'

The value of the treasure which, with the help of his Huguenot partner, Drake had seized at gunpoint from Spain amounted to nearly a sixth of the then annual revenue of the English Crown;* and, of the half-share of it brought back to England, nearly a twelfth. At the time of his arrival Elizabeth was engaged in one of her diplomatic balancing acts, trying to negotiate a rapprochement with her royal brother-in-law of Spain, who, like her, was reluctant, when it came to the point, to commit himself to the unpredictable extremities and expenses of war. The heroic resistance being put up under William of Orange and the Protestant northern and coastal provinces of the Netherlands and their fierce 'Sea Beggars' to Alva's increasingly costly campaign of frightfulness, as well as the revulsion felt at it by many Catholics, had by now caused King Philip to contemplate a less drastic means of reducing his rebellious subjects. At the end of 1573 he replaced the pitiless and uncompromising duke by a gentler and more politic Viceroy, Don Luis Requesens. And this had awoken in Elizabeth hopes, never wholly dormant, that her fanatically devout brother-in-law might, after all, be persuaded to accept the reasonable compromise over the Netherlands she had so sensibly been proposing. It was scarcely, therefore, surprising that, in view of the indignant protests of the Spanish authorities who were demanding Drake's head, the triumphant end of the opening round of his private war with Spain was viewed with considerably less favour in the Queen's Council

* Estimated by Sir John Neale, including the amount raised by parliamentary and other taxation, at about £250,000 a year. J. E. Neale, *Queen Elizabeth*, 284.

77

than in his native Devon. For some months, for all his sudden accession of wealth, Drake found it advisable to disappear almost as completely as he had done in the palm-fringed shores of the Caribbean. And, though during the next three years many of his fellow countrymen, hoping to make their fortunes as he had done, set out on privateering expeditions of their own in that sea, Drake was not among them.

When he resurfaced in 1575 it was in command of a ship, the *Falcon*, on the coast of Ireland, where Walter Devereux, Earl of Essex, was trying to plant part of that chaotic land with English and Welsh settlers. Many of the leading West Country families – Grenvilles, Gilberts, St Legers, Carews, Courtenays, Raleghs and Champernownes – were engaged in the attempt to colonize and pacify the rebellious island, which was still in much the same state of perpetual tribal warfare and anarchy as England had been a thousand years before. But Drake's stay there was brief. Faced by evidence that the newly appointed Viceroy of the Netherlands, Philip's bastard half-brother, Don John of Austria – victor of the great Mediterranean battle against the Turkish fleet at Lepanto – was contemplating an invasion of England from Antwerp in favour of Mary Queen of Scots, whom he hoped to marry, and angered by the arbitrary seizure of a London merchant's ship in a Spanish port and by papal and Spanish intrigues in Ireland, Elizabeth had decided to teach her brother-in-law a lesson. And the means she chose was the self-confident little Devonshire sea-captain who had made a fortune and avenged his own and Hawkins's wrongs by plundering King Philip's forbidden Caribbean dominions.

It was the new Secretary of State, Sir Francis Walsingham – champion, with Leicester, of the war party in the Council and a fanatical Protestant – who introduced him to the Queen. The meeting was an immediate success, for the two, as has been said, were of a kind. 'Drake,' she is reputed to have told him, 'I would gladly be revenged on the King of Spain for divers injuries I have received.' What exactly was agreed between them is uncertain, for the full royal instructions for Drake's mission were never committed to paper. But he was to sail with the Queen's commission in command of a secret semi-official joint stock venture in which she herself, together with Leicester, Walsingham, Sir Christopher Hatton – captain of her Bodyguard – John Hawkins and Lord Howard of Effingham, the hereditary Lord Admiral, were all shareholders.

It was given out that the destination of the expedition was Egypt, to open a new overland trade in East Indian spices through the Turkish port of Alexandria, in rivalry to the existing Venetian land and Portuguese sea routes. Yet though the seamen and soldiers enlisting for the voyage were told this, the gentlemen volunteers, who flocked to serve under Drake with his Midas touch, were led to understand that the voyage's real objective was the discovery of a vast new southern continent – Terra Australis. Rumoured to be rich in gold, it was believed to lie somewhere south of the stormy straits into the Pacific Ocean which the great Portuguese circumnavigator, Magellan, had found and negotiated for Spain sixty years earlier. Owing, however, to their immense distance from Europe and their navigational dangers, no one had since used them, the Spanish masters of Peru preferring the far shorter overland route across the Panama and Darien Isthmus. Now, by following Magellan's course through these remote and perilous straits, Drake was to find and annex this undiscovered continent and its fabled riches for the English Crown.

It is doubtful, however, if either Drake or the Queen – both realists with feet firmly on the ground – set much store on this hypothetical continent, imagined by the Devonshire magnate, Sir Richard Grenville of Buckland Abbey, as part of his lifelong dream of planting a new English nation beyond the ocean. Dominating Drake's clear pragmatic mind was his memory of the calm, sunlit Pacific glimpsed with his lieutenant, John Oxenham, from the tree-top in Darien, and his prayer that God would 'give him life and leave to sail an English ship once upon those waters'. That, and the knowledge, garnered from the Cimaroons, that the Spaniards, secure in their monopoly of their supposedly inaccessible ocean, were shipping the mineral wealth of Peru up the Pacific to the Isthmus in unarmed vessels – for no naval cannon had yet been cast there – to finance the 'bloody steps' of their European armies' march to universal monarchy. And these included the future subjection of a heretic England, like the Netherlands, to the dungeons and purging stake-fires of the Inquisition.

Though it was the essence of the partnership between the Queen and her avenging corsair that she should be free to disown him if reasons of state demanded – a condition unquestioningly and proudly accepted by him – there seems no reason to doubt that all alternatives for the expedition were discussed between them, though not all were committed to paper. Among these were a voyage up a plunder-ripe

Pacific coast and the arrival of his little fleet off Panama, 4,000 miles north of the Magellan Straits, to help the Cimaroons and the English corsairs from the Atlantic, drive the Spaniards from the Isthmus, so compelling King Philip, deprived of his chief source of military revenue, to desist from his despotic courses in the Low Countries. Already John Oxenham had invested his share of the captured Darien treasure to equip a ship for the Isthmus and had sailed in it from Plymouth with fifty-seven men and equipment to build and launch a pinnace in the undefended waters of the Pacific – an intention of which Drake, who conferred with him before he left, was almost certainly aware.

It seems, however, to have been stipulated by the Queen that nothing about the possibility of Drake's attacking Spanish treasure in the Pacific should be communicated to Lord Burghley, who, though a staunch Protestant, was leader of the peace party in the Council which, as distinct from the war-hawks, Leicester, Walsingham and Hatton, wanted, like the Queen indeed herself, to avoid driving Spain into open war. It was also agreed between her and Drake that there should be no needless taking of Spanish life: she because she wished to give Philip as little grounds as possible for resorting to war, and Drake because, like her, he was by nature humane and, though he hated Spain, idolatry and the Inquisition, had no quarrel with individual Spaniards other than the Viceroy of Mexico. And though their ultimate objectives differed – hers a bargaining position of strength to make her stubborn brother-in-law see sense, his the defeat by the new ocean sea-power of an inflated Colossus whose wealth from the Peruvian mines was 'troubling all the earth' – their immediate aim was the same.

Yet the sling and stone with which the English David was once again preparing to challenge the Spanish Goliath seemed ridiculously small. It consisted only of Drake's flagship, the *Pelican*, of little more than a hundred tons with eighteen guns, the *Elizabeth* of eighty tons with sixteen guns, commanded by Captain John Winter – a nephew of the Queen's veteran Admiral-at-Sea, Sir William Winter – and three even smaller vessels, the *Marigold*, *Swan* and *Christopher*. With this minute force and a company of one hundred and fifty men and fourteen boys, Drake sailed from Plymouth on November 15th 1577. Driven into Falmouth by a storm and forced to return to Plymouth to refit, it was not till the middle of December that he finally got away from England. After watering on the Barbary coast and calling at the Cape Verde Islands, where an invaluable captured Portuguese pilot elected to join him, he was sixty-three days without sight of land before striking Brazil on April 5th. 'During which long passage where nothing but sea beneath us and air above us was to be seen,' recalled one of the company, 'our eyes did behold the wonderful works of God in his creatures, which He hath made innumerable, both small and great beasts, in the great and wide sea.' Afterwards the voyagers were becalmed in a dense fog on the coast of what today is the Argentine, where at one point, taking soundings in a dinghy, Drake himself was nearly lost. Here they encountered dancing giants and flocks of ostriches and were attacked by savages with poisoned arrows. Twice scattered by storms, it took the little fleet many weeks, beating against adverse winds and assailed by nameless terrors, before it was able to reassemble at the end of June, in the wild, desolate bay of St Julian, 10,000 miles from England. Here, sixty years earlier, Magellan had refitted before entering the Straits which bear his name, after quelling a mutiny and hanging two of its ringleaders.

Drake now faced the same experience. Among the gentlemen adventurers who had sailed with him was a former member of the Earl of Essex's household with whom he had become friends while serving together in Ireland. A courtier of distinguished manners, who had fought as a soldier in the Low Countries, Thomas Doughty belonged to a world of culture and sophistication which Drake, a simple provincial sailor, had never before encountered. With all his charm, however, like many courtiers Doughty was an adventurer and intriguer. Drake had trusted and loved him, but during the long voyage south had found his trust misplaced. For Doughty tried to undermine his authority, stirring up trouble between the gentlemen adventurers and the rough sailors they despised. While, amid the storms and darkness of a Patagonian midwinter, the expedition prepared for the passage of the Straits, Drake came to believe that his false friend was fomenting a mutiny with the intention of changing its destination or forcing it to return to England. Suspecting him of having revealed his and the Queen's secret to Burghley and, by doing so, alerted the Spaniards, Drake had him arrested and, impanelling a jury, tried and sentenced him to death for mutiny. Yet before Doughty paid the penalty for his treachery on an improvised block close to the remains of Magellan's gallows, the two old friends dined and took the Sacrament together, bidding each other farewell in

Christian reconciliation.

After the execution, Drake addressed himself to restoring the morale and discipline of his command, shaken as it was by doubts and factions. One day, when all hands were assembled for Sunday service, he announced that he himself would preach the sermon. Rating the sailors for their contempt of the gentlemen adventurers, and the latter for shirking the work of the ship, he continued, 'I must have the gentleman to haul and draw with the mariner, and the mariner with the gentleman. I would know him that would refuse to set his hand to a rope, but' – after a pause – 'I know there is not any such here.' Then he revealed the full purpose of the voyage, stressing its immense difficulties and dangers, and offered a ship to all whose hearts failed them and who wished to return to England. Then, as no one took advantage of his offer, he went on: 'You come, then, of your own will: on you it depends to make the voyage renowned or to end a reproach to our country and a laughing-stock to the enemy. Let us show ourselves to be all of a company.' Twenty years later Shakespeare – at that time still a Stratford grammar schoolboy – paraphrased Drake's sermon in the speech he put into the mouth of Henry V before Agincourt:

> 'What's he that wishes so? . . .
> Rather proclaim it, Westmoreland, through my host,
> That he which hath no stomach for this fight,
> Let him depart; his passport shall be made,
> And crowns for convoy put into his purse:
> We would not die in that man's company
> That fears his fellowship to die with us.'

On August 17th 1578, with his three fighting ships, *Pelican, Elizabeth,* and *Marigold,* the small fry having been broken up for firewood during the fleet's midwinter sojourn in the Patagonian wilderness, Drake entered the Magellan Straits. Before doing so, he renamed his flagship the *Golden Hind,* after the crest of Sir Christopher Hatton, one of his chief backers at the Queen's Court. Negotiating, with the loss of six men, the intricate and perilous three hundred and sixty miles of icy mountain-bound Straits, in sixteen days – half the time taken by Magellan – he reached the Pacific on September 6th, only to be struck by a tremendous storm, which, scattering his little squadron, drove him far to the south. For fifty-six days the gale persisted. During its course the *Marigold* was engulfed with all hands and the *Elizabeth* driven back into the Atlantic and forced to return to England. Only the flagship remained, its indomitable commander and her crew subsisting on a diet of putrid penguin meat with which they had fortunately victualled the *Golden Hind* from an island during her passage through the Straits.*

In the aftermath of the storm, Drake made two discoveries. One was that Grenville's southern continent did not exist, at least where the cartographers supposed; the other that the mountains and islands south of the Magellan Straits ended only in ocean and that, beyond the southern extremity of America, the Atlantic and Pacific flowed into one another. When he had revictualled and refitted his solitary and storm-battered ship, he set out northwards up the four thousand mile Pacific coast of South America. In January 1578, he reached the most southerly Spanish settlement at Valparaiso Bay, where he surprised and plundered the unsuspecting shipping lying in the little roadstead and took on board a consignment of gold and Chilean wine.

Then began that amazing voyage up the Peruvian coast where no English ship had ever sailed before, with all the wealth of Spanish South America dropping like ripe plums into his hold. It was a revolutionary demonstration of what sea-power could do in an oceanic age – a new force to be reckoned with, of which Drake was the first pioneer. For at that moment in time and place it required only one ocean-going ship with a double broadside – the microcosm of a fleet-in-being in an ocean where few vessels mounted so much as a single gun – to make Drake temporarily master of the Pacific, rather as Cortes and Pizarro, and their few hundred conquistadores, with their unfamiliar weapons and horses, had conquered for Spain, half a century earlier, the empires of the Aztecs and Incas. Being free to strike wherever he chose, and enjoying complete initiative and surprise, he took care, as he moved up the coast, to sink or immobilize every vessel which could carry warning of his coming. Capturing ship after ship and helping themselves to whatever they chose or needed, his crew entered into the spirit of the game, laughing and frollicking their way northwards, the playboys and terror alike of the western world.

In the middle of February they reached Callao, the port of Lima, capital of Peru, and seat of its Viceroy. Here they plundered and set

---

* 'The 24 of August we arrived at an island in the Straits where we found great store of fowl which could not fly, of the bigness of geese; whereof we killed in less than one day 3,000, and victualled ourselves thoroughly therewith.' R. Hakluyt, *Principal Navigations.*

adrift, as the Spanish crews fled ashore, every ship in the harbour. Here, too, from their prisoners – all of whom Drake treated with his habitual kindness and released unharmed before he left – they learnt that Oxenham's adventure had ended in disaster, and that he and his two chief officers were awaiting death in the dungeons of the Inquisition at Lima. The rest of his crew, it appeared, had been hanged at Panama as pirates. For, though during the year when Drake's expedition had been fitting out at Plymouth, Oxenham had done what he intended, building a pinnace on the far side of the Isthmus and launching it in the Pacific to raid the Pearl Islands and capture a bark laden with gold for Panama, by the year's end he had lost all he had gained, including his own freedom and the lives of his crew. A brave, humane man, sparing and releasing, like Drake, his prisoners and restraining his savage allies, the Cimaroons, from massacre, he lacked his former commander's genius, charisma and flawless timing and perfectionism. Careless about security, without the imagination to anticipate his enemy's mind and movements, and failing to seize time by the forelock as Drake had always done, he had been surprised and captured by the Spanish governor of Darien, who, alerted by the reappearance of English corsairs in the Isthmus, had taken precautionary and punitive measures against the Cimaroons.

With only a single ship left and no hope of co-operation from the Cimaroons, any idea of an attack on Panama from the Pacific was at an end. But before he left Callao, Drake learnt that a heavily-laden treasure ship had sailed for the Isthmus fourteen days before. While the Viceroy, hurrying down from Lima, mobilized every soldier on the coast for an attack on the intruder, the *Golden Hind* vanished over the northern horizon. A fortnight later, on March 1st 1579, Drake's fourteen-year-old page and cousin, keeping a look-out from the maintop, won the golden chain promised to the first seaman to sight the quarry. That night, with her mizzen mast brought down by a warning shot and her crew overpowered by a swarm of English sailors with cutlasses, the astonished captain of the *Nuestra Senora de la Concepcion* surrendered to a broad-shouldered, short-bearded man with magnetic eyes who, doffing his casque with grave courtesy, bade him 'accept with patience what is the usage of war'. For the next six days the two ships lay side by side on the calm sunlit Pacific, while emeralds, jewels and precious stones, thirteen chests full of reals of plate, eighty pounds weight of gold, and twenty-six tons of silver were transferred to the *Golden Hind*. Meanwhile, the Spanish captain was entertained in Drake's cabin as an honoured guest and, when the operation was over, he and his crew, with many little acts of kindness and courtesy from their captors, were allowed to resume their voyage in peace, less, however, as the Spanish authorities ruefully informed their sovereign, 362,000 pesos worth of treasure.

Three weeks later, on April 4th, far to the north off the Guatemalan coast, Drake captured another vessel, laden with Chinese silks and porcelain and owned by a Spanish nobleman of high birth, Don Francisco de Zarato, a cousin of Spain's senior grandee, the Duke of Medina Sidonia. From him we have a picture of Drake, by whom he was entertained for three days, in a letter sent after his release to the Viceroy of Mexico, describing his experiences at the hands of this strange corsair who boasted that he carried the Queen of England's commission and wore a gold sea-cap given him by her and a green silk scarf embroidered by her Maids of Honour with the words, 'The Lord guide and preserve thee until the ende'.

'He received me with a show of kindness and took me to his cabin where he bade me be seated and said, "I am a friend of those who tell me the truth, but of those who do not I get out of humour." . . . He is about thirty-five years old, of small size, with a reddish beard, and is one of the greatest sailors living, both from his skill and his power of commanding. He ordered me to sit next to him and began giving me food from his own plate, telling me not to grieve, that my life and property were safe. I kissed his hands for this . . . Certain trifles of mine having taken his fancy, he had them brought to his ship and gave me, in exchange for them, a falchion' -- a broadsword – 'and a small brazier of silver, and I can assure your Excellency that he lost nothing by the bargain. On his return to his vessel he asked me to pardon him for taking the trifles, but that they were for his wife.'

Don Francisco also described the excellent discipline Drake kept:

'When our ship was sacked, no man dared take anything without his orders. He shows them great favour, but punishes the least fault. . . . Each one takes particular pains to keep his arquebus clean. He treats them with affection and they him with respect. He also carries painters who paint for him pictures of the coast in exact colours. He carries trained carpenters and artisans, so as to be able to careen the ship at any time. He has with him nine or ten gentlemen, younger sons of leading men in England who form his council. He calls them together on every occasion and hears what they have to say, but he is not bound by their advice . . . He has no privacy: those I mentioned all dine at his table. He is served on silver dishes with gold borders and gilded garlands, in which are his arms. He carries all possible dainties and perfumed waters: he said that many of these had been given him by the Queen. He dines and sups to the music of viols . . .'*

By this time the entire Pacific coast of Spanish America was in uproar, its outraged authorities hastily casting cannon† and repairing immobilized ships in order to seek the heretic intruder in the Gulf of Panama or, alternatively, intercept his homeward voyage, thousands of miles to the south, on the way back to the storm-swept Magellan Straits. But Drake – 'the master thief of the unknown world' as the Spaniards called him – was at neither. For, having taken from a ship, engaged on their new China trade between Mexico and the Philippines, charts and sailing directions for the Pacific passage, he had resolved to complete his mission by circumnavigating the globe like Magellan, and return home by way of the rich spice islands and the Portuguese seaway round Africa.

First, however, leaving Spanish waters far behind, he sailed north up the American coast for a brief perfunctory search for the Pacific entrance to the supposed 'North West' passage or Strait of Anian – so dear to contemporary English cartographers, like the equally imaginary Terra Australis, whose non-existence he had already proved. Then, buffeted by icy storms, he turned back into the sunshine.

Before leaving America, somewhere north of the coast of what today is California, and hundreds of miles from the nearest Spanish settlement, Drake found a 'fair and good bay' whose white cliffs reminded him of England. Here, to careen and give the *Golden Hind* a much needed overhaul, he built a make-shift dock in which to unload and reload the treasure from her crowded hold. While doing so he established his usual happy relations with the native Indians. 'Our General,' wrote the young gentleman adventurer, Francis Preedy, to whom we owe the chief first-hand account of the voyage, 'according to his natural and accustomed humanity, courteously entreated them and liberally bestowed on them necessary things to cover their nakedness.' They seem to have regarded the 'palefaces' who had descended on them from the sea as visitants from a higher plane,

---

* Hakluyt, cit. A. L. Rowse, *The Expansion of Elizabethan England*, 185.

† A few days after Drake's appearance at Callao, Oxenham and his fellow prisoners at Lima had been closely interrogated by the Viceroy's officials as to their knowledge of casting cannon.

listened entranced to their psalm singing and scripture reading,* and invested Drake, whom they tried, to his embarrassment, to worship, with a chieftain's crown of feathers and the lordship of their country, which he accepted on behalf of his royal mistress, proclaiming it an English dominion in her name. He christened it New Albion and erected a monument and inscription for the guidance of future settlers and voyagers. Then, towards the end of July, the refreshed circumnavigators set out on the long haul across the Pacific. 'The natives,' wrote Preedy, 'frequented our company to the hour of our departure, which departure seemed so grievous unto them that their joy was turned to sorrow. They entreated us that, being absent, we would remember them.'

It was sixty-eight days before the heavily-laden little ship first sighted land again in the Philippine Sea and nearly three months before she reached the Moluccas, centre of the sea-borne European spice-trade – at that time a closely guarded monopoly of the Portuguese, who had established a fort and factory in the islands. But at Ternate Drake found a friendly sultan who was at war with them, purchased from him six tons of cloves – even more valuable on the European market at that time than gold or silver – and negotiated a verbal treaty which was to become regarded as a starting-point for English sea-borne trade with the Orient. Then on January 9th 1580, while still negotiating the intricate maze of uncharted equatorial islands and swift treacherous currents which lay between the Pacific and Indian oceans, the *Golden Hind*, and the expedition with it, all but came to an end on a submerged reef on which, for twenty hours, she lay grounded. But, always cheerful and resolute in adversity, Drake refused to despair; 'as he had always hitherto showed himself courageous and of good conscience in the mercy and protection of God,' wrote one of his officers, 'so now he continued in the same.' After he had called all hands to prayer and lightened the ship by jettisoning half the guns and three tons of cloves, the wind suddenly changed, and the *Golden Hind* slid gently off the reef unharmed.

It was not till March, after a refit in Java, that Drake and his crew at last got clear of the treacherous Floris Sea and Indonesian Archipelago and reached the open Indian Ocean. The first Englishman ever to

* 'In the time of prayers, singing of psalms and reading of certain chapters in the Bible, they sat very attentively, and at every pause, with one voice cried "Oh", greatly rejoicing in our exercises. Yea, they took such pleasure in our singing of psalms that, whenever they resorted to us, their first request was commonly this "Gnath", by which they entreated us that we would sing.' Hakluyt, *Principal Navigations*.

cross it, as, in the course of his miraculous voyage, he had been of both the South Atlantic and Pacific, he rounded the Cape of Good Hope on June 18th – 'a most stately thing and the fairest cape we saw in the whole circumference of the earth'. Stopping only to water at Sierra Leone on July 22nd, and reaching far out into the Atlantic to pick up the westerlies, he cast anchor in Plymouth Sound on September 26th 1580. Of the one hundred and sixty-four who had sailed with him from Plymouth nearly three years before, only fifty-one remained. Yet in the whole of his avenging foray in Spanish waters, not a single Spanish life had been taken.

But a vast amount of Spanish treasure had been – enough to support Philip's armies in the Netherlands for many months and even more, taking into account the fantastic interest rates Spain had to pay for the loans borrowed, on the strength of her bullion shipments, from Italian, German and Flemish bankers under its extravagant and procrastinating financial system. It seemed a heavy punishment and penalty to suffer for the treacherous attack on Hawkins and his crews at San Juan de Ulloa. And the imperial dynast in the Escorial had reacted furiously to the news of Drake's Pacific depradations as it had filtered through to Spain and Europe in the autumn of 1579. His ambassador had demanded his piratical head in the, as he supposed, unlikely event of his ever getting back to England.

When therefore the triumphant circumnavigator arrived safe and sound with his captured treasure, Mendoza's fury doubled. Nor did Drake himself know what sort of reception he was likely to receive from the Queen, with whose enigmatic commission he had sailed before robbing her fellow sovereign so outrageously. He did not even know whether she was alive and reigning until a fishing boat, hailed off Cawsand, reassured his fears, for he had had no news from home for nearly three years. What were Elizabeth's present relations with Spain and what the balance of forces in her councils he had still to learn. Using the pretext, therefore, of an outbreak of plague in Plymouth, he lay for a week off St Nicholas Island without landing until a messenger, despatched post haste to his friends at Court, together with some jewels for the Queen, could let him know how he stood.

He need not have worried. For he could not have arrived at a more opportune moment. Mendoza's complaints about his misdeeds in the outer oceans had merely been met by the Queen's bland insistence that Spain had no right to forbid, under pain of imprisonment or death, their use to her subjects who were therefore perfectly entitled in self-defence to take the law into their own hands, 'seeing,' as she put it, 'that the use of the sea and air is common to all.' Moreover, as she had made it abundantly clear to the ambassador, she had far more serious grievances of her own about Philip's interference in the affairs of her Irish kingdom, where a rising in Munster had been fomented by papal emissaries and Jesuits with Spanish arms and backing. And in the very week of Drake's arrival she had received news that six hundred Spaniards had landed there, presumably with her brother-in-law's authority, as part of an expedition sent by Rome to aid her rebellious Catholic subjects. She flatly refused to discuss the subject of Spanish injuries in the Pacific so long as a single Spanish soldier remained on Irish soil and until she had received a full apology for their being there.*

Moreover, King Philip had committed a far more serious breach of international propriety that summer. Following the fall of the young King of Portugal in the disastrous battle of Alcazar-el-Kebir in the Moroccan desert, and the death, only a year later, of his aged celibate successor, the direct line of the House of Aviz had come to an end in January 1580 while the *Golden Hind* was still edging her course through the islands of the Portuguese East Indies. Among those with a claim to the vacant throne was Philip of Spain. But Portugal had been a separate kingdom for more than four centuries, and her people were jealous of their independence and proud of the rich trading and colonial empire their explorers had founded on the shores of Africa, Brazil and the Orient. It seemed, therefore, as morally questionable as high-handed for the ruler of Spain to invade his little crusading neighbour with a huge army under the dreaded Duke of Alva and forcibly expel the successful claimant, Don Antonio, from the throne, of which, with popular Portuguese assent, he had taken possession six months earlier.

For Elizabeth and England, Philip's annexation of Portugal had tremendous implications. It all but doubled the size and wealth of Spain's already huge global empire, making it by far the most powerful state in Christendom, and carrying King Philip far along the road to universal dominion. And it brought him, not only the

* They did not remain there long, receiving short shrift from Elizabeth's Lord Deputy, Lord Grey de Wilton, a fanatic Protestant, who had them all massacred on the grounds that they had no right to levy war in the name of the Pope – one 'who was without authority from God or man: a detestable shaveling, the right Antichrist'.

riches of the spice islands, the mines of Brazil and the sea-borne trade round Africa with the East, but a means of commanding the oceans which, as Drake had proved, had hitherto eluded Spain – a military but not as yet, save in the enclosed galley-ruled waters of the Mediterranean, an invincible naval power. For Portugal possessed an ocean-going fleet of twelve of the world's finest fighting galleons, the great Atlantic port of Lisbon and the ocean-staging islands of Cape Verde and the Azores. All these were now at Spain's command.

Coming in the same month as the news of this prodigious Spanish *fait accompli*, Drake's return with his treasure, his treaty with the Sultan of Ternate, and the wonderful story of his world-encircling voyage seemed providential. A resounding answer to Alva's sinister march on Lisbon, it made every English heart glow with pride. Never in international relations had so much been achieved by the resource and daring of one man. When, with a long train of packhorses laden with jewels, Drake arrived in London that October, he found himself the hero of the Court and nation. The value of his treasure in the money of the day amounted to a million and half sterling or more than a third of the annual produce of King Philip's American mines.* Those who had invested in his voyage, including its principal shareholder the Queen, received a fourteen-fold capital return. Before having the treasure in the *Golden Hind* officially valued to be shipped to London and lodged in the Tower, a grateful Elizabeth – in a letter under her sign-manual 'to be kept to himself alone' – instructed the royal Commissioner in Devon to allow Drake to retain £10,000 worth of bullion, equivalent to roughly a million in present-day money, so making him one of the richest men in the kingdom and ensuring that, even if Philip succeeded in reclaiming any part of his lost hoard, her little privateer should keep what his courage and genius had earned him. Meanwhile depositions were taken from every survivor of the crew to prove that no Spaniard had suffered unnecessary violence during the voyage, unlike the unfortunate English seamen who had been hanged or sent to the galleys by King Philip's officers or burnt by the Spanish Inquisition, as John Oxenham was that October at Lima.

Such was Drake's popularity with his royal mistress – like everyone else agog to hear the story of his adventures – that, on his arrival at Court, she gave him a private audience lasting six hours and, on another occasion, sent for him no fewer than nine times in the course of a day. Poor Mendoza was beside himself with rage, describing, in

* J. B. Black, *The Reign of Elizabeth*, 210.

vivid letters to his master, the Queen walking in the garden in deep converse with the offending pirate or appearing in Court on New Year's Day in a new crown set with five magnificent – Peruvian – emeralds. The climax to the infamous voyage came on April 4th 1581, when, coming down the river in her gilded barge, Elizabeth was entertained by Drake, 'a right magnifico now,' to a superb banquet – 'finer than any had ever been seen in England since King Henry,' the ambassador reported – in the state cabin of the *Golden Hind* at her moorings at Deptford. Afterwards, telling her host that she had brought a golden sword with which to cut off his head, she handed it to the French Ambassador – so implicating that diplomat and his country in her defiance of King Philip's demands for redress – bidding him knight the erring circumnavigator on his own quarter deck.*

---

* Nearly four hundred years later, the author saw Elizabeth II knight the single-handed circumnavigator, Sir Francis Chichester, on the riverside terrace of the Royal Naval College, Greenwich.

Chapter Four
PEACE OR WAR

'The rose is red, the leaves are green,
God save Elizabeth, our noble Queen.'

Lines scribbled in 1589 by a Westminster
schoolboy, in a Latin text-book

Drake's voyage round the world was a climacteric in the evolution of England as a nation. It was the starting-point for the next three and a half centuries of her history. Already, thanks to her Queen's inspired leadership, the champion of the threatened Protestant cause in Europe, her roving sea-captain's miraculous achievement had staked her little kingdom's claim to the freedom of the world's oceans. Together, in their very different ways, Elizabeth and Drake had raised it from the nadir of weakness, disunion and peril into which it had fallen to a repute greater than any it had known since the days of Henry V, when its archers had laid low the chivalry of Europe's mightiest kingdom. Like them, coming from outside the warlike feudal and knightly caste which for half a millennium had monopolized command of arms in the Christian West, the humbly-born Drake had proved himself both a fighting commander and a strategist of the highest genius. Almost alone he had seen how to win control of the outer oceans and realized the fatal communications gap between Spain's monopolist empire in the Americas and its arid, poverty-stricken homeland. Never commanding much more than a hundred men, and seldom that, he had made rings round her proud and stately colonial chivalry and, despite her prodigious conquests of the past sixty years, had held her pretensions to military invincibility up to ridicule. With his practical experience of fighting Spain at sea, he saw how her imperial power could be broken for ever. In the summer after his return, he sought permission to fit out a new expedition to repeat, with a whole fleet instead of a single ship, his plundering voyage up the defenceless Peruvian coast, to rouse Spain's conquered helots to throw off her hated rule before, once more encircling the globe and joining forces with his remote ally, the Sultan of Ternate, to wrest the trade of the spice islands from King Philip's Portuguese vassals.

Till now, both the shrewd stateswoman on the throne and the self-made seaman of genius who had sailed to the ends of the world in her name had been seeking the same thing: the rejection of Spain's arrogant claim to a monopoly of trade in the outer oceans. Yet to the Queen the ultimate end she sought was not the destruction of the Spanish empire – something far beyond her means or ambition – but the preservation of the unifying peace which for close on a quarter of a century she had given her realm and on which its reviving strength and wealth depended.* She wished to avoid war – not, as the event was to show, at all costs, but at all reasonable costs. And as she believed that, in the last resort, her fellow sovereign in the Escorial had the same distaste for the uncertainty and waste of war as her frugal and sensible self, she had no wish to goad him to extremities. A woman, a realist and a politique, by nature tolerant and open-minded and totally dedicated to the peace and well-being of her country, she found it hard to believe that to Philip – a religious devotee and a bureaucratic perfectionist – the peace and well-being of his subjects mattered less than the enforced imposition on all mankind of the orthodox Faith with which he had increasingly come to identify his own exclusive right to rule and ordain.

It was inevitable that the Queen's judgment, not Drake's, should prevail, for her control of foreign policy was absolute. Even the wise Burghley, though he might doubt and caution, could never challenge it. There was talk for a time in Court and City circles of sending the great corsair on a less ambitious voyage to take over the Portuguese island of Terceira in the Azores, which had declared for Don Antonio, as a future base from which to cut the Plate Fleet's communications with America. But nothing came of it, for the Portuguese pretender, wearying of Elizabeth's delays and hesitations, decided to rely on French aid, instead of English, to restore him to his lost dominion. And, with the people of Portugal submitting, however reluctantly, to Alva's occupying army, a major, and seemingly irreversible, step had been taken towards the fulfilment of the Spanish poet, Hernando de Acuna's dream of – *un Monarca, un Imperia y una Espana.*

---

* 'For nearly a quarter of a century, the Queen's sedate and prudent government kept this country out of foreign war, during which time its resources were nourished and increased.' A. L. Rowse, *The Expansion of Elizabethan England*, 238.

Instead, Elizabeth continued, as before, to thwart her brother-in-law in such small ways as lay within her power. In August 1581 he was still threatening her with war to recover his plundered treasure. But she reduced him to reason, or, at least, hesitation, not by using Drake to harry his distant ocean realms again and enrage him still further, but by playing her old diplomatic card of an Anglo-French marriage treaty. For such an alliance, with both shores of the English Channel in hostile hands, would completely cut Spain's communications with the Netherlands and make it impossible for her to supply her armies there. That October Alençon – 'François the Constant' – revisited England at Elizabeth's invitation to renew his courtship, upon which Philip withdrew his threats, proposed a mutual forgiveness of all past offences and offered the incorrigible Queen a renewal of their ancient friendship. To both monarchs the war in the Netherlands seemed far more important than anything that could happen in the remote waters round America; Philip because his father's favourite patrimony and the triumph of the Catholic cause in Europe were at stake, Elizabeth because a Spanish victory there would not only finally close her people's traditional continental export market for their cloth, but release a victorious army for an invasion of her realm across the narrow seas. Seeing in Antwerp, like Napoleon two centuries later, a pistol pointed at the head of England, she continued to supply her restless French suitor with large, though not over large, loans – financed out of Drake's Pacific plunder – to induce him to pluck her chestnuts out of the fire and sustain the Protestant cause in the Low Countries without her having to intervene herself and so provoke her Spanish brother-in-law into war.

For, while Drake had been circumnavigating the world, the conflict in the Netherlands had continued to take the see-saw course which – short of a return to the old peaceful and tolerant pre-Philipian relations between the Spanish Crown and its non-Spanish subjects – best served Elizabeth's and England's ends of allowing neither Spain nor France to dominate them. At one moment in 1576, the brutal and horrifying sack of Antwerp and other Flemish cities by Spain's unpaid and mutinous soldiers had temporarily united all seventeen provinces under William of Orange against their Spanish rulers. Since then the military and diplomatic genius of young Alexander Farnese of Parma, Philip's natural nephew, who succeeded the dead Don John of Austria as Governor-General and, later, as Viceroy of the Netherlands, had been gradually winning back most of the country, except Protestant and maritime Holland and Zeeland, from Orange's insurgent rule, still leaving Elizabeth as a neutral arbiter between them. 'Thus sate she,' wrote the contemporary historian, William Camden, 'an heroical princess and umpire betwixt the Spaniards, the French and the States, so as she might well have used that saying of her father, *Cui adhaero praeset* – "the party to which I adhere getteth the upper hand".' For he saw her, as she saw herself, as the tongue of the scales in the balance of European power.

So it came about, as a result of this precarious stalemate, that for the next few years England's greatest sea-captain remained on shore, purchasing from Sir Richard Grenville the great monastic estate of Buckland Abbey, representing a Cornish constituency in Parliament, and, later, serving as Mayor of Plymouth, in which capacity, with his usual enterprise and generosity, he later helped to provide the port with a piped water supply from Dartmoor. When in 1582 a privately promoted expedition – to which both he, Leicester, Burghley, Walsingham, Hatton and the Muscovy Company all subscribed – sailed for the Moluccas to set up a trading factory to exploit his unwritten treaty with the Sultan of Ternate, its command was entrusted to a brother-in-law of John Hawkins, Edward Fenton. A courtier and soldier of fortune, Fenton had been engaged under the Yorkshire explorer and ex-privateer, Martin Frobisher, in some much publicized but unsuccessful, searches for gold on the frozen shores of northern Canada, where the latter had been trying to find the elusive North-West passage to the Pacific. But Fenton was no Drake, and the expedition proved a dismal failure, never getting further than Brazil. Meanwhile, consolidating their new Portuguese possessions and their control of Portugal's ocean-going navy, the Spaniards under their most experienced admiral, the Marquis of Santa Cruz – a hero of the great Mediterranean galley victory of Lepanto – won off Terceira in the Azores a decisive engagement against a French fleet seeking to restore Don Antonio to his throne. It left Spain with no rival in the Atlantic but England, and encouraged the victorious admiral to urge his royal master to prepare a massive invasion armada to overwhelm the troublesome islanders.

With France split by civil war, England now alone stood between King Philip and the dominion of western Christendom. But, still at peace under their pacific Queen, the islanders were already beginning to buckle on the wooden armour of their sovereign's fleet of war. Ever since Elizabeth's accession in England's forlorn and defenceless

state after the fall of Calais – lost through her then weakness at sea –
the growth of her naval strength had been a slow but continuous
process. 'Bend your force and credit and device to maintain and
increase your Navy,' the English ambassador in Paris, Sir Nicholas
Throgmorton, had written as long ago as 1560 – when the young
Queen and Cecil were staking everything on saving the nascent
Scottish Reformation from the French by a winter blockade of the
Forth – 'for in this time, considering all the circumstances, it is the
flower of England's garland'. And in the very month in which Drake
had set out on his voyage round the world, his former chief and
partner, John Hawkins of Plymouth, the most experienced ocean-
going trader of his generation, succeeded his father-in-law, Benjamin
Gonson, as Treasurer of the Navy Board – the official body which,
since its creation by Henry VIII, administered the royal ships and
dockyards. His appointment was the result of a paper which he had
prepared for Lord Treasurer Burghley entitled 'Abuses in the
Admiralty touching Her Majesty's Navy'.* In it he had exposed the
time-honoured cheats which were causing the Crown to spend twice
as much in building and maintaining its ships as was necessary. In
many cases the Queen was paying officers and dockyard officials for
vessels whose timbers she herself had already provided from the
royal forests. Naval stores were habitually sold to line the pockets of
officers and dockyard officials; clerks were paid double wages; worn
out and decayed materials charged as though they were new. For
almost everything the Navy needed the Queen was grossly over-
charged. By eliminating all this corruption, or as much of it as was
possible in a universally corrupt age, Hawkins – a practical and
businesslike administrator with a lifelong experience of ships and the
sea – was able during the next few years to double the efficiency of the
Navy without increasing the amount his frugal-minded royal mistress
was prepared and able to devote to it.

The underlying purpose which inspired Hawkins's paper and his
subsequent work as Treasurer of the Royal Navy was the transforma-
tion of what was still a home-waters fleet, built and maintained to
protect and patrol the seas immediately around England and Ireland,
into one capable of operating, and remaining at sea, like Drake and
his fellow buccaneers, thousands of miles from her shores. For this
purpose, as he knew from personal experience, the huge castellated
carracks, with their heavy superstructures of towering poop and

* *Lansdowne Mss.* 113 ff, 45–7, cit. J. A. Williamson, *Hawkins of Plymouth*, 251.

97

forecastle, which had been the pride of the early Tudor Navy and its continental rivals, could be almost as dangerous in Atlantic gales to their own crews as to the enemies they were designed to overpower. The most effective warships in heavy weather were those offering as small a target to wave and shot as possible – slim, seaworthy, fast, handy and easy to sail and manoeuvre. In place of the thousand ton, and even fifteen-hundred ton, floating castles of the past, made for summer campaigns in gentler seas, which till now had been the pride of royal shipwrights, Hawkins and the new English deep-water seamen favoured much smaller craft, 'not of so great bulk,' as Francis Bacon put it, 'but of a more nimble motion, and more serviceable'. Long in proportion to their beam in a ratio of three-and-a-half to one on the water-line, they could stay at sea in any weather and, because of their smaller size, were easier to maintain in dock, being so much the less liable to conceal dry rot in their timbers. Hawkins's ideal was the *Revenge*, of 450 tons, laid down in 1575, which, with its speed and hitting power, Drake regarded as the perfect fighting galleon and was, in war, to choose as his flagship. Its last fight in 1591 under Sir Richard Grenville was to constitute one of the great sea-epics of all time.

> 'Ship after ship, the whole night long,
>   their high-built galleons came,
> Ship after ship, the whole night long,
>   with her battle-thunder and flame;
> Ship after ship, the whole night long,
>   drew back with her dead and her shame.'

Apart from shipbuilding, supplies and dockyards, there were two other matters with which John Hawkins concerned himself during the ten crucial years when, as Treasurer of the Navy Board, he fought to overcome the inertia and excessive conservatism of the past and the time-honoured knavery and corruption of royal officers and contractors. One was guns, than which there had been none better in the world than those made in England under Cecil's fostering care of her native industry. In those years the gunfounders of Sussex, Kent and Surrey were acknowledged to be the best in Europe. So good were their guns that during Hawkins's Treasurership their export had to be forbidden to prevent their falling into Spanish hands. The gun most favoured by Hawkins and his colleagues was the culverin – lighter to carry, quicker in firing and with a longer range than the heavier cannon hitherto in use. Firing an iron shot weighing seventeen pounds, it had an extreme, if far from accurate, range of from a mile and a half to two miles – little less than that of the guns of Nelson's fleet at Trafalgar. And the English gunners were as famous as their guns – 'sober, wakeful, lusty, hardy, patient and quick-spirited.'

The other branch of naval administration where Hawkins's reforms proved revolutionary was that of manning. Instead of crowding as many men into the Queen's ships as possible, his experience, like Drake's, of ocean voyages had taught him the advantage of sailing and fighting with as few as possible. One of the handicaps imposed by the top-heavy superstructures in ship design of the past was the over-crowding involved in manning fore and aft towers with soldiers and gunners in readiness to board or sweep the crowded decks of their opponents with their small-arms. The broadside fire of long-range culverins made such floating towers as unnecessary and useless as the shore-warriors who filled them. The ships Hawkins built or con-verted were cheaper to man and victual and freer from the fevers, dysentery and typhus which swept through the overcrowded insanitary decks of their predecessors. The ideal complement of the *Revenge* and her successors was one hundred and fifty sailors, twenty-four gunners and seventy-six soldiers, or two hundred and fifty in all – a manning scale of a man for every two tons, or enough to sail and fight with maximum efficiency, compared with almost a man for every one and a half tons in the past. This allowed ships to remain at sea for much longer without having to revictual, and helped to reduce the incidence of scurvy. It also made it possible for Hawkins – who by now was financing the maintenance of the Royal Navy for a fixed annual contractual sum of £5,714 a year – to secure in 1585 a rise of the seaman's basic pay from 6s 8d to 10s a month.* Above all, it enabled England to use to the full her supreme naval asset – a highly skilled hereditary seafaring population, bred from boyhood to navigating stormy waters, without having to dilute it with unneces-sary soldiers and the untrained flotsam and jetsam of inland towns.

Little of this escaped Ambassador Mendoza's watchful eye. During the years following Drake's return from the Pacific, he warned his master that the English were building new war ships without cessation. Nor was it only at sea that the islanders were looking to their arms – hitherto so powerless on land against the disciplined Spanish, Swiss, Italian and German mercenaries employed by the great supranational

* S. T. Bindoff, *Tudor England*, 269.

dynasties of Hapsburg and Valois, with their sophisticated weapons and new battle techniques. Since the outbreak of the rebellion in the Netherlands, growing numbers of young English and Welsh volunteers had been fighting beside their Dutch and Flemish co-religionists. In 1572 Sir Humphrey Gilbert, who had learnt his soldiering in Ireland – and ten years later was to go down in an Atlantic storm to death and history as the pioneer of North American colonization – formed the first English regiment in the Low Countries with the aid of a staunch, but unassuming, warrior from Glamorgan named Thomas Morgan. It was the first time English soldiers had fought together in any larger unit than a company against the huge dreaded Spanish *tercios* which had so long, 'at push of pike', carried all before them on the battlefields of the Continent.

They were followed by others, like the six Norris brothers, sons of Lord Norris of Rycote, all but one of whom were to die in the Queen's service.* Though their Dutch employers and fellow fighters for freedom were receiving little support as yet from the cautious and frugal Queen, who was now once more trying to negotiate a peaceful settlement with Philip's Commander-in-Chief, the courteous young Duke of Parma, these volunteers helped, in a melancholy terrain of rivers and marshes, to prove that, given the right military framework, their native isle still bred soldiers second to none in hardihood, valour and stoical humour. 'This is the hand which cut the pudding at dinner,' jested John Carey, throwing it on the mess-table after it had been severed by a cannon-ball. Such men formed a bridge in time between the archers of Crecy and Agincourt and their scarlet-coated descendants who fought and conquered under Marlborough and Wellington. And, during the late fifteen-seventies and fifteen-eighties, while young Englishmen, many of them cadets of famous families, were learning to be soldiers in a foreign war, at home the first frail attempts were being made to transform the primitive organization of the country's local militia – still armed with bills and bows – into some semblance of a modern fighting force.

Yet it was neither naval armada nor invading army which presented the greatest threat to England's peace as her Queen, in the autumn of 1582, entered on her fiftieth year. It was the threat to her life. That

* The kneeling and armoured effigies of two of them, 'Black' John and Tom Norris, sculpted by Epiphanius Evesham, can be seen in Westminster Abbey. 'My own Crow,' Elizabeth wrote to comfort her old friend, their mother, 'we were loath to write … lest we should give you fresh occasion of sorrow, but could not forbear, knowing your past resolution in like mishaps and your religious obedience to Him whose strokes are unavoidable'. J. E. Neale, *Elizabeth*, 217.

spring, an all but successful attempt by Spanish agents had been made to assassinate William of Orange – the chief obstacle, after Elizabeth herself, to the triumph of the Counter-Reformation in Europe. Though for weeks his life was despaired of, the prince recovered. But while the prize offered by Spain on William's head was high, that for the assassination of the childless Queen of England was even higher. For if she were to fall to an assassin's knife or bullet, her Catholic cousin, the Queen of Scots, would automatically succeed to her vacant throne. And during that summer a messenger of Mendoza, the Spanish Ambassador, disguised as a dentist, had been stopped crossing the Scottish frontier. A letter, hidden at the back of a mirror, was found among his possessions, which, in the hands of Secretary Walsingham's cipher-breakers, during a year of following clues and tapping Mary's secret correspondence, led to the discovery of a conspiracy – in which Mary herself, the Spanish Ambassador, King Philip and the Pope were all involved. As the prelude to a joint Catholic rising and Spanish invasion – designated by the code name, 'Enterprise of England' – Elizabeth was to be struck down by a devoted former retainer of Mary Queen of Scots, a young Catholic of good family named Francis Throgmorton, nephew of the former royal ambassador to France, Sir Nicholas Throgmorton.

Arrested and put to the torture, Throgmorton confessed all, reproaching himself before his terrible traitor's death that he had disclosed the secrets of her who was 'the dearest thing to him in the world'. For, in her correspondence with those who were plotting to kill Elizabeth, Mary had implicated herself to the hilt. Nor did Throgmorton's death remove the standing threat to the Queen's life and, with it, of the country's peace and security. At any moment some other unknown hand might set in motion the fearful train of consequences which the kingdom's foes, external and internal, had been planning. Only a week or two before Throgmorton's arrest a young Warwickshire Catholic gentleman – also caught and hanged – had set off to London with a pistol, boasting in his cups that he was about to compass the death of the Queen and 'hoped to see her head set on a pole, for she was a serpent and a viper'. And no one knew how many Catholics, ostensibly loyal and law-abiding subjects, might not, on the orders of the head of their Church in Rome, seek a heavenly crown by over-throwing an earthly one.

For in the year in which Drake returned from the Pacific the first Jesuit missionaries landed in England, sworn to face martyrdom in their dedicated task of winning back their countrymen to the Faith. They had already been preceded by other returning Catholic exiles who, since England's apostasy after the death of Mary Tudor, had been educated for the priesthood at English seminaries at Douai and Rome and indoctrinated with the belief that the noblest service they could do for their country was to embrace martyrdom – 'that glorious conquest of human nature' – in order to redeem its deluded people from heresy and eternal damnation. Most of those who, bravely defying Parliament's ban on Catholic priests, returned to England, did so, not to kill its Protestant sovereign, but to minister to their fellow Catholics – deprived by law of the offices and consolations of their Faith. But two successive Popes had let it be known that merit for the faithful could be won by ridding the world of a heretic Queen. Ten years after Pius V had issued his Bull excommunicating Elizabeth and releasing her subjects from their allegiance, in December 1580 his successor, Gregory XIII, authorized an unequivocal reply by the Papal Secretary to an enquiry about the permissibility of taking her life. 'Since that guilty woman of England rules over two such noble kingdoms of Christendom and is the cause of so much injury to the Catholic faith and loss of so many million souls, there is no doubt that whosoever sends her out of the world, with the pious intention of doing God service, not only does not sin, but gains merit.'

The result of this dedicated priestly invasion was twofold. The laws against the practice of Catholic rites in England – at first, in a universally intolerant age, so mildly interpreted by her young Queen – were far more strictly enforced. The very existence of a Roman priest in England was now made treason by Parliament and punishable by death. As a result, the home of many a loyal and law-abiding Catholic subject became an illegal fortress where, sheltered in minute hiding places or priest holes made behind panelling or under floor-boards,★ visiting priests could lie concealed while carrying out their perilous ministrations of spiritual comfort and guidance to the local Catholics or 'recusants', as they became called. For the immediate effect of the exposure of the Throgmorton plot against the Queen's life was to spark off a national panic. In its course, to allay and canalize Protestant fears, the Council drew up a Bond of Association by which, in the event of the Queen's assassination, all loyal subjects were asked to pledge themselves to take the life, by any means available and without

★ The most historic of all can be seen in the little Staffordshire house of Boscobel where Charles II was hidden after his flight from Worcester.

benefit of law, of any person claiming succession to the throne by virtue of such treasonable crime – that is, of Mary Queen of Scots. This Bond, with its resort to lynch law and the blood hunt, was widely subscribed to – in Yorkshire alone over seven thousand seals were received. It was subsequently submitted to Parliament for legalization when it met in November. Only as a result of Elizabeth's refusal to countenance the death of anyone, even her own murderer, without due trial was it modified by a provision for the setting up instead of a special tribunal to try any claimant to the vacant throne benefiting by the Queen's assassination. And all Jesuits and Catholic priests were ordered by Parliament to leave the country within forty days and their presence in England thereafter to be punished as treason.

★   ★   ★

Long before Parliament met, the revelations of the Throgmorton plot had led to a drastic tightening of the ring round the hapless but incorrigibly intriguing Mary who, with her little court and household, was removed from the chivalrous custodianship of the Earl of Shrewsbury to Tutbury Castle and the close charge of a stern Puritan, Sir Amyas Paulet. It caused, too, the departure from England of her fellow conspirator, the Spanish Ambassador. On January 9th 1584, Mendoza was given fifteen days to leave the country whose sovereign he had sought to destroy. 'The insolence of these people,' he wrote indignantly to the Spanish Secretary of State, 'has brought me to a state in which my only desire to live is for the purpose of avenging myself upon them. I pray that God may let it be soon and will give me grace to be His instrument of vengeance.'★ Yet though his parting words, as he ended his ten years' diplomatic mission, were 'Don Bernardino de Mendoza was not born to disturb countries but to conquer them,' neither King Philip nor Elizabeth were yet fully prepared to resort to the final arbitrament of war.

Instead, the undeclared war between them in the Netherlands continued, with Elizabeth, in order to keep it alive, continuing to give the necessary minimum of financial aid to the rebel Protestant cause, and the young Spanish Governor General, Alexander Farnese of Parma, by a combination of conciliatory diplomacy towards the southern and mainly Catholic provinces and of successive victories in the field, gradually narrowing the area controlled by William of

★ J. B. Black, *The Reign of Elizabeth*, 315.

Orange and the Dutch Calvinists and sea-faring northern irreconcil-ables. In March 1584, he won back the capital, Brussels, and, during the spring and early summer, the rich Flemish cities of Ypres and Bruges. Then, on July 10th at Delft, in response to the reward offered for William of Orange's life, an assassin's bullet, fired at point-blank range, won the King of Spain his greatest, and, as it seemed, culminat-ing, triumph over the patriot leader and statesman whose twelve years' defiance of tyranny as Stadtholder of Holland, Zeeland, and Utrecht, had alone kept the rebellion in being.

With the death of William 'the Silent' – the faithful Father Wilhel-mus of Dutch legend and national memory – the Protestant cause in the Netherlands seemed doomed. For with his army of 60,000 mercenaries, its discipline now restored, Parma was driving ever deeper into the heart of Flanders and Brabant, taking town after town, either by battle and siege or by the politic lenience he offered to all but persistent heretics. For, thanks to the young Governor-General's genius and wisdom, the revolt of the once United Provinces was ceasing to be national and becoming again merely Protestant, and, as such, increasingly confined to the north and seaboard. No help for the failing rebel cause could any longer be looked for from Elizabeth's old suitor, the French Duke of Anjou – the former Alençon – whom she had subsidized to keep the rebellion alive without her own and England's intervention and whom Orange had installed as Duke of Brabant and Count of Flanders. For, an inveterate intriguer and double-dealer, Anjou had long alienated the Protestant elements in the country, and, succumbing to typhus, had died, a discredited man, only a few weeks before the tragedy of Delft. His death ended the possibility of any further help from a bitterly divided France, leaving, as it did, the reversion of its crown to the Huguenot Henry of Navarre. To Anjou's brother, the weak and frivolous Philip III, last of the Valois line, the despairing Netherlanders vainly offered their throne, only to have their offer rejected. For, with the threat of a Protestant succession precipitating a new French civil war, effective power in France for the moment passed to the Catholic champion, the Duke of Guise, who, making a secret alliance with Philip of Spain, called in a Spanish army to keep out the heretic heir-presump-tive, Henry of Navarre.

With Ghent, last of the rebel Flemish cities of Flanders, falling to Parma in September 1584, the Spaniards closed in on the great port and commercial centre of Antwerp. That winter, while in England

Parliament debated the measures to deter would-be assassins of the
Queen, Parma built an enormous dam across half a mile of tidal water
to cut off all access to the doomed city from the sea and any hope of its
relief by the Dutch 'sea-beggars' from the north. By the summer of
1585, as starvation began to bite and the last appeal to the French king
failed, it became clear that nothing could save the Protestant cause in
the Netherlands but the open intervention of England. And no one
in Europe believed that the English would dare to challenge the immense military and – with the Portuguese navy joined to Spain's –
naval power of Philip's all-conquering empire.

Yet as the summer drew on, it was beginning to look as though the
English might do so after all. At the end of May relations between
the two countries were exacerbated by a sudden and treacherous
embargo placed by the Spanish King on English grain ships unloading
in the ports of northern Spain, where a failure of the previous year's
harvest had caused a famine. The master and crew of one of the ships
ordered to be seized had resisted and, overcoming the boarding party,
sailed for England, carrying with them the Spanish functionary
supervising the arrests. On arrival, papers concealed in his boots
revealed that the seizure of the ships had been made on King Philip's
personal orders, in order to provide shipping for a future invasion of
England. The indignation provoked by this revelation of Spain's
intentions coincided with the arrival of commissioners from the
Netherlands to beg Elizabeth's help for besieged and starving Antwerp.

The sovereignty they offered and implored her to take she rejected,
as she had done William of Orange's offer of ten years before. But
Antwerp was at its last gasp, and, once it fell, only Holland and
Zeeland, behind their sea barriers, would be able to hold out against
Parma's triumphant armies. Unless England's help was speedily
forthcoming, the resistance of the remaining United Provinces and,
with it, of the reformed Faith in the Netherlands, would be at an end,
and Parma's victorious troops could be freed for an invasion of
England. Reluctant as her Queen was to commit her country to war,
and all that it implied, she saw that the consequences for her people of
a refusal to do so would be worse. Just as she and Cecil had faced the
enormous risk of war in their country's hour of extreme weakness a
quarter of a century before to save Scotland's Reformation and
independence, they now acted to save those of the Low Countries,
and for the same reason. Burghley summed it up in a memorandum
to his royal mistress;

'Although her Majesty should thereby enter into a war presently, yet were she better to do it now, while she may make the same out of her realm, having the help of the people of Holland and before the King of Spain shall have consummated his conquests, . . . whereby he shall be so provoked with pride, solicited by the Pope and tempted by the Queen's own subjects, and shall be so strong by sea and so free from all other actions and quarrels, yea, shall be so formidable to all the rest of Christendom, as that her Majesty shall no wise be able with her own power . . . to withstand his attempts, but shall be forced to give place to his insatiable malice.'*

So at her riverside palace, where fifty-two years earlier Elizabeth had been born, the die was cast. Though it was too late to save Antwerp, which capitulated from starvation on August 7th, by the terms of the Treaty of Greenwich, signed three days later, England agreed to provide an army of 4,000 foot – later raised to 5,000 – and 1,000 horse. In addition she undertook to advance the United Provinces £125,000 a year to support the war, more than half, that is, the ordinary revenue of her Crown. In return, the States were to allow the English to occupy the ports of Flushing and Brill as pledges for the loan.†

In a formal 'Declaration of the courses moving the Queen of England to give aid to the Defence of the People afflicted and oppressed in the Low Countries' issued that autumn, Elizabeth and Burghley set out the reasons for their intervening. It expressly refrained from any formal declaration of war, even referring to King Philip as the Queen's 'ally' and paying a noble tribute to his Viceroy, the Duke of Parma, as one 'who hath dealt in a more honourable and gracious sort in the charge committed unto him than any other that hath ever gone before him or is likely to succeed after him.' Disclaiming any wish to extend the Queen's dominions, it maintained that her sole purpose in sending aid 'to the natural people of those countries' with which England had so long been associated in trade and friendship, was 'to defend them and their towns from sacking and desolation, and thereby to procure them safety . . . to enjoy their ancient liberties for them and their posterity'. She had acted only because 'we did manifestly see in what danger ourselves, our countries and people might shortly be if in convenient time we did not speedily otherwise regard to prevent or stay the same'.

* A. L. Rowse, The Expansion of Elizabethan England, 241–2.
† J. E. Neale, E.H.R. 1930, Elizabeth and the Netherlands, 375.

PEACE OR WAR

In this famous Declaration – compared by a modern historian to the American Declaration of Independence as 'one of the noblest state papers ever written'* – Elizabeth laid down what was to remain a ruling principle of English policy for three and a half centuries: the independence of the Low Countries and a 'common cause' with all prepared to defend it against any despotic power seeking to absorb it. 'All this time of my reign,' she was to recall in Parliament a decade later, when the war with Spain she had tried so long to avoid had become the inescapable background of her life, 'I have not sought to advance my territories and enlarge my dominions . . . My mind was never to invade my neighbours or to usurp over any. I am contented to reign over mine own and to rule as a just prince.' For what was right for her own people, she held, must be right for other peoples. Against the supranational claims of imperial Spain to succeed, and extend, the supranational claims of the medieval Church, Elizabeth set herself and England as the champion of all 'natural' peoples who wished to govern themselves through their own laws and princes.

★   ★   ★

The freedom of the Netherlands was not the only principle for which Elizabeth's England contended. The other was the freedom of the seas against Spain's claim to deny the use of outer ocean and its shores beyond an arbitrary line drawn by papal decree. In 1584, after the expulsion of Mendoza, the Queen had at last given the arch opponent of that claim, Sir Francis Drake, leave to undertake a second circumnavigation of the world, for which he had vainly pleaded three years earlier. Financed by a joint stock subscription by the Queen and other leaders of the Court and City, a fleet of eleven warships, four barks and twenty pinnaces, manned by 1,600 picked sailors and soldiers, was to sail under Drake's command to ravage once more the Pacific coasts of Peru and Panama, recross that ocean and, following up his treaty with the Sultan of Ternate, take over from Spain the Portuguese 'factories' in the East Indies, so securing for England the trade of the spice islands.

Had the expedition sailed and succeeded it might have anticipated by fourteen years the foundation of the East India Company and, possibly by a century, the beginnings of England's commercial

* C. R. Markham, *The Fighting Years*, 69.

107

ascendancy in the Far East. But King Philip's seizure of the English grain ships in the Basque ports in the summer of 1585 changed its destination. Instead, it was deflected to release the captured ships and, then by way of the Cape Verde Islands, descend on the Spanish possessions in the Caribbean to cut the flow of American treasure across the Atlantic which was financing the suppression of the Dutch rebellion and the projected invasion of England. Before sailing from Plymouth in September, it was reinforced by twelve companies of soldiers, bringing its total complement to 2,300 men. Under Drake, as the Queen's Admiral and General, was the Yorkshire ex-privateer and Arctic explorer, Martin Frobisher, as vice-admiral, and Walsingham's son-in-law, Christopher Carleill – a brilliant young veteran of the Netherlands and French wars of religion – as lieutenant-general.

Up to the last moment it was feared that the Queen, still hoping to avoid a final breach with Spain, might stop the voyage. Even the usually cautious Burghley sent a secret warning to Drake to act quickly. He need not have worried, for, without waiting for the completion of the fleet's victualling, the great seaman was already off the Spanish coast. With only a fraction of England's naval strength, he occupied Vigo bay and proceeded, as though in his native Devon, to provision his ships at the expense of the Spanish authorities who, with their slow and cumbersome communications, were powerless to prevent him. Then, having dealt a shattering blow to King Philip's prestige, he sailed for the Cape Verde Islands, whose capital, Santiago, he sacked and burnt. During the Atlantic crossing, however, a fatal fever, contracted in the islands, caused the death of three hundred of his men, or nearly a seventh of his scanty force. Yet, it did not prevent him, in two brilliant amphibious operations, from storming and capturing – on New Year's Day 1586 – the capital of the West Indies, Hispaniola, and then, in February, in the face of a strong garrison, the supposedly impregnable fortress and harbour of Cartagena, capital of the Spanish Main. Both operations were superbly directed, raising Drake's reputation to a new height, most of all among his enemies who now regarded him as invincible – a man, as one of them put it, 'equal to any undertaking'. By the simple subject peoples whom Spain had conquered or enslaved he was regarded as liberator and saviour; a captured Spaniard reported that 'Drake behaved with such humanity to the Indians and negroes that they all love him.'★

★ *Cal. S.P. Venetian, 1581–91*, p. 155, cit. A. L. Rowse, *The Expansion of Elizabethan England.*

PEACE OR WAR

As in his Pacific voyage of seven years before, owing to the man-power losses sustained on its outward course Drake was unable to achieve his supreme ambition of capturing the Panama isthmus and so cutting at its weakest point the supply-line between Spain's silver mines in Peru and her conquering armies in Europe. To have taken, let alone held, it with the few hundred soldiers left him would have strained his slender resources far too far. Nor did he succeed in capturing a single treasure ship, still less the Plate Fleet which it had been hoped in England might have fallen into his hands. For, having taken advantage of the respite afforded by his long enforced sojourn at home, the Spaniards were now much better able to defend them-selves in their ocean colonies than they had been. As a result the expedition brought no financial profit to its promoters, who re-covered only three-quarters of the capital they had invested in it. Yet the damage inflicted by Drake on King Philip's preparations for invading England was incalculable. Among the trophies he brought home were 240 captured cannon, at a time when the Spaniards were still only learning to make their own. And when the news of the capture of Hispaniola and Cartagena reached the money-markets of Europe, King Philip's credit plummeted. 'The Bank of Seville is broke,' noted Lord Treasurer Burghley, formerly so dubious about the consequences of Drake's ocean ventures, 'the Bank of Valencia also very likely. It will be such a cooling to King Philip as never happened to him since he was King of Spain.' For that monarch's financial problems of paying Parma's 60,000 mercenaries and buying naval stores, provisions and munitions from half the countries of Europe for an invasion of England had been increased out of all measure by the action of a few hundred men under a great naval commander four thousand miles away. What Drake had regained for his country was the initiative at sea which his royal mistress had thrown away by keeping him so long on shore. It was its recovery which caused Spain's 'General of the Ocean Sea', the Marquis of Santa Cruz, to hasten with the flower of his navy across the Atlantic to save the Caribbean from Drake's ravages, so shutting, at his master's urgent command, the stable door after the horse was out. 'Truly,' wrote Lord Burghley, 'Sir Francis Drake is a fearful man to the King of Spain.'

★   ★   ★

Yet King Philip was not to be deterred from his purpose. It had taken long to bring him to the sticking-point, and he was now resolved to deal, once and for all, with the menace of England and its heretic Queen – the wasting ulcer at the heart of the Catholic polity in the West. Yet the Queen who so plagued him was still hoping for peace with him, both for herself and the Netherlands. The cost and frustrations of the defensive war she had so bravely, but reluctantly, undertaken in the one place where, to a landswoman's eye,* it could alone be decisive, was proving all she had feared and more. She was vexed out of patience by the factious and greedy demands of the intolerant and ever-quarrelling Dutch magnates and burghers and the Calvinist fanatics, who together formed the hard core of resistance to Parma's armies and for whose sake she was making such onerous financial sacrifices. And the commander of the forces she had sent to their aid – her old flame, Lord Leicester, now grown stout and choleric – was not only no match for Parma in the field, but had caused her deep distress by flying in the teeth of her instructions and, intoxicated by the enthusiastic reception at his first landing in the Netherlands, had accepted from the States General the grandiloquent title of 'His Excellency' and the nominal Governorship of the rebellious Provinces – an authority which, for her country's sake, Elizabeth herself had deliberately refused. That 'a creature' of hers, as she wrote in an indignant letter to Leicester, 'raised up by ourself, and extraordinarily favoured by us above any other subject,' should flout her commandments in this way was intolerable and, after her public Declaration, had gravely impugned her honour with her fellow Sovereigns. To make matters worse, his wife, Lettice, whom Elizabeth detested, was reported to be about to join him 'with such a train of ladies and gentlewomen and such rich coaches, litters and side-saddles, as her Majesty had none such, and . . . as should far surpass her Majesty's court.' Only Burghley's entreaties to his infuriated royal mistress saved Leicester from the humiliation of having to renounce his offending titles publicly.

Nor was Leicester's insubordination and the ill-success of his arms the only problem facing the Queen that summer. A few days after Drake's return from the Caribbean, a new storm broke round the head of her embarrassing captive, Mary Queen of Scots. In July 1586 a treaty had just been signed at Berwick under which Mary's twenty-year-old son, James VI, accepted a pension from the English Queen in

* So far as is known the nearest she had then been to the sea was her riverside palace at Greenwich.

return for a permanent Scottish alliance. Early that August it became known that his mother had been implicated in yet another plot against Elizabeth's life. The public fury and panic knew no bounds; the church bells were rung, bonfires lit, and mobs, singing Protestant psalms and demanding Mary's immediate death and that of the 'hellish priests' believed to be plotting Elizabeth's assassination, paraded the London streets. In a sense it had all been partly brought about by the ultra-Protestant Secretary of State, Sir Francis Walsingham, who, a few months earlier, had apprehended a secret Catholic agent sent to England to try to re-open a correspondence with the captive Scottish queen, then under strict surveillance at Chartley in Staffordshire. Faced by the rack, the agent had been 'turned round' by his English captors and employed by them to open a 'secret' way for Mary – who since the Throgmorton plot had been living virtually incommunicado at Tutbury without any correspondence with the outer world – to receive and send letters, all of which were now intercepted and, before being sent on to their destinations, deciphered by Walsingham's code-breakers. Through the medium of a small waterproof case slipped through the bung-hole of the ingoing and outgoing kegs which supplied Mary's household with beer, a voluminous cipher correspondence developed between the captive Queen and her Catholic sympathizers at home and abroad, every word of which became immediately known to the Government. It led to the discovery of an elaborate plot to assassinate Elizabeth as the prelude to a Catholic rising and a Spanish invasion – all part of King Philip's secret 'Enterprise of England' and centring round a seminary priest and a rich young Derbyshire landowner of ancient family, named Anthony Babington, formerly a page of Mary's at Sheffield Castle. A dozen or more young Catholic gentlemen, under Babington's lead, had made a pact to win a martyr's crown by despatching Elizabeth and rescuing Mary from captivity. They had even had their picture painted together to commemorate their impending heroism, while Mary herself, favoured with a long letter from Babington describing exactly how they proposed to dispose of her royal cousin, replied, enthusiastically approving and adding a few helpful suggestions of her own. Poor woman, after twenty years of imprisonment and frustration, she had little else on which to employ her time and her very considerable talents for intrigue.

Caught red-handed, the conspirators, amid wild scenes of popular rejoicing, suffered the terrible penalties for high treason in St Giles's

Fields on September 20th and 21st. Accompanied by rumours that the French of the now triumphant Catholic League – the residuary heirs, as it were, of the Massacre of St Bartholomew – had landed in Sussex and that a Spanish invasion fleet was about to sail from a Breton port, the parliamentary commission of peers, privy councillors and judges appointed by Parliament after the Throgmorton Plot to try the beneficiary of any attempt to assassinate the Queen, arrived on October 11th at Fotheringay where Mary had been taken for trial. Her bold denial of guilt in face of her own damning correspondence availed her nothing, and, 'with one assent', the Commission adjudged her guilty. Yet it took more than three months, despite much impassioned petitioning by Parliament, which met on October 29th, and another outburst of popular panic, with widespread rumours of Elizabeth's death and a Spanish landing in Wales, before the Queen could bring herself to sign the death warrant and thus make herself guilty of her cousin's and fellow sovereign's blood. For, in the last resort, she alone, not Parliament, possessed the constitutional power to end poor Mary's life.

On the morning of February 8th, in the hall of Fotheringay Castle, the dethroned Queen of Scots, Dowager Queen of France and heir-presumptive to the English throne, paid the final penalty of her tragic life for having placed her feelings as a woman before her duties as a Queen. Her noble dignity in the hour of defeat and death foreshadowed that of another Stuart sovereign sixty-two years later, her grandson Charles I. As the axe fell, a small pet dog, concealed in her skirts, emerged whimpering and lay in a pool of blood between her severed head and body. Afterwards, as the news reached London and bonfires were lit for joy in every street, Elizabeth alone remained inconsolable, refusing to eat or sleep, and even repudiating the unfortunate official who had despatched the death warrant after she had signed it.

★　　★　　★

With the end of Mary's suicidal readiness to provide the means for Jesuit and Catholic missionaries to win back England to their Faith through assassination, insurrection and foreign invasion, there died Elizabeth's last hopes of a reconciliation between the Catholic and Protestant princes of the European family, of which both she and the dead Scottish Queen were members. With it died, too, that tolerant and sensible religious uniformity for all her subjects under the aegis of a moderate and lenient reformed Church – not wholly divorced from the beliefs and ritual of their long Christian past – within which, at the start of her reign, she had sought to unite them. For by now the vast majority of her Protestant subjects were at one in a passionate hatred of Rome and all its works – born of the Smithfield fires, the massacres in the Netherlands and Huguenot France, the cruelties suffered by English seamen at the hands of the Inquisition and the repeated attempts, authorized by two successive Popes, to murder an adored Queen in order to replace her by a foreign idolater popularly supposed to have murdered her own husband. This divided the Catholic minority, even those most loyal to the Queen, from the rest of the nation, causing them to be suspected as traitors and politically penalized. Though only their priests, who, with the coming of war, were forbidden the realm, suffered serious physical, as distinct from financial, persecution, many of these, as suspected fomenters of treason, suffered martyrdom in the course of their spiritual mission.* Thanks, however, to the Queen, the persecution of Catholics in England never, even at the height of the life and death struggle with Spain, became anything like as cruel as that of heretics in Catholic countries abroad. Yet it was far removed from the merciful ideal which Elizabeth had tried so hard to establish. The fierce crusading fanaticism of the Counter-Reformation, enforced as it was by foreign arms, had evoked in the majority of Protestant Englishmen, with their love of gospel-reading, sermons and psalm-singing, a growing intolerance of everything which smacked of Rome, superstition and priestly authority, so playing into the hands of that fanatic minority of extreme Puritan zealots which to Elizabeth, with her moderation and good sense, was anathema.

By transmitting to her Protestant son her hereditary claim to the succession of the English throne – which the dead Queen before her execution bequeathed to Philip – Mary's death removed the incentive for a Catholic assassination of Elizabeth. For, while protesting volubly at his mother's decapitation, the young King of Scotland, who was not Darnley's son for nothing, remained tacitly, but cannily, committed to the English alliance and the substantial pension from

---

* Rather under three hundred of them perished in the last thirty years of Elizabeth's reign compared with the same number of Protestants burnt in three years under her predecessor, Mary Tudor.

Elizabeth he had so recently accepted for it.★ Disappointed of a rising of English Catholics and a diversion by Scottish ones against the heretic Queen's northern border, for his 'Enterprise of England' King Philip was now entirely on his own. 'As the affair is so much in God's service,' he had written when Babington's plan had been submitted to him, 'it certainly deserves to be supported, and we must hope that our Lord will prosper it.' As the Lord had not yet done so, the devout royal autocrat, in his crusade against the troublesome islanders, now claimed the succession to their throne for himself and his family as he had done that of Portugal. His descent from John of Gaunt's daughter Philippa, gave him a better right to it, he reckoned, than any other Catholic claiment, and no one in his eyes but a Catholic had any right to occupy it at all.

★ 'How fond and inconstant I were,' he wrote to Leicester at the time of Mary's sentence, 'if I should prefer my mother to the title, let all men judge. My religion ever moved me to hate her course, although my honour constrains me to insist for her life.' cit. J. E. Neale, *Queen Elizabeth*, 278.

Chapter Five

PREPARATIONS FOR INVASION

'The first article of the Tudor creed was that a united England
was an invincible England.'

S. T. Bindoff

'Come the three corners of the world in arms,
And we shall shock them. Nought shall make us rue
If England to itself do rest but true.'

Shakespeare

After his victories over the French in the Azores, the Marquis of
Santa Cruz – Spain's General of the Ocean Sea – had placed before his
royal master a plan for a titanic punitive Armada against Elizabeth's
heretic kingdom. It was to consist of 556 vessels, including 196 battle
or capital ships, together with forty fly boats and 200 flat-bottomed
barges carried on board the larger ships, the whole manned by 94,222
men, more than two-thirds of them soldiers.★ With this immense
force he guaranteed to sweep England's Navy from the seas and land
an army or armies at any point on her shores. It would make Spain
unchallenged mistress of the Atlantic, English Channel and North
Sea, as her victory at Lepanto had made her of the Mediterranean.

But the estimated cost of this self-contained amphibious enterprise
was staggering. It involved the provision of 373,337 cwt of biscuit,
22,800 cwt of bacon, 21,500 cwt of cheese, 16,040 cwt of salt beef,
23,200 barrels of tunny-fish, 66,000 bushels of peas, beans and rice,
50,000 strings of garlic, more than five million gallons of wine, with
20,000 pipes of water for the horses and mules. The ships – half of
which had still to be built – and their guns, ammunition and stores
had to be collected from every quarter of Philip's world-wide
dominions. It would cost more than even all the treasures of Mexico

★ Michael Lewis, *The Spanish Armada*, 55–7.

115

and Peru and the monopoly of the East Indian spice trade could meet. Eager though he was to subdue England, it was too much for the King's careful, calculating mind to contemplate, or for his slow patience to bear. For he was no longer prepared to wait even a year before settling accounts with Elizabeth.

Instead, Philip decided to reduce the size of the naval part of the enterprise, where his existing resources were limited, and to increase the military part which were relatively unlimited. He already had to his hand in Flanders the finest army in the world under the command of its first soldier, situated on the nearest coast to England and only a day's sail, or single tide, from her shores. And though, like his predecessor and fellow soldier, the Duke of Alva, Parma was not in favour of a war against the English, who commanded his vital sea supply-route through the Channel – at least until he had completed his reconquest of the Netherlands and secured the use of the ports of Antwerp and Flushing – in order to please his royal uncle and master, on whose favour all his wordly hopes depended, he had once, as part of an earlier plan for releasing Mary Queen of Scots, rashly suggested the possibility of a sneak barge invasion of England across the narrow seas when conditions of weather and tide were favourable and its defenders' attentions were deflected elsewhere.

Recalling this, the King, therefore, opted for a smaller and more manageable Armada, striking up the Channel from the Atlantic under Santa Cruz, in conjunction with a simultaneous descent on England's low-lying south-eastern coast by 30,000 troops under Parma, who were to cross the North Sea in flat-bottom barges collected from the rivers and canals of Flanders. How these two widely separated forces were to co-operate in the face of weather and tide, not to mention the watching English fleet in the Dover strait, was never wholly clear, despite Philip's meticulous and detailed calculations and directions on every other point. But the numerical odds in their favour seemed overwhelming. And in every port, from the Mediterranean to the Baltic, shipyards were now set to work and vast quantities of naval stores and equipment bought and shipped to the Tagus, where Santa Cruz's armada was to assemble. For Philip was resolved at all costs to strike down England in the summer of 1587.

During the winter which saw Mary Queen of Scots' trial and death, it became impossible any longer to ignore the enormous concentration of naval force building up beyond the Bay of Biscay, or to doubt its purpose. 'The like preparation was never heard nor known,' Drake warned his royal mistress, 'as the King of Spain hath and daily maketh to invade England.' In the closing days of 1586, while the threat of assassination was still hanging over her head, the Council had authorized the immediate preparation of a preventative expedition to sail in the spring to impede and, if possible, delay the concentration of this vast threatening force. Financed in the usual English way as a private joint stock venture – for, with the war in the Netherlands on her hands, the Queen's normal income was strained to the utmost – its command was entrusted to Drake, who, like his old associate and fellow Devonian, John Hawkins, Treasurer of the Navy, was insistent – novel though the idea was – that the place to defend England was on the enemy coast and not on her own. For having begun their seafaring lives as private traders in the outer oceans, and, when trade was forbidden them by the Spanish monopolists, earned their living as privateers on the enemy's colonial coasts, they had graduated in a school of naval warfare very different from that of the home-waters royal navies of Europe. And, though untaught in any school save that of practical experience in seamanship, Drake was a creative genius who had formed in his mind strategic and tactical conceptions far in advance of his time, which, in coming centuries were to govern the theory and practice of the great sea captains of the classic age of British sea power. These were to defend their island base by seeking out would-be invaders off their own ports and challenging and destroying them wherever found.

Though the main body of such of her Navy as the Queen could at present afford to man, mobilize and maintain, was based, as in the past, in the Medway and Thames estuary to guard against an invasion from the Netherlands, Drake's flying ocean force, fitting out at Plymouth, was the most powerful yet entrusted to him. It consisted of twenty-three warships and pinnaces, with ten companies of soldiers for shore operations. Four of the finest ships of Hawkins's new-built Navy, including Drake's flagship, the *Bonaventure*, were provided by the Queen herself – the principal shareholder. Other subscribers were the Lord Admiral, the London merchants of the Levant Company, who contributed seven heavily-armed Levanters accustomed to fighting their way through the pirate-ridden Mediterranean, and Drake himself, who added three more auxiliaries. His instructions were exceptionally wide. He was to intercept, capture or destroy all naval vessels or supply ships found on the Spanish coast – 'to impeach,' as they put it, 'the joining together of the King of Spain's fleets out of their several ports, to keep victuals from them, to follow them in case they should . . . come forward towards England or Ireland.' He was even empowered to 'distress the ships within the havens themselves.'

He wasted no time. As two years before in his Caribbean expedition, he was off even before he had fully completed victualling, sailing from Plymouth at the beginning of April 1587. It was well that he did so, for his pacific Sovereign, once more hoping for a negotiated peace in the Netherlands, was still refusing to believe in the seriousness of her hitherto temporizing brother-in-law's intentions. Among the State papers in the Record Office is a draft of a later order from the Council which seems to have just failed to reach Drake before he sailed, going back on his previous instructions and ordering him to 'forbear to enter forcibly into any of the King's havens, or to offer any violence to any of his towns or shipping within his harbours, or to do any act of hostility upon the land.' Either it never reached him or, if it did, he acted as if it had arrived too late.

For by then Drake was already at sea. 'There was never more likely in any fleet of a more loving agreement than we hope the one of the other, I thank God,' he had written to Walsingham before sailing. 'I find no man but as all members of one body to stand for our gracious Queen and country against Anti-Christ and his members . . . If your honour did now see the fleet under sail and knew with what resolution men's minds do enter into this action, so you would judge a small force would not divide them . . . Each wind commands me away, our ship is under sail. God grant we may so live in His fear as the enemy may have cause to say that God doth fight for her Majesty as well abroad as at home.'*

What Drake did there was daring in the extreme. The bulk of the vast battle fleet which was intended that summer to strike down England was already at Lisbon, awaiting new guns, behind the forts guarding the narrow entrance to the Tagus estuary. Any attack on this, even if possible, was expressly forbidden to Drake by a Government still not officially at war with the Spanish/Portuguese empire and still hoping for a negotiated settlement in the Netherlands. But Drake knew that there was a secondary concentration of shipping intended for the Armada still at Cadiz, Spain's chief Atlantic port, and, resolved to strike hard, he made straight for it. Arriving off the port on April 19th, after battling for five days with a south-westerly gale, he called an immediate Council of War. It was a long-established

* A. L. Rowse, *The Expansion of Elizabethan England*, 264.

custom of the Navy for Councils of War to act only on a majority decision of the captains present, but Drake would have none of it. Ignoring the objections of his Vice-Admiral, William Borough – a highly experienced officer and a member of the Navy Board – he ordered an immediate attack and led the fleet straight into Cadiz road. Here a large concentration was guarded by shore batteries and defended by what has always been regarded as invincible in enclosed waters – a squadron of long shark-like galleys, with heavy iron-shod rams for sinking any vessel which crossed their path, independent of wind and tide and propelled at incredible speed by the great sweeps of oars of chained galley-slaves spurred on by the overseer's whip.

With a favouring wind the English fleet bore straight down on the crowded shipping in the harbour. Immediately the galleys went into the attack, expecting to sink or board the rash intruders. Before they could reach them, they were met by a devastating fire from the massed guns of the *Bonaventure* which, sweeping their enslaved oarsmen's benches, quickly immobilized them and drove them back for shelter under the shore batteries.

There were about eighty Spanish ships in the port. Except for the smaller fry which were able to take refuge in shoal waters where the English could not follow them, all those ready to sail were seized and taken out to sea by prize crews, while the remainder, after being plundered, were burnt. So were the painfully collected stores destined for the Armada. Then the invaders fell on the inner harbour, where a huge galleon belonging to the General of the Ocean Sea himself was awaiting its complement of guns. It, also, was boarded and burnt. Meanwhile the English Vice-Admiral, fearful of being caught wind-bound in the inner harbour, took his ship out to sea and tried to persuade others to follow him. For this Drake, hot-tempered and peremptory when disobeyed, had him tried by court martial and sentenced to death, though the sentence – very properly, for Borough was a good and loyal, if conventional, naval officer – was never carried out.

Yet when the wind did, in fact, drop, and the dreaded galleys, seizing their opportunity, returned to the attack, they were again driven back in rout by the English gunners. Altogether 13,000 tons of shipping were destroyed before Drake withdrew, having inflicted an intolerable humiliation on earth's greatest monarch in his own chief Atlantic harbour. 'We sank,' Drake wrote in his report, 'a Biscayan of 1,200 tons, burnt a ship of 1,500 tons belonging to the

Marquis of Santa Cruz, and thirty-one ships more of from 1,000 to 200 tons, carried away with us four laden with provisions, and departed thence at our pleasure with as much honour as we could wish.'

Anticipating by more than two hundred years the classic naval strategy of Jervis and Nelson in the same waters, Drake now moved up the coast to Cape St Vincent, round which all traffic bound for Lisbon from the Mediterranean and the ports of eastern Spain and Italy was bound to pass.★ Here, to afford his fleet a protected anchorage, he landed his troops and, taking personal command, stormed the cliff castle of Sagres where, in the fifteenth century, John of Gaunt's grandson, Prince Henry the Navigator, had directed the Portuguese discoveries which, by opening the way round southern Africa to the golden East, changed the future of the world.

Here, while challenging and taunting the indignant Santa Cruz to come out and fight against his all-destroying guns, Drake maintained a close blockade of the Portuguese coast, seizing the catches of tunny fish which were to provision the waiting Armada and capturing and destroying 1,700 tons of hoops and pipestaves on which it was going to depend for supplies of water. Only when his ships, overcrowded with their complement of soldiers, ran out of victuals was he finally forced to desist, hunger driving at least one of his little fleet to mutiny. Then, with what force remained to him, he suddenly struck out far into the Atlantic and, on reaching the Azores, sighted and captured a huge Portuguese carrack returning from the East Indies with a cargo of silks and spices. Its subsequent sale in England doubled the capital invested in the expedition. When, after Drake's return to Plymouth on June 26th, rumour of the carrack's capture reached King Philip, it caused him, in his rage and anxiety, to send part of the great fleet arming in the Tagus half way across the Atlantic in order to save his threatened treasure ships. By doing so it made it impossible for the Armada to sail before the winter.

Drake's exploit made him the most famous man in the world. Men said he had singed the King of Spain's beard. The Spaniards

★ 'As long as it shall please God to give us provisions to eat and drink,' Drake wrote to Walsingham, 'and that our ships and wind and weather will permit us, you shall surely hear of us near this Cape St Vincent . . . If there were here six more of her Majesty's good ships of the second sort, we should be the better able to keep the forces from joining.' *C.M.H.* III, 305. It was the same shortage of 'good ships of the second sort' – that is, frigates and cruisers – which was to cause Nelson to miss the French fleet and Bonaparte's transports on their way to Egypt in 1798.

believed him to be a wizard who had traded his soul to the Devil for a magic mirror which enabled him to see the movements of his enemies wherever they were and so destroy them at will. 'El Draque', the dragon, they called him, viewing him with a mixture of fear and admiration. Even the Pope, Sixtus V, praised him. 'Just look at Drake,' he commented when the news reached him. 'Who is he? What forces has he? . . . We are sorry to say it, but we have a poor opinion of this Spanish Armada, and fear some disaster.' 'She certainly is a great Queen,' he said of the heretic princess in whose name these deeds were done. 'Were she only a Catholic she would be our dearly beloved. Just look how well she governs! She is only a woman, only mistress of half an island, and yet she makes herself feared by Spain, by France, by the Empire, by all.'*

'There must be a beginning of any great matter,' Drake had written from Cape St Vincent, 'but the continuing of the same to the end until it be thoroughly finished yieldeth the true glory.' Yet, almost alone, the Queen refused to be impressed by his achievement. Far from letting him return to his commanding station off the Portuguese/Spanish coast to finish the blockade he had begun, she not only refused him permission, but berated him soundly for what he had done at Cadiz. For that summer she had again opened negotiations with the Duke of Parma, not only in the hope of relieving her over-strained Treasury from the bottomless cost of maintaining an army in the Netherlands in support of her unco-operative and ungrateful Dutch allies, but, even more, of inducing her royal brother-in-law to overlook all the insults and injuries she and her maritime subjects had inflicted on him, so reverting to their old familiar diplomatic Box and Cox relationship of the past twenty-nine years. For there seemed no other way left to preserve for her realm and people the healing and enriching peace she had given them for the past quarter of a century.

And, though much glory, even when unwanted, had attended her arms at sea, it was very far from having done so under Leicester's command on land. And it was proving infinitely more expensive. The long sequence of petty defeats and retreats at Parma's hands had been redeemed only by the stubborn courage of individual English soldiers. A year earlier there had fallen in a cavalry skirmish near Zutphen the most brilliant and universally admired of all Elizabeth's younger subjects, the poet and courtier, Sir Philip Sidney – Leicester's step-son and Walsingham's son-in-law. Son of the Lord President of

* J. E. Neale, *Queen Elizabeth*, 284.

Wales and Lord Deputy of Ireland, the most accomplished writer
England had known since the great medieval court poet, Geoffrey
Chaucer, and, in the eyes of the princely rulers of Europe, almost one
of their own exalted family circle – Philip of Spain was his godfather –
with his virtue, genius and scholarship he was, at thirty-two, the
bright star of the English Protestant renaissance. Though Governor
of Flushing – the vital port which an English garrison was denying
Parma – and Leicester's General of Horse, he could not refrain from
venturing his life in the field. As, mortally wounded, he was borne
from it, he won for himself an immortality surpassing even that of his
famous *Defence of Poesie* and *Arcadia*. 'For being thirsty from excess
of bleeding,' his friend, Fulke Greville, wrote, 'he called for a drink,
but, as he was putting the bottle to his mouth, he saw a poor soldier
carried along, who had eaten his last at that same feast, ghastly casting
his eyes at the bottle. Which Sir Philip, perceiving, took it from his
hand before he drank and delivered it to the poor man with these
words, "Thy necessity is yet greater than mine". And when he had
pledged the poor soldier, he was presently carried to Arnhem.'

As for the cost of that unrewarding campaign for another people's
liberty, there seemed no end to the corruption and inefficiency –
universal in that age – of the military administration and the waste of
all the Queen's careful frugality. In its first year alone the war in the
Low Countries had swallowed nearly half her peacetime revenue.
And though she had already contributed far more than she had
promised and had sent a further 5,000 troops to the Netherlands to
take the place of those who had fallen or died, such was the habitual
fraud and dishonesty of nearly all engaged in public administration,
that the men were still unpaid and in rags. 'It is continually alleged,'
she complained, 'that great sums are due; yet why such sums are due,
or to whom they are due, and who are paid and who not paid . . . is
never certified.' No wonder she hated war, and, most of all, the wasteful and uncertain business of land warfare. 'It is a sieve,' she said, 'that
spends as it receives to little purpose.'

Despite this, so long as any in that unhappy land were prepared to
continue fighting for their independence from Spanish tyranny and
intolerance, Elizabeth would not abandon them by recalling her
troops and subsidies. Yet she felt that if she could only persuade
Parma – so akin to herself with his subtle, brilliant Italian intelligence
and good sense – to give the warring peoples he was seeking both to
conquer and conciliate, some measure of independent unity and peace

under his own rule in place of that of his despotic and bigoted Spanish uncle, it might prove possible, even at the eleventh hour, both to end the tragic sixteen years' rebellion and simultaneously avert a further and fatal escalation of the naval war with Spain.

Throughout the winter and early months of 1588, while the waiting Armada in the Tagus was recovering from the wounds Drake had inflicted on it, the peace commissioners, whom the Queen had sent to Flanders to negotiate with Parma continued, therefore, to maintain that those wounds had never been intended and had only occurred because Drake had exceeded his instructions, incurring thereby her grave displeasure. All her hopes of peace now centred on being able to persuade Philip's Viceroy to end the war and rebellion by assuming, with her help and mediation, the sovereignty for himself of a reunited and independent Netherlands. But tempting though her inducement was to Parma – for all his vice-regal honours a petty Italian princeling and royal bastard, to boot, to whom such sovereignty would have meant much – he was first and foremost a loyal servant of his uncle and employer, the King of Spain, who had no intention of allowing him to conclude a peace with Elizabeth on such terms or of letting her off the fate he had now prepared for her. The negotiations were therefore only permitted to continue until the Armada and Parma himself were ready to strike. And though Parma wanted nothing so much as to be free to complete his reconquest, so brilliantly begun, of the Netherlands, and had no faith at all in his inexorable master's unrealistic proposal to embark his fine army in an unseaworthy fleet of flat-bottomed canal barges, he continued obediently to spin out the peace negotiations with Elizabeth's commissioners. And all the while he continued secretly – or as secretly, that is, as was compatible with building and widening canals to link the country's waterways to the Flemish coast – to prepare and organize his part in the impending invasion.

For King Philip was now adamant. In his unremitting devotions and bureaucratic labours in his remote monastic cell in the Escorial, he was convinced he was being divinely guided, step by step, to the means – now preparing in the Tagus and in the canals of Flanders – for completing, with avenging fire and sword, the sacred work entrusted to him of reuniting western Christendom, begun thirty-four years ago by his marriage to his sterile cousin, Mary Tudor. Interrupted by Mary's untimely and childless death and the disastrous succession of her red-headed heretic half-sister to the throne of a kingdom which, since the Queen of Scots's death, he now felt was his by hereditary right, he was, at long last, through the blessing and intercession of the Saints, about to launch a crusade to redeem its stiff-necked people from heresy and eternal damnation. Armed *cap à pied* and mounted on his antiquated steed, the Rosinante of a faithful, pious and still half medieval Iberian land, the Spanish royal Don Quixote, not wholly disinterestedly – for there was a good deal of Sancho Panza in him – prepared to level his huge, cumbersome and formidable lance against the windmill of Elizabeth's maritime and Protestant England.

So it came about that, when the Captain General of the Ocean Sea returned from his Atlantic wild-goose chase to the Azores after the elusive Drake, his inexorable master – still resolved to launch his 'Enterprise of England' before the end of the year – ordered him to take the Armada to sea in the heart of the winter gales. Only when warned by Santa Cruz that this would be to court certain disaster, was he reluctantly persuaded to wait till the spring of 1588 – a year which soothsayers had long predicted would be one of ill omen and disaster.

That February, worn out by so many discouragements, Santa Cruz died, possibly of typhus which was raging among the overcrowded crews and soldiery of the waiting Armada, but more probably of exhaustion – for he was sixty-three – and despair at his inability to meet his sovereign's demands. The country, to whom, since his exploits at Lepanto and Terceira, the old seaman had become something of a national hero, was deeply shocked. But the crusading King, undeterred, promptly replaced him as Admiral-in-Chief of the Armada by the senior Grandee of Spain, the Duke of Medina Sidonia – a man of the highest birth and character but without the slightest experience of the sea or naval affairs. After pleading his reluctance to accept an assignment for which he was so manifestly unfitted,[*] he obeyed his sovereign's command in the spirit of devoted Christian dedication and obedience, which, with personal pride and honour, was the highest ideal of Spain's crusading chivalry. 'If you fail,' the King wrote, 'you fail, but the cause being that of God you will not fail.' Sacred banners, crucifixes, images of the saints, holy relics,

---

[*] 'The force is so great and the undertaking so important that it would not be right for a person like myself, possessing no experience of seafaring or of war, to take charge of it . . . I possess neither aptitude, ability, health nor fortune for the expedition.' Letter of Duke of Medina Sidonia to King Philip's secretary. cit. Edward Grierson, *The Fatal Inheritance*, 259.

shrivings and confessionals, companies of preaching friars and priests, and the prayers of an entire nations were to make good any possible deficiencies in the Armada's sea-worthiness, sailing qualities and provisioning.

Yet, by any standards, it was a deeply impressive force, 'the greatest Navy,' in Francis Bacon's words, 'that ever swam upon the sea.' Of its hundred and thirty sail, twenty-four were the giant new galleons of the Castilian Indies Guard and the huge fighting carracks of the Portuguese Royal Navy. The largest warships in existence, they were supplemented by four Neapolitan galleasses, each propelled, as well as by sail, by three hundred slave oarsmen and capable, under the spur of the whip, of sudden and tremendous speed. Forty-one others were large converted merchantmen or line-of-battle auxiliaries, with new fighting superstructures and armouries of heavy guns.

For, though the number of battleships was less than half the number envisaged in Santa Cruz's estimate of two years before, in one respect the 1588 Armada was a more formidable force than the abandoned one of 1586. Paradoxically it owed this to Drake's very success at Cadiz in the previous spring. For, such was the devastation he wrought there with the guns of Hawkins's new *Bonaventure* that everyone, from King Philip downwards, had realized that it would be suicide for the Armada to take to sea without a far heavier armament than that originally contemplated. Instead, therefore, of 1,150 guns distributed among 556 ships, it was equipped with 2,341, including nearly five hundred large cannon firing roundshot of up to 60 lb, far heavier, that is, than any employed in the English Navy. For whereas the latter relied on long-ranging culverins capable of firing a 17 lb iron shot a mile or more, the Spaniards, trusting to their vast superiority in soldiers and relying on the classic Mediterranean tactics of grappling and boarding their adversaries, had used the year of waiting by collecting, from every quarter available, every heavy gun they could secure. Their object was to batter the lighter and swifter English ships to a standstill by a tremendous bombardment at short-range of their masts, spars and sails, so depriving them of superior sailing-power and leaving them at the mercy of their grappling irons and boarding troops.

Equiped with this powerful new ordnance, the fighting ships of the Armada were manned by 13,000 highly trained soldiers or nearly twice as many as the seamen who handled and navigated the ships and, in a Spanish fleet, were regarded as subordinate to the military.

Apart from thirty-two pinnaces and light craft, and four galleys compared with the forty in Santa Cruz's original plan the rest of the fleet consisted of twenty-five hulks – storeships and transports – carrying equipment and replacements and 6,000 veteran troops intended to reinforce Parma's waiting army. For twelve hundred miles away, beyond the Biscay Bay and the English Channel, under King Philip's revised plan another 20,000 veterans were waiting for the arrival of the great fleet which was to ensure their passage to England and enable them to overthrow the usurping royal heretic and place a Spanish princess on her throne.

Meanwhile, as it grew clear that the negotiations in Flanders between the Queen's commissioners and Parma were merely a blind to conceal the imminence of Spain's intentions, the main English regular fleet, until now in cold storage to conserve the country's slender financial resources, was at last being mobilized and manned. At its head was the hereditary Lord Admiral, Lord Howard of Effingham – the fourth of his family to serve in that office. For in that intensely aristocratic age no one but a great nobleman accustomed to command and obedience was considered capable of controlling the jealousies and rivalries of the rough sea captains under him. A member of the Council and a cousin of the Queen, unlike Medina Sidonia he was not without some, though no great, naval experience. Fifty-two years of age and a Protestant, he was a modest, courteous but clear-headed and highly honourable man, with a strong sense of duty and responsibility to those under him.

Taking up his command in December, Howard quickly made his authority felt. At first, true to custom, he established his headquarters and that of his fleet in the Thames estuary in support of the squadron patrolling the Dover Strait and Flemish coast against Parma's threatened invasion. But he quickly came round to the view of the more experienced *avant garde* seamen who had learnt their business fighting Spain as privateers on the far side of the Atlantic, that the best defence for the country at sea was to attack. Their supreme prototype was Drake, now appointed Howard's Vice-Admiral and second-in-command, and at the moment in charge of an advance force of five Royal Navy warships and twenty or thirty armed West Country and London merchantmen at Plymouth. 'The opinion of Sir Francis Drake, Mr Frobisher and others that be men of the greatest judgment and experience,' Howard wrote to the Council, 'is that the surest way to meet with the Spanish fleet is upon their coast, or in any harbour of their own, and there to defeat them . . . I confess my error at that time, which was otherwise, but I did, and will, yield ever to them of greater experience.'★

All April, as the abortive Flemish peace negotiations drew to their inevitable conclusion, Drake, fretting with impatience at Plymouth, bombarded the Queen and Council with requests for leave to attack the Armada. 'I assure your Majesty,' he wrote on the 13th, 'I have not in my lifetime known better men and possessed with gallanter minds. than your Majesty's people are for the most part which are here gathered together voluntarily to put their hands and hearts to the finishing of this great piece of work. Wherein we are all persuaded that God, the giver of all victories, will in mercy look upon your most excellent Majesty and us, your poor subjects, who for the defence of your Majesty, our religion and native country, have resolutely vowed the hazard of our lives.'

'The advantage of time and place in all martial actions is half a victory, which being lost is irrecoverable,' Drake continued, 'wherefore, if your Majesty will command me away with those ships that are here already and the rest to follow with all possible expedition I hold it in my poor opinion the surest and best course . . . Touching my poor opinion how strong your Majesty's fleet should be to encounter this great force of the enemy, God increase your most excellent Majesty's forces both by sea and land daily, for this I surely think: there was never any force so strong as there is now ready or making ready against your Majesty and true religion.' 'If a good peace for your Majesty,' he wrote again on the 28th, 'be not forthwith concluded (which I as much as any man desireth) then these great preparations of the Spaniard may be speedily prevented . . . by sending your forces to encounter theirs, somewhat far off and more near their own coast, which will be the better cheap for your Majesty and people, and much the dearer for the enemy.' But, fearful lest her too aggressive seamen, in their desire to attack the enemy on his own coasts, should leave hers unguarded, the Queen and her Council refrained from giving the required permission.

★   ★   ★

That April, in a splendid religious ceremony at Lisbon, the Cardinal Patriarch and Viceroy of Portugal, representing King Philip – still

★ A. L. Rowse, *The Expansion of Elizabethan England*, 269.

praying and planning in the Escorial – presented to the Duke of Medina Sidonia, as he knelt before the high altar of the Cathedral, the Standard of the Armada. Blessed by the Pope, it was afterwards, to a salute from three hundred guns, raised to the mainmast of the Duke's flagship, the *San Martin*. Owing, however, to stormy weather, it was not till May 19th, more than a month later,* that the great fleet finally got to sea with its hundred and thirty ships and 30,000 men.

Four days later, on May 23rd, Lord Howard of Effingham, leading in the *Ark Royal*, took the main English fleet of thirteen battleships and supernumaries into Plymouth, Drake, vested with the Vice-Admiral's standard, going out to greet him with his Western Squadron of five battleships and twenty-three other craft. Three hundred miles to the east, five other English battleships and sixteen smaller craft, under Lord Seymour and Admiral Sir William Winter, remained, reluctantly, in the Downs to patrol the Narrows and, with the help of the Dutch 'sea-beggars', blockade the Flemish invasion ports of Dunkirk and Sluys. 'Our ships doth show themselves like gallants here,' wrote stout old Sir William Winter, 'I assure you it will do a man's heart good to behold them. And would to God the Prince of Parma were upon the seas with all his forces, and we in view of them!'† It was this squadron's presence which made nonsense of King Philip's sanguine hope that, during the main English fleet's absence in the west, Parma's troops, packed in their flat-bottomed river barges, might be able to slip across the North Sea to the Essex coast.

Here an amateur army under Lord Leicester was already waiting to receive them, while a boom and Thames defence works were being put urgently in hand. For the country was arming fast. In every southern county militiamen and volunteers were forming under the Deputy Lieutenants and the young veterans who had learnt their soldiering in the Netherlands. 'Black' Sir John Norris, who had won his spurs wherever Englishmen – in Flanders, France and Ireland – had fought in the past fifteen years, was in charge of the coastal defences from Kent to Dorset; 3,000 men under Sir George Carey were hurried to the Isle of Wight, believed to be a major Spanish objective; and the two West Country paladins, Sir Walter Ralegh and Sir Richard Grenville, laying aside their plans for colonizing Virginia, took over the joint defence of Devon and Cornwall. By

---

* May 29th/30th by the new style calendar used by Spain, but not – until the eighteenth century – by England.

† J. A. Williamson, *Hawkins of Plymouth*, 300.

June 25,000 troops were in being in Essex to defend the coasts against the dreaded *tercios*, while another 14,000 under Lord Hunsdon had assembled in Kent for the personal defence of the Queen. The last, however, for all their enthusiasm, found some difficulty in exercising their function, as Elizabeth refused either to remove from her riverside palace at Greenwich or take notice of their presence. For she did not consider she needed protection.

Meanwhile the Armada had run into difficulties, as it was driven far to the south and then struggled northwards against adverse winds up the Portuguese coast. For the number of experienced seamen to work so large a fleet, compared with the multitude of soldiers, nobles, priests and friars and other passengers aboard, was insufficient to cope with the exceptionally stormy conditions of that early summer. The victuals, which had been assembled in such immense quantities, and with such difficulty as a result of Drake's blockade in the previous spring, were already going bad, the water butts leaking, the wine soured, the meat, cheese and fish putrid in their barrels of unseasoned wood. After three weeks of trying to keep his unwieldy ships in station and his crowded and dysentry-ridden crews in heart, Medina Sidonia had at last reached Finisterre by June 9th when his vast straggling fleet was struck by a heavy south-westerly gale. The admiral and his leading ships managed to round the cape and take shelter in Corunna, while the remainder were driven far off course, some as far north as the Scillies.

The poor Duke was by now in such despair over his impossible assignment that, once ashore, he found the courage – and, in the face of that grave, resolved and inexorable despot in his remote monastic fortress, it required a good deal – to advise the King to abandon his venture. Thirty-three of his ships or a quarter of his total force were at that moment missing on the high seas – a prey to tempest and, worse than tempest, fear of the dreaded sea-wizard, Drake. Stores were running out, and most of the Duke's storm-tossed ships were in need of urgent repairs. 'I am bound to confess,' he wrote, and he included himself, 'I see very few, or hardly any, of those in the Armada with any knowledge or ability to perform the duties entrusted to them.'

But Philip, who was always at his best in adversity, remained imperturbable. Wracked with gout and in perpetual pain, he bade his faint-hearted lieutenant be of good heart, repair his ships, revictual the fleet and trust in God, who would never allow a work of such importance to fail, provided its human instruments were worthy of it. And to meet the emergency and overcome the shortages, he sent his executive secretary to Galicia, with over-riding powers to requisition everything needed to revictual and get the battered Armada out to sea again. Above all, he repeated, as he had so often done before, the detailed directions which the Duke was to follow and which he held were certain to lead to victory: that is, to press forward at all costs through the English Channel to his goal on the Flemish coast, where Parma would be awaiting him, turning aside for no other object, and only fighting on the way if attacked. The one thing the King failed to make clear was what he was to do when he got there, other than hand over 6,000 of his troops to the Duke of Parma and secure a passage for the latter's army to England. Parma, who knew infinitely more about commanding armies than Medina Sidonia did fleets, was also favoured with the same flow of peremptory orders; should the English fleet move to Plymouth and the Western approaches, if he was able in its absence to slip across the Channel before the Armada's arrival, he was to do so at once and boldly. Otherwise he was to wait on the coast till it arrived, embarking his troops in the meantime, and spinning out the pretended peace negotiations with Elizabeth's commissioners to lull her into a sense of false security. In vain Parma pointed out that flat-bottomed barges could only hope to cross the North Sea in a dead calm, and that, so long as English and Dutch warships continued to blockade his only available invasion ports, Sluys and Dunkirk, they could never cross at all.

Meanwhile all England waited breathlessly for news of the Armada. Not till June 18th, four weeks after the latter had sailed from the Tagus, was the nation officially informed through a proclamation to the Lord Lieutenants that it was at sea. All the country knew for certain was that a powerful army, which had long terrorized the Netherlands, was waiting, under the greatest commander of the age on the Flemish coast, for a chance to invade; and that the largest fleet ever assembled was at large in the Atlantic to enable it to do so. Actually, at that moment, its head was sheltering from storms at Corunna, and the remainder of the Armada was still scattered about the Bay of Biscay trying to reform. Those whom its movements most concerned, and whose business it was to find it, were themselves windbound at Plymouth under the Lord Admiral and the little group of world-famous sea captains who were his assistants. By his tact, consideration, firmness and courtesy, and complete selflessness,

Lord Howard had already welded them into a band of brothers and a single directing command; all he and they needed was a chance to find the enemy. 'There is here,' Howard wrote to Burghley, 'the gallantest company of captains, soldiers and mariners that I think was ever seen in England.'* Twice they had set out to attack the Armada on the Spanish coast, but had only been forced to return by gales and adverse winds, which were also holding up the victualling ships from London on which their ability to remain at sea depended. 'Such summer season saw I never the like,' wrote Seymour from his station in the Downs, 'what for storms and variable unsettled winds.' They were equally handicapped by the Queen's not unnatural reluctance, with the two invasion threats hanging over her realm, to let them go far from its shores lest the Armada should slip past them. What she preferred was to have them what she called 'plying up and down' the Channel and Western Approaches: 'a thing,' commented the Lord Admiral, 'impossible.' Yet, no more than she, was he able to know where the still invisible enemy intended to strike: in the Channel, in Ireland, in Scotland or even, encircling the British Isles, in the North Sea. He himself, a member of the Council and, therefore unlike Drake, well acquainted with contemporary European politics, suspected that it might be along the French coast in search of a harbour, somewhere north of the Huguenot stronghold of La Rochelle, which the Guises and their Catholic League supporters, then in the ascendant in faction-torn France, might be able to offer to the Armada as a friendly base from which to launch its invasion of England† – from a purely strategic point of view, probably the Spaniards' best course. For this reason Howard cast his defensive net as wide as possible, spreading his patrolling forces across the hundred miles of the Soundings from Scilly to Ushant, whenever the south-westerly gales of that stormy June and the arrival at Plymouth of long-awaited victualling ships from the Thames enabled him to do so.

For uncertainty over the supply of provisions was proving as much a handicap to England's sea defenders as the putrid state of the Armada's long-assembled six months' store of food and drink had proved to the Spaniards. It arose partly from the difficulties experi-

* 'I must let you know,' Howard wrote to Walsingham, 'how lovingly and kindly Sir Francis Drake beareth himself, and also how dutifully to her Majesty's service and unto me, being in the place I am in; which I pray you he may receive thanks for, by some private letter from you.' cit. A. M. Hadfield, *Time to finish the Game*, 109.

† He wrote to Walsingham to this effect on June 22nd 1588. A. M. Hadfield, *Time to Finish the Game*, 110.

enced by the Royal Navy's inadequate victualling-system – geared to supplying a fleet traditionally based on the Thames estuary – in serving one based on far-away Plymouth. It sprang even more from the Queen's habitual parsimony and her reluctance to let her aggressively-minded seamen venture more than a day's sail from England's threatened shores. That they could only do so at the expense of being forced almost immediately to return to harbour to avert starvation, had already prevented Drake from forestalling the threatened invasion by doing to the Armada in its own harbours what he had partially done at Cadiz in the previous year.

For that quick imaginative perception, linked to a lifetime's experience of sea, ships and seamen, which the Spaniards attributed to his possession of a magic mirror, enabled him, even before the news reached England, to realize that the Armada, scattered and dispersed by storms, was sheltering and refitting in the havens of north-west Spain. If, with a northerly wind behind them, the English could catch it wind-bound in harbour before it resumed its interrupted voyage, with their fast, easily manoeuvreable and heavily gunned warships, they would be able to damage it beyond hope of repair and, by doing so, save their country from invasion before King Philip's fleet could even catch sight of its shores. Every piece of news reaching England confirmed Drake's belief as to what had happened. Late in June a Cornish bark, bound for France, had sighted nine great ships between Scilly and Ushant with huge red crusaders' crosses on their sails; the captain of another West Country coastal trader was chased by a fleet of fifteen sail and, escaping from them, had landed in Cornwall and ridden post-haste with his tidings to Plymouth.

So it came about that when on July 7th – with the fleet strung out across the northern entrance to the Bay of Biscay – the wind suddenly changed to the north, Drake persuaded Howard to seize the opportunity and strike south with all speed. They were short of rations but he knew that, once on the Spanish coast, he would be able to repeat his expedient of two years before and victual the fleet from Galician farms and granaries. But when the English were within a day's sail of Corunna the wind suddenly changed again and blew strongly from the south. There was no point in trying to beat against it, for in their unvictualled state, long before they could hope to reach their target, they would run out of food and starve. There would also be the appalling risk that the Armada, taking advantage of the change of wind, might put to sea and reach the English Channel before them. There was nothing for it but to return to Plymouth at once to revictual. This, in no happy temper, they accordingly did, reaching the Sound, after two days battling with a gale, on July 12th.

Early on the day on which the battered English fleet reached Plymouth, the Armada, reassembled, refitted and revictualled, put to sea again after its month in harbour. For the next four days the vast crusading fleet, with a southerly wind behind it, sailed northwards in calm sunshine across the Biscay bay. Provisioned with fresh food and water and its crews confessed, shrived and given the Blessed Sacrament, everyone was in good heart. The sight of the huge concourse of ships stretching from horizon to horizon, and the complete absence of any enemy or, indeed, a ship of any kind, inspired a new confidence in all aboard. Every morning, as was customary in a Spanish fleet, the ships' boys sang the sacred salutation of 'Good Morrow' at the foot of the mainmast, and, every evening at sunset, the 'Ave Maria, Salve Regina'. For every day of the week an appropriately pious watchword was set, Jesus for Sunday, and, for the other days, the Holy Ghost, the Holy Trinity, St James, All Angels, All Saints and Our Lady. As the Duke of Medina Sidonia, interpreting his master's faith and that of all Spain, put it, 'the object of our expedition . . . is to regain countries to the Church now oppressed by the enemies of the true Faith.'

By the night of July 15–16th, the great fleet was off Ushant, where it ran into lowering and heavy weather, which swamped its four Mediterranean galleys, forcing them to run for safety to the nearby French coast, where two of them were shipwrecked, their Mohammedan and Protestant galley-slaves escaping in the general confusion. Here, too, Medina Sidonia put ashore one of his captains to travel overland to the Netherlands – where he arrived eight days later – to warn Parma that he was on his way. For the next two days the storm continued and the Armada was once more temporarily dispersed, about forty of its ships being driven to the north by the south-westerly gale.

But on the 18th, a Thursday, the weather came fair again, and the fleet resumed its northward journey towards the Scillies, all its missing ships rejoining it by nightfall. On the same day a letter from the Lord Warden of the Cinque Ports reached the Secretary of State, Sir Francis Walsingham, to warn him that Spanish and Italian troops of Parma's army had been seen embarking at Dunkirk. The Viceroy himself wrote on that very day to let King Philip know that his invasion boats and barges had all assembled at Nieuport by the canals which he had had dug that winter to carry them to the invasion coast. And, as on the 19th, the Armada continued its course north-wards in calm and halcyon weather, at its Admiral's orders it closed into battle formation.

Chapter Six

THE INVINCIBLE ARMADA

'Attend all ye who list to hear our noble England's praise;
I tell of the thrice famous deeds she wrought in ancient days,
When that great fleet invincible against her bore in vain
The richest spoils of Mexico, the stoutest hearts of Spain.'

Macaulay: Ballad of the Armada

'To invade by sea upon a perilous coast, being neither in
possession of any part nor succoured by any party, may
better fit a man presuming on his fortune than enriched
with understanding. Such was the enterprise of Philip II
upon England in the year 1588, who had belike never heard
of this counsel of Artabanus to Xerxes, or forgotten it.'

Sir Walter Ralegh: History of the World

At first light on Friday July 19th, Captain Thomas Fleming, patrolling off the Lizard in the 80 ton pinnace *Golden Hind*, sighted on the far southern horizon an ever-growing concourse of sails. Knowing well what it portended, he made as fast as he could for Plymouth, a hundred miles away. At about four that afternoon, he found the Lord Admiral on the Hoe playing bowls with Drake. 'We have time to finish the game,' the latter is reputed to have said as he stooped to bowl, 'and beat the Spaniards too.' What there was no time for was to finish the revictualling of the fleet, which meant that the English had to go into battle without sufficient food and water for a prolonged campaign. Yet disastrous as such a handicap could prove, to remain in harbour an hour longer than necessary with the Armada bearing down on Plymouth before a south-westerly wind was to court certain destruction. There was no alternative but to get to sea as fast as possible. About the same time as the English admirals were alerted to their danger, fifty miles away watchers on the Spanish flagship caught their first glimpse of the far line of the Lizard, three leagues to the north, and of the land they had come to conquer.

All that evening and night, caught revictualling in harbour on a lee shore, the English crews worked fiercely and unrestingly to warp their ships out to sea against wind and tide before the enemy could attack. As darkness fell, on every height along the Cornish and Devonshire coasts, and far inland, the warning beacons were lit. It was the awaited signal to carry to every part of England the news that the Invincible Armada was off her shores, ready to land the grim Spanish soldiers who, during the past twenty years, had brought massacre, fire and rape to half the cities of the Netherlands.

'Night sank upon the dusky beach, and on the purple sea,
Such night in England ne'er had been, nor e'ere again shall be . . .
For swift to east and swift to west the ghastly war-flame spread,
High on St Michael's Mount it shone: it shone on Beachy Head.
Far on the deep the Spaniards saw, along each southern shire,
Cape beyond cape, in endless range, those twinkling points of fire.'

They marked the end of the twenty-five years of halcyon peace and security which Queen Elizabeth had given a formerly divided and imperilled people. They expressed, too, the unity and proud sense of nationhood which her rule had evoked. In every shire, as the summons went out, a whole nation sprang to arms to defend its Queen and realm.

'With his white hair unbonneted, the stout old sheriff comes:
Behind him march the halberdiers; before him sound the drums;
His yeomen round the market cross make clear an ample space;
For there behoves him to set up the standard of Her Grace.'

By dawn on that Saturday, July 20th, the wind being at south-west, almost the entire English fleet, by a superb exercise of professional skill and disciplined improvization, had got itself out of Plymouth. All morning, close-hauled against the wind, its ships beat from the Sound to the open sea, in the Lord Admiral's phrase, 'very hardly'. By midday he had fifty-four of them close to the Eddystone rocks. Only a few vessels, caught in the midst of victualling, were still warping themselves out of harbour. An irreparable disaster had been averted.

Meanwhile the Spaniards, still twenty miles to windward and unaware that the English fleet lay in their path, were debating whether to attack Plymouth and, with their massive boarding troops, overwhelm any helpless English vessels lying there. But though they did not know it, the opportunity had already passed. And, though his subordinate admirals were strongly in favour of an attack on the port, Medina Sidonia felt bound by King Philip's instructions to fight only if there was no other way he could secure the all-important passage of Parma's army to England. Avoiding all diversions, therefore, in obedience to royal orders he proposed to press steadily up the Channel towards the Straits of Dover where, three hundred miles to the east, he believed the main English fleet was waiting to bar his junction with the Viceroy. There, and there only, was he empowered to fight except in self-defence.

That night the Armada anchored in the close battle formation in which it was to sail and defend itself until it reached its destination. To observers from the shore it resembled an enormous crescent stretching far out to sea. In reality it constituted a vast square or round floating laager, with the flagship and largest fighting galleons in front to sweep aside opposition, while other warships on either flank and in the rear protected its soft centre, which was packed with transports and store-ships as in some enormous mobile harbour. This was in keeping with traditional Spanish naval technique, based on long experience of fighting in the enclosed waters of the Mediterranean by combatants applying to battles at sea the military rules appropriate to those fought on land.

During the night, which was moonlit but hazy, shadowy forms were observed passing across the Armada's front towards the open ocean beyond it. Others were seen moving westwards between its inshore flank and the Cornish coast. Only when day dawned was it realized that a surprised and outnumbered English fleet, after weathering it out at sea, had crossed the Spaniards' front without being seen, and then, in the hours of darkness, had outflanked and infiltrated behind them and was now cruising a mile or so to windward. By a feat of seamanship so remarkable that the Spanish pilots and sailors could hardly credit it, Drake and his fellow admirals, in the course of a brief summer's night, had captured the weather-gauge and, at the expense of leaving the Channel and southern English coastline open to the Armada, had placed themselves in a commanding and controlling position in its rear. Instead of defensively barring its course towards the Straits and Parma's waiting army, staking his country's survival on a novel principle of naval warfare – evolved and taught by the world-famous circumnavigator who was now the Lord Admiral's chief of staff and deputy fleet commander – Howard had deliberately uncovered what he had been sent to defend. By doing so he had regained the initiative. Outnumbered in capital ships by nearly two to one – for part of the new-built battle-fleet was at the other end of the English Channel guarding the narrow seas against Parma – he was in a position to call the tune and make the Armada dance to it. For the revolutionary technique of ocean warfare which Drake and his fellow privateers had mastered in their ocean forays and taught their countrymen, and which Hawkins had so prophetically applied in building their new warships, was to make the wind England's servant and, anticipating and adapting to its ever-changing moods – whether Ariel or Caliban – use it in battle as an ally.

The two fleets confronting one another – or rather drawn up behind one another, both facing east up the English Channel – presented a remarkable contrast. Obscuring the sight of the sea's surface for several square miles lay a dense mass of a hundred and thirty Spanish ships, some of them of a thousand tons or more, with huge black hulls, towering masts and superstructures, and coloured sails emblazoned with the Catholic mythology of a thousand years. Their decks were packed with soldiers waiting to board, while great grappling-irons hung from their yard arms to enable them to do so. As the contemporary Elizabethan historian, William Camden, put it, 'the English descried the Spanish ships, with lofty turrets like castles in front, like a half moon, the wings thereof spreading out about the length of seven miles, sailing very slowly though with full sails, the winds being, as it were, tired with carrying them and the ocean groaning with their weight.'

In contrast, scarcely half their height, with white sails bearing St George's Cross and hulls painted in geometrical patterns of green and white – their Queen's colours – the scattered English battleships, hovering in the Armada's rear, looked almost puny by comparison. Lying low in the water, with guns bristling from their portholes, they yet had a trim, business-like and, to Spanish eyes, rather sinister look.

The first action fought in mid-ocean between two major sailing fleets was now about to begin. In pursuance of their King's and Admiral's express orders, the Spaniards' purpose was to retain their close defensive formation, so protecting within it the unarmed hulks and transports carrying the troops and supplies which were to join with Parma's waiting army to invade England, while continuing steadily eastwards towards their distant destination on the Flemish coast three hundred miles ahead, beyond the Dover Strait. The object of the smaller, less organized and far less impressive-looking force to windward of the Armada was to use its greater sailing skill and manoeuvreability and its, till now, proved superiority in gun-power, to break up the Spaniards' defensive formation and destroy in the open sea their capacity to land an army on English soil. For this they relied on their ships' formidable broadsides with which Drake had reduced to helpless impotence and surrender so many isolated Spanish ships in the Caribbean and Pacific, and more recently demonstrated on the coasts of Spain itself – notably in Cadiz harbour – their terrifying punishing power.

Having the weather-gauge, which they had so quickly and unexpectedly seized from their enemy during the past twenty-four hours, the English began the engagement by attacking the weather division of the slow eastward-moving Armada. They did so not as a single fleet but in little groups of ships – led by Howard, Drake and Hawkins or often without a leader at all – making for the nearest enemy vessel or group of vessels and subjecting them to their gunfire, firing about five shots to one of their adversaries. As ship after ship, sailing in line ahead, poured successive broadsides on to one after another of the outlying Spanish ships, and then, tacking and returning, repeated the same punishment with the other broadside, the weaker ships of the Spanish weather-squadron began to give ground and fall back on the Armada's crowded centre.

But at this point the English received an unwelcome surprise from the unsuspected power of the new heavy-shotted cannon with which the Armada had been secretly equipped during the waiting months after Drake's spectacular gunnery success at Cadiz. Two Spanish ships in particular, both commanded by grandees of high lineage, the *San Juan* – flagship of the veteran Don Juan Martinez de Recalde of Bilbao, commanding the Biscayan squadron of the rearguard – and that of his vice-admiral, though heavily outnumbered and resisting with great gallantry, made it clear, whenever their assailants came too near, that the 50 lb iron round-shot from their new heavy battering pieces were capable of totally destroying the rigging on which the English ships depended for their superior mobility, so leaving them at the mercy of the grappling irons and massed boarding troops to which the Spaniards traditionally looked for victory. It was for this, realizing the superiority of the finely-handled English culverins firing their 17 lb shot at long-range, that King Philip had re-equipped his fighting galleons with far heavier cannon and shot. 'It must be borne in mind,' he had written, 'that the enemy's object will be to fight at long distance in consequence of his advantage in artillery . . . The aim of our men, on the contrary, must be to bring him to close quarters and to grapple with him.' During the Armada's year of waiting in the Tagus he had therefore given its average fighting-ship a broadside, at short-range, of twice the weight of the average English long-range broadside, and provided the fleet with no less than 123,790 cannon-balls and 517,500 lbs of gunpowder.*

Realizing that to press home their attack against such devastating – and unexpected – weight of fire-power would be suicidal, the English fell back on their hereditary skill in seamanship and the greater manoeuvrability of their ships to keep out of range, confining their own bombardment of their foes to the longer ranges at which their culverins, with their much lighter shot, could safely operate. At this distance, though out of reach of the destructive power of the short-range heavy Spanish cannon, the English, notwithstanding the greater accuracy and speed of fire of their practised gunners, could make no impact at all on the stout hulls of their adversaries. Both participants in the furious and isolated gun battles which raged all morning were thus unable to make any decisive impression on their opponents, despite a prodigious expenditure of noise and ammunition, particularly on the English side, whose rate of fire was far more rapid than that of the less skilful and experienced Iberian gunners. The Spaniards suffered more casualties, mostly among the soldiers drawn up on their crowded decks waiting to board; the English, keeping to a safe distance, hardly any at all.

While this was happening, some of the greatest fighting galleons of the unengaged Spanish vanguard, led by Medina Sidonia's flagship, the 1,000 ton *San Martin*, had been coming to the assistance of Recalde's hard-pressed ships. To do so they had had to leave their stations in the Armada's closely-packed formation, and travel round its circumference to reach the embattled rearguard. Like the retreat of some of the weaker brethren into the Armada's soft and crowded centre, this caused a good deal of confusion, including a collision between two galleons of the Andalusian squadron, causing one of them – the *Nuestra Señora del Rosario*, flagship of its admiral, Don Pedro de Valdez – to lose her foremast and bowsprit. About the same time, another great galleon, the *San Salvador*, vice-flagship of the

* Michael Lewis, *The Spanish Armada*, 74, 79, 134–5.

Guipuscoan squadron, carrying the Paymaster General of the Armada and part of the royal treasure, was rocked by an enormous explosion, which destroyed both its stern decks and killed two hundred of its crew, burning and wounding many more. It was rumoured that a conscripted Dutchman had avenged himself and his countrymen by throwing a lighted fuse into a powder-barrel before jumping overboard. Rendered unmanageable by fire, the *San Salvador*, like the damaged *Nuestra Señora*, had to be towed into the Armada's safe centre, where its treasure and surviving crew could be taken off and trans-shipped.

At one o'clock, the Spanish formation proving virtually unbreakable, alarmed at the rapidity with which his gunners were exhausting his fleet's inadequate reserves of ammunition Howard wisely called off the action. Neither side could claim a victory. The nine hundred or so heavy battering-pieces with which King Philip had equipped the Armada had failed to immobilize a single English ship or subject it to the close in-fighting and boarding which had won the great Spanish galley victories of Lepanto and Terceira, and through which he had hoped to crush the English by sheer weight of numbers and courage of his highly-trained and disciplined soldiers. In the course of a four hours' engagement, the Spaniards had discovered the impossibility of getting to close grips with the elusive islanders in the face of their long-range broadsides and the ease and speed with which they could manoeuvre their vessels in and out of range. 'Their ships being very nimble,' Medina Sidonia reported to the King after the action, 'and of such good steerage, they did with them whatever they desired.'

On the other hand, the English had found the tenacity and endurance of Spain's proud martial chivalry far greater than that of the easy-going Spanish colonials whom they had encountered and routed in the tropics. Nor, though for a short while they had dented, had they been able to break the close defensive cordon round the Armada's soft centre, any more than their hitherto triumphant guns had proved able at long-range to penetrate its galleons' stout sides. 'As far as we can perceive,' Drake reported, 'they are determined to sell their lives with blows.' 'I will not trouble you with any long letter,' Howard wrote that afternoon to Walsingham. 'We are at this present otherwise occupied than in writing. At nine of the clock we gave them fight which continued till one . . . We durst not venture to put in among them, their fleet being so strong.' The sting of his letter lay in its tail. 'Sir, for the love of God and our country, let us have with some speed some great shot of all bigness and some powder with it; for this service will continue long.'

One thing at least the English had achieved by that morning's exploratory and indecisive engagement. With the wind behind them, they had imperceptibly pushed the Spaniards past the entrance to Plymouth, to the great relief of its Mayor and people, anxiously watching and listening to the battle from the Hoe. Yet the price still to be paid for the English admirals' revolutionary tactic of seizing the weather-gauge by placing themselves behind the advancing Armada was that it still left the whole coastline of the English Channel wide open to the invading army, carried in its transports in the centre of that threatening forest of masts and sails. It was, therefore, essential to keep it moving and not allow it to seize a harbour or bay where it could disgorge its ravaging troops. For the English could not know that this was precisely what the directing despot in the Escorial had expressly forbidden his Commander-in-Chief until he could reach the Flemish coast and effect his junction with the Duke of Parma.

Nor were they aware that on that very afternoon, at a Council of War in the *San Martin*'s cabin, the Spanish admirals were urging this very course on the Duke of Medina Sidonia. One in particular – the staunch old seaman, Juan Martinez de Recalde, a hero of Terceira and a former commander of the Indies Fleet – argued passionately for providing the Armada with a secure base at the western end of the English Channel, where it could refit and be reinforced for future operations. For both he and the English admirals were well aware that one such potential base – the broad sheltered anchorage of Torbay* – lay only a short distance ahead on the Armada's port bow. Yet the conscientious Duke would not deviate from his master's orders or contemplate any halting place on his perilous crusade except, at the urgent instance of his admirals, the Isle of Wight two hundred miles ahead, which, in earlier instructions, King Philip – though it was still a hundred miles short of Parma's waiting army on the Flemish coast – had suggested the fleet might seize on its way.

During that afternoon and evening – one of Councils of War in both fleets – the vast Armada, followed and shepherded at a safe distance by the English, was moving slowly eastwards along the Devonshire coast. All attempts to take the crippled *Nuestra Señora*

* Where just a century later, in 1688, the future King William III landed with an invading army.

in tow had failed, and, as the officer whom King Philip had appointed to advise the inexperienced Commander-in-Chief on navigational matters was insistent that the close formation of the Armada, on which its security against English attacks depended, could not be maintained if it shortened sail for her, the crippled flagship of the Andalusian squadron had to be abandoned. As night was falling, a galleon and one of the fast galleasses, together with a pinnace, were detailed to stay with her and take off her treasure, crew and admiral. But the latter, Don Pedro de Valdez – a cousin of the flag officer of the same name who had advised Medina Sidonia to leave the luckless ship to her fate – refused to sully his honour by leaving her. So it came about that during the night, after being accidentally sighted by a small English auxiliary which proceeded to shadow the *Nuestra Señora* and her cluster of escorts, the latter, fearful of being found at daybreak and cut off by the pursuing English, abandoned her and made off to rejoin the Armada. It so happened that during that night Drake, following Howard's flagship in the *Revenge*, saw some shadowy ships moving in the opposite direction and, suspecting they might be Spaniards trying to repeat his manoeuvre of the previous night and regain the weather gauge, slipped out of his place in the line to follow and thwart them. Dawn, however, showed them to be a convoy of German merchantmen proceeding down Channel on their lawful occasions. In seeking to regain his place in the pursuing fleet, he accidentally encountered the abandoned Spanish derelict. Upon which, summoned by the *Revenge* to yield, Don Pedro de Valdes surrendered without a fight to the one man – the dreaded 'El Draque' – to whom even the proudest and bravest Spaniard felt it no shame to submit. Thus, with Drake's usual good fortune, he was able, at the very outset of the campaign, to capture, complete with its treasure, admiral and crew of 460 and 46 guns, a major Spanish galleon. Frobisher, who hated him and his good fortune, subsequently maintained that he had deliberately left his place in the line to snap up the abandoned prize. But as Drake at the time could not possibly have known of her fate and whereabouts – for, unlike the Spaniards in their close disciplined formation, the English had no means of communicating with one another at night except by lanterns – the charge was manifestly ridiculous. Both the *Nuestra Señora* and the burnt out and abandoned *San Salvador* were subsequently towed into English ports, where the latter's hold unexpectedly yielded up a providential store of 1,000 iron shot and two hundred barrels of high-grade powder, which was sent post haste after the English fleet, then running dangerously short of both.

Though, thanks to King Philip's meticulous care, the Armada had been lavishly equipped with everything, once a landing had been effected, to finance a permanent occupation of the British Isles as part of his Catholic Atlantic empire, thanks to the same all-commanding eye its tactical directives had been so strictly set that they allowed of no possible deviation. The Armada thus proceeded on the exact course ordained for it by its creator without turning aside to land its formidable and superbly equipped troops in the Torbay anchorage in its path. So precisely did its obedient Commander-in-Chief and his chief naval adviser – a disagreeable martinet named Diego Flores de Valdez, much disliked by his fellow admirals but in high favour with King Philip – observe the royal instructions that they sent a pinnace of officers of the Provost's Corps round the fleet to ensure that every ship was keeping its exact station in the rigid military formation ordained for it, with orders, and a hangman and gallows in attendance, to string up summarily any captain who got out of alignment. None, however, did so. Nor at this stage did Providence – favouring the Armada's sacred mission with a week of flawless, storm-free weather – nor the heretic islanders, with their shortage of ammunition, put a spoke in the Escorial's wheel, the English following the huge, impregnable floating fortress, vainly hoping for further stragglers to attack, as it made its slow majestic way eastwards across Lyme Bay in the summer sunshine of Monday, July 22nd. All the time a continuous stream of small ships and boats poured out from the little Dorset ports of Lyme, Charmouth and Bridport, bringing the English fleet volunteers, supplies of food, fresh vegetables and ammunition, as fast as the shore authorities could collect or requisition them, while spectators, peering anxiously seawards through the summer haze, crowded the low hills above the Chesil Beach and West Bay.

During the short moonlit night of July 22nd the Armada and Howard's shadowing fleet passed to the south of the long projecting peninsula of Portland Bill, to the immediate east of which, as dawn broke on Tuesday the 23rd, both fleets found themselves becalmed. By then the south-west wind which had followed them from the Atlantic had dropped and was succeeded by a gentle breeze from the north-east, giving the Spaniards the windward station which Howard and Drake had seized from them three nights earlier. Half a dozen

ships on the English inshore flank, lying close to the Portland cliffs and
led by the hot-tempered Martin Frobisher in the 1,000 ton *Triumph* –
the largest vessel in the English fleet – were as a result dangerously
exposed to attack. Seeing an opportunity to apply the battering and
boarding process which was the Spanish recipe for victory at sea,
Medina Sidonia sent in his four swift giant Neapolitan galleasses,
each propelled by three hundred galley slaves, to encircle the wind-
bound English ships and enable their waiting soldiery to board them.
But Frobisher, who was never happier than in a fight, poured such an
intensity of fire on the galleasses' rowing-decks, killing and wounding
so many of their oarsmen and smashing their long sweeps, that they
were forced to take to their sails, which made them so clumsy as to be
virtually unmanageable.

Meanwhile the inshore fight between the two fleets became general.
Both flagships were heavily engaged, the *San Martin*, which had
gone to the galleasses' assistance, being attacked by the *Ark Royal*
and six other English ships. Yet though the Spanish flagship lost
fifty of her crew from the English gunfire, had her water butts holed
and fifty shots lodged – but only lodged – in her huge sides, the range
between the contestants, as more and more Spanish galleons joined
the mêlée, grew steadily less. And, as the danger of close fighting and
boarding increased, the overwhelming superiority of the invaders'
military manpower pointed to only one, and that a disastrous, ending.

At that moment Drake, from the battle's seaward flank, entered the
fight with dramatic effect. Knowing, from long experience of the
English Channel winds and weather, how in a summer's day an early
offshore breeze could suddenly veer at midday to a sea-wind from
the south or west, he had anticipated the change by beating out to
sea while Howard and Frobisher were so dangerously engaged near
Portland Bill. Then, when the wind behind him changed, with fifty
ships, great and small, he swept down on the mêlée out of the clouds
of battle smoke to rescue his hard-pressed chief and comrades,
threatening not only to break the embattled Armada in two, but to
cut it off from the east and the open Channel up which it was moving
towards its junction with Parma. At once, abandoning his attempt to
close on Howard and Frobisher, Medina Sidonia, obedient to his
royal master's instructions, reformed his fleet's ranks so as to resume
its purely defensive role. The engagement continued till five o'clock,
when, not daring to press home their attack to point-blank range
against the retreating enemy's heavy guns, and themselves running

increasingly short of ammunition – for they were even reduced to firing plough-chains from the Dorset farms instead of shot – the English called off the fight. With the battered, but proud, *San Martin* leading, the Armada resumed its progress eastwards.

During Wednesday the 24th the two fleets, the English still at a respectful distance behind the Spaniards like sheep-dogs shepherding an enormous flock of rams and sheep, drifted in the light south-west breeze past Lulworth and the Purbeck cliffs towards the distant Isle of Wight. Here, under its temporary Governor, Sir George Carey, the islanders, reinforced by three thousand militiamen and volunteers from the mainland, were preparing to sell their lives dearly on the beaches to save their farms and villages from the fate of the Netherlands. Meanwhile, determined at all costs to keep the Armada moving past the island anchorages and thwarted so far in every attempt to break up its close formation, in a Council of War in the *Ark Royal*'s cabin the English admirals decided to match the Spaniards' discipline in battle with a battle order of their own, though a naval, not a military one. Instead of leaving their ships to fight individually and group themselves as they pleased, as in the battles of Plymouth and Portland, they agreed to confront the Spaniards next day in four separate squadrons, commanded by Howard himself, Drake, Hawkins and Frobisher, and to which every ship, great or small, naval or auxiliary, should belong, and from whom all captains and masters should take orders by signal or word of mouth. It was the first time in England's sea history that such a course had been taken.

Dawn on Thursday July 25th found both fleets becalmed near the south point of the Isle of Wight. Guarding the eastern entrance to the Solent and the flat north-east coast of the island most exposed to a large-scale landing – and where the French had landed forty years before – was Frobisher's squadron, led by him in the *Triumph*. Once more the fiery Yorkshireman – Drake's rival and bitterest critic – put up a magnificent fight. At one moment the *Triumph* was attacked by three galleons and was in imminent danger of being boarded. Lowering eleven of his boats to tow his imperilled flagship into what wind there was, Frobisher's gunners just managed to keep the attackers at bay until a light breeze from the west got up and the great ship, with all her guns blazing, escaped from the net closing round her.

During the calm the *Ark Royal*, which had gone to Frobisher's assistance, had also been attacked by three of the Neapolitan galleasses which, emerging from the Armada's centre at high speed, with all their hundreds of oars flashing, surrounded and tried to board her. But once again, as at Portland two days earlier, just as the Spaniards with their grappling-irons and massed storm-troops, saw victory almost within their grasp, the situation was again transformed by Drake's seaward squadron. Anticipating the midday change of wind, to avail himself of which he had beaten out to sea, he burst on the battle from the south, possibly with Hawkins's squadron to aid him, sweeping the Spaniards away from their prey and the island beaches and threatening to drive the Armada's weather flank on to the dangerous Ower Banks between the Isle of Wight and Selsey Bill. To prevent his embattled fleet from being cut in two, Medina Sidonia and his leading galleons were forced to abandon both their potential prey and the invasion beaches and withdraw, still fighting, eastwards. Gradually the whole mass of the Armada began once more to move up Channel, carrying with it, to the relief of the militiamen and volunteers guarding the threatened island, the thousands of waiting soldiers who might so easily have captured it.

A little before three in the afternoon the rival admirals by tacit agreement broke off the action. Both sides were glad of the respite. For the Spaniards had had all they could take, and the English were almost out of ammunition. One Spanish hulk, the *Santa Ana*, heavily holed and in serious difficulty, dropped away to the south, making during the night for the French coast, where she became a total wreck. Both fleets spent the rest of the day recovering, their crews making good the damage to sails, hulls and rigging, and the two commanders-in-chief writing urgently to their backers on shore. Howard wrote to the Earl of Sussex, Governor of Portsmouth, imploring him to send him all the shot, powder and victuals he could command. Meanwhile Medina Sidonia was writing to the Duke of Parma, warning him to be ready to embark his troops the moment the Armada appeared off the Flemish coast, and requesting two shiploads of powder and shot and as many small fly-boats as possible to help him force the evasive English into close encounter so that he could board and overwhelm them with his superior weight and numbers.

With only eighty miles to cover before the Straits of Dover, King Philip's strategy was about to be put to the test. There a small but powerful English squadron, under Lord Seymour and Admiral Sir William Winter, was guarding the narrow tidal waters which lay between the approaching Armada and the little shallow North Sea ports of Dunkirk and Nieuport, where Parma's invasion troops and barges were blockaded by two patrolling flotillas of fierce Dutch 'sea beggars', eager to cut the throats of every Spanish soldier who ventured within reach. If, in the face of weather, tide and any further attack by Howard's shadowing fleet, the Armada could preserve its unbroken formation and, brushing aside the light English and Dutch forces in its way, anchor off the Flemish coast, it could take into its safe protected centre the open flat-bottomed river-barges and boats assembled there to carry Parma's waiting troops to England. Then, joined to those from Spain already in the crowded transports, they could together be ferried across the North Sea to land, under cover of the Armada's guns, on the flat Essex shores north of the Thames estuary. Commanded by the greatest captain of the age, an army of nearly 30,000 professional veterans could then march on London, with nothing to stay them but a loose, ill-equipped assemblade of half-trained militiamen and volunteers.

Everything, therefore, would turn on what happened in the next few days. Having failed in three successive battles to break the Armada's defensive formation and, despite a prodigious expenditure of ammunition, to sink a single Spanish ship, the English admirals knew that, unless they could now force a victory over what had so far proved invincible, nothing could save their country from invasion and from all which that portended for their dear ones, homes, Queen and religion. They had little time left in which to strike, for, if the weather held and the wind stayed in the west, the Armada could be on the Flemish coast within the next two or three days. It was now a week since they had left Plymouth Sound, and, despite supplies continually hurried out to them in small craft from every Hampshire, Sussex and Kentish port, they were growing short of food and had only ammunition enough for one more battle on the scale of the last three. And they knew that, unlike Spain, with the inexhaustible wealth of the Indies and the Pacific behind her, their small country was without financial reserves. For all her Queen's careful parsimony, she could not continue indefinitely to maintain a fully manned fleet and militia army with an invasion Armada remaining intact in northern waters.

In the Spanish fleet, unknown to the English admirals, even graver doubts and anxieties prevailed. For, though none of their ships had been sunk in battle, they had suffered far heavier damage by long-range gunfire than their smaller, more weatherly and better handled opponents. And the morale of their officers and crews had suffered far more than their ships from their humiliating failure, despite their superiority in size and numbers, to bring the English to grips. The need for a port or some safe harbourage, in which to repair and refit, was clear now to every seaman in the Armada. When Medina Sidonia's despatches at least reached the Escorial, forgetting what he had so imperiously ordained and the impracticability of what Parma had repeatedly, so far as he dared, warned him, even King Philip minuted, 'I do not see how they are to effect a juncture if they have no port to do it in.'

As for the unfortunate Viceroy, assailed by Medina Sidonia's almost desperate overland emissaries apprising him of the Armada's imminent arrival on the Flemish coast, with the only two small ports he possessed, Dunkirk and Nieuport, both blockaded by the Dutch sea-rebels, he could do nothing until the Spanish fleet appeared on the coast and drove the blockaders away. He had always felt that his royal master should wait before launching the Armada until he had had time to expel the English and Dutch from Flushing and the islands blocking Antwerp and the Scheldt, and so secured at least one reasonably-sized port where the embarkation of his troops could be conducted in safety. Nor, with his sound military judgement, could he regard with anything but profound apprehension the prospect of embarking his fine army – the best in Europe – in a flotilla of unseaworthy open boats and entrusting it to an amphibious operation fraught with so many risks and uncertainties. Like Alva before him, he had never wanted a breach with England, with her geographical stranglehold on Spain's sea communications with the Low Countries, until he had completed their subjection and regained possession of the seafaring heretic northern maritime provinces of the Netherlands, which, given time, he was confident he could do. With his fine strategic brain, he was also almost unique in the Spanish camp in his awareness of the full significance of sea power in the new oceanic world which his Italian countrymen, in the service of Spain and Portugal had helped a century earlier to discover, and which Drake and the English corsairs had since so brilliantly exploited. And he was aware how far-seeing Elizabeth and Cecil had been in their intervention on behalf of the Dutch insurgents, and how fatal an interruption to his master's plans the occupation and defence of Flushing by an English garrison was proving.

It was, therefore, in anything but a hopeful frame of mind that he received at Bruges on Sunday July 28th an urgent summons from Medina Sidonia, despatched overland on the previous evening from the Armada off Calais, where, at the end of its ten days' voyage up the English Channel, it had just cast anchor. 'If you cannot bring out all your fleet,' the Admiral wrote, 'send me the forty or fifty fly-boats I asked for yesterday, as with this aid I shall be able to resist the enemy's fleet until your Excellency can come out with the rest, and we can then go together and take some port where this Armada can enter in safety.' For, having obediently brought his great fleet, with all its treasure and its thousands of invincible soldiers, to anchor off a neutral French port twenty miles short of the Flemish border, this hapless landsman-at-sea seemed to be expecting the Viceroy, who had no fleet but only an army, to help him find the non-existent port for lack of which all King Philip's carefully laid plans looked like foundering. For both the genealogically immaculately-descended first Grandee of Spain and the irregularly born Italian princeling of military genius had been entrusted with the impossible task of reconciling the physical world of land and sea with the pious illusions of a devout and bureaucratically minded master, living in a cloud-cuckoo world of his own imagination ruled over by the Catholic saints and the Blessed Virgin Mary. Instead, they had to wrestle with the awkward terrestrial facts brought about by the policies of an anything but blessed English virgin – a bastard and usurper at that, as King Philip now maintained – whose skilful seamen were resolved to contest to the death the mastery of the narrow seas, and whose amateur but stubborn soldiers so inconveniently occupied in Flushing the one port which could have afforded the Armada the invasion base it so desperately needed.

So it came about that, in the afternoon of Saturday July 27th, having covered the eighty sea-miles from the Isle of Wight and deliberately avoided the English side of the Dover Strait, warned by his pilots of dangerous shoals immediately ahead along the French and Flemish coast Medina Sidonia anchored off the French port of Calais. Here, by courtesy of its neutral but Catholic governor, he could communicate quickly and directly with the Duke of Parma. Immediately afterwards the English fleet, which had continued to shadow the Armada, anchored about a mile to windward and sea-ward of it, having, with its habitual expertise, avoided overshooting its quarry and so losing the wind, as the Spanish admirals had vainly hoped it would. Shortly afterwards, just as dusk was falling, it was joined from England by the remainder of the Royal Navy under Lord Seymour and the veteran Sir William Winter, whose fine seamanship in blockading the Firth of Forth thirty years before in the opening days of Elizabeth's reign, had saved the nascent Scottish Reformation from the French.

After the Battle of the Isle of Wight, the Council, its mind concentrated on the menace of the invading army assembled opposite the Thames estuary, sent an urgent despatch to Seymour, then cruising off Dungeness, ordering him 'to bend himself to stop the issue of the Duke of Parma's forces from Dunkirk'. But on Saturday afternoon, while he was revictualling in the Downs on his way to do so, he received an urgent summons from the Lord Admiral bidding him join him off Calais. This, spoiling for a fight, he and Winter immediately did, with their eight battleships and thirty or so armed merchantmen and auxiliaries.

The entire Royal Navy was now concentrated under the Lord Admiral. His new accession of strength brought the number though not the size, of the ships under his command to even more than that of the Armada. As the two admirals went aboard the flagship for a Council of War, there was a nip of autumn in the air, and more than a hint that the lovely summer weather of the past ten days was about to change. With Parma's waiting army at Dunkirk only a few hours away there was no doubt in the minds of those present what had to be done. If only the Spanish fleet's defensive formation could be broken, there would be a chance of destroying or crippling it before it could take in Parma's invasion barges. There was no time to be lost. It was, therefore, decided that, if the Armada made no move next day, the English should rout it out at night with fireships – the classic way of moving a fleet of wooden ships anchored on a lee shore.

During the Sunday, July 28th, both fleets rested, their crews observing their Catholic and Protestant forms of worship. But among the English, who had now been joined by many members of the Queen's Court – including Sir Walter Ralegh, the young earls of Oxford, Cumberland and Northumberland, Charles Blount the future Lord Mountjoy, and both Burghley's sons, Thomas and Robert Cecil – all thoughts turned to the battle to be fought on the morrow for their country's existence, and to the preparations for launching the fireships. It had been intended to have them prepared at Dover, but when it was realized that these could not arrive in time, they were taken from the swarm of small ships which had joined the fleet from almost every port in southern England. Both Drake and Hawkins contributed vessels of their own. All eight, screened from Spanish view, were stacked high with firewood and barrels of pitch, and armed with guns, pointed at the enemy, which would go off simultaneously as soon as the flames reached their primings.

At midnight a single gun was fired from the *Ark Royal*. Manned by volunteer crews, with dinghies in tow to evacuate them, the fireships set off in line abreast, aimed at the centre of the Armada. With both wind and tide running fast behind them, as that raging forest of fire bore down on the Spanish flagship and the great fighting galleons around it, a wild panic broke out. Though Medina Sidonia himself kept his head and his own flagship took orderly evasive action, in most of his ships the frightened captains and crews cut their cables, abandoned their anchors and put to sea in utter confusion. Many collided in the dark, and the flagship of the Neapolitan galleasses broke her rudder and ran aground. She was subsequently stormed and sacked, as she lay helpless on the beach, by successive waves of English and French plunderers.

Daybreak, on Monday July 29th, found the Armada drifting a few miles to the east of Gravelines, its formation lost. Scattered over a large area of sea, unable to anchor, Medina Sidonia in the *San Martin* tried desperately to rally and reform its ranks. It was the moment for which the English had been waiting. Weighing anchor at first light, they went into the attack in four squadrons, led by Drake, Hawkins and Frobisher, and Seymour and Winter with the newly joined squadron of the Narrow Seas. Howard, for once, entered the battle late, having been delayed attending to the destruction of the galleasses' grounded flagship.

For fifty miles to the east of Calais there stretched off the Flemish coast a line of concealed sandbanks known as the Banks of Zeeland, which every Spanish pilot was now seeking to avoid. Along its northern and menacing fringe the Battle of Gravelines, as it became known to history, was fought. To Drake, whose seafaring life had begun at the age of eleven as an apprentice on a Thames estuary hoy trading with Newcastle and the Netherlands, the swirling tides, currents, shoals, winds and sudden fogs of this treacherous stretch of water had been his earliest teachers, remaining deeply impressed on his memory. It was he who led the attack from the west on the Spanish rear. Passing and repassing the defending galleons in line ahead, the ships of his squadron led by the *Revenge*, firing their deadly broadsides, subjected the enemy to the heaviest fire yet experienced by them. The main target of attack was Medina Sidonia's flagship, the giant *San Martin*, which, though the English were unable to sink her owing to the strength of her sides, they battered so long and mercilessly that nearly half her crew were killed and her decks strewn with dead and dying. In the end, despite the courage of her seamen and soldiers, she became almost incapable of replying – a fact which helps to explain the astonishing lowness of the English casualties. For in the whole campaign against the Armada, including the culminating Battle of Gravelines, less than a hundred Englishmen lost their lives in action, and, owing to their superb seamanship, not even a single ship of theirs was sunk or boarded.

In dense clouds of smoke and amid deafening noise, the other English commanders, Hawkins in *Victory*, Frobisher in *Triumph*, Seymour in *Rainbow*, Winter in *Vanguard*, Howard in *Ark Royal*, Fenton in *Mary Rose* and the eighty-nine-year-old captain of the *Dreadnought*, Cheshire Sir George Beeston* – knighted three days earlier on the deck of the Lord Admiral's flagship with Frobisher and Hawkins – fell on the Spaniards' shaken ships like a pack of famished wolves. The *San Martin*, her fellow flagships and the great galleons of Castile and Portugal, defending the unprotected hulks and transports of the now broken Armada, bore the brunt of the day's fighting. But their captains' and crews' heroism was in vain. For their supply of round-shot was running out, and, as it did so, their assailants, fighting furiously, shortened the range, and, for the first time since the campaign began, the light shot of the long English culverins began to penetrate the hulls of the Spanish battleships. One great galleon, holed, withdrew behind the half-breached screen of what remained of the Armada's protected centre and there sank, while three others in like plight became total wrecks, drifting out of the fight onto the Banks of Zeeland or the Flemish coast beyond, where they subsequently surrendered to the English garrison of Flushing, or were boarded and massacred by the merciless Dutch 'sea beggars'.

By the end of the day, not a single Spanish galleon remained capable of fighting. Their stout structures and the morale of their crews were alike shattered. Their hulls, repeatedly holed, were leaking, their sails torn to shreds, their stores and water-casks ruined or broken, and their holds a shambles of dying or wounded men, horses and sheep.

* His memorial is in Bunbury church, where it is recorded that he ended 'his life of honour' in 1601 at the age of 102. G. Ormerod, *History of Cheshire*, II, 142.

At about six o'clock in the evening, after nine hours of battle, which for the Spaniards had long become a massacre, they 'bore away' north-eastwards, a huddled and broken mass, to escape the terrible English guns.

By this time the victors, unconscious of what in their desperation they had achieved, had literally shot their bolt, having run completely out of ammunition. The sound of firing, which had continued all day, suddenly died away. Listeners on the Flemish coast, realizing that a victory had been won but not knowing by whom, awaited the expected appearance of the triumphant Armada. Parma's soldiers stood to arms all night beside their barges at Dunkirk and Nieuport, waiting all next day for the sight of that forest of masts on the horizon, within the ring of whose protection they were to embark for their perilous voyage to England. And at Flushing, and in the islands fringing the mouth of the Scheldt, the anxious Dutch wondered if at any moment a victorious Spanish fleet would appear to seize the haven it needed and so break from the sea the resistance their watery provinces had maintained on land for more than sixteen years.

But, on that fateful evening of July 29th 1588, as the guns ceased to sound and the vanquished sought refuge in the open sea to the north, and the victors, their stores of shot and powder exhausted, fell asleep beside their guns, the wind, which had shifted into the north-west, freshened into gale and began to blow the broken Armada back towards the dreaded Zeeland Banks on to which the English had striven all day to drive them. All through the night their danger grew as the doomed and shattered galleons struggled to escape. When dawn broke on Tuesday, 30th, their crews could see the white waves breaking over the shoals, towards which they were being helplessly driven. Already their pilots, who had been sounding all night, reported that the depth beneath them was down to seven fathoms and diminishing every hour. As their larger ships drew only six fathoms, the whole Armada seemed certain to be dashed to pieces on the hidden sand banks. So grave was their situation that, as the only hope of saving the lives of the 20,000 men still on board, a pinnace was prepared to carry an offer of surrender from the battered *San Martin* to the English Commander-in-chief. But this proved too much for the Spanish sense of honour, and, according to one account, one of the admirals at the Council of War, the valiant Don Miguel de Oquendo, threatened to throw his fellow admiral, the hated Don Diego Flores de Valdez who had proposed this shameful course, into the sea.

Then at eleven o'clock, a miracle occurred. One of the Catholic saints, who had been charged in King Philip's and his people's prayers with the protection of the Armada, intervened at the last moment to save it. It was St Lawrence's Day, and, as every Spaniard aboard believed, it was St Lawrence's doing which now caused the wind so suddenly to shift to the south-west. Miraculously the drift on to the sandbanks ceased, and, as the great ships, the wind filling their tattered sails, turned northwards again towards the open sea, those, who an hour before had expected to die, thanked God and St Lawrence for sparing them to live to another day. How soon for most of them that day would come, and how horrifying the death reserved for them would be, was mercifully not revealed.

The English, who that morning had expected the wind to finish the work of destruction they had begun, but had been unable themselves to complete it for lack of shot and powder, watched with dismay their defeated enemy sail so unexpectedly out of the jaws of death into which they had so nearly driven them. There were still some hundred and twenty Spanish sail – only a dozen or so less than there had been when they were sighted near the Lizard. They were still afloat and free, if they could or would, to find a harbour and base, in Scotland, Scandinavia or North Germany from which to threaten England anew. Thwarted of their prey, sadly and hungrily the victors – for they were almost as bare of victuals as they were of ammunition – set out to follow and shadow them. For though they knew they had done their utmost, they still had no idea of the extent of the damage they had inflicted on their foes and how great a victory they had won.

On the evening after the battle the Lord Admiral wrote to Walsingham:

'We have chased them in fight until this evening late and distressed them much. But their fleet consisteth of mighty ships and great strength; yet we doubt not, by God's good assistance to oppress them. . . . Their force is wonderfully great and strong, and yet we pluck their feathers by little and little. I pray to God that the powers on the land be strong enough to answer so present a force.'

But Drake, who had a much clearer idea of the damage he and his ships had wrought, wrote more sanguinely:

'God has given us so good a day in forcing the enemy so far to leeward as I hope in God the Prince of Parma and the Duke of Sidonia shall not

155

shake hands this few days; and whensoever they shall meet, I believe
neither of them will greatly rejoice. . . . I assure your Honour this day's
service hath much appalled the enemy.'

Yet, as Howard had put it, 'all the world never saw such a force as
theirs was', and it was still at sea.

Still less did the rulers and people of England realize the magnitude
of their sailors' victory. Alerted to their peril since the beginning of
the year by news of the digging of canals and the concentration of
invasion barges on the Flemish coast, the Armada's appearance off
their shores and its unimpeded voyage up the Channel had awoken
an intensity of alarm and patriotic fervour in every part of the country.
The news in London of yet another battle which had left the Spanish
fleet still at large, while Parma's victorious army of the Netherlands,
bent on invasion, lay only a single tide away, made everyone feel that
a landing was imminent and that the Armada's sortie into the North
Sea was only a feint to allow the dreaded *tercios* to cross while the
English fleet was following it. So probable did this seem that urgent
orders were sent by the Council for Seymour's squadron of the
Narrow Seas to leave the pursuing fleet and resume its watch off the
Thames estuary and its blockade of Parma's invasion ports. Meanwhile Howard's ships, hungry and munitionless, followed Medina
Sidonia northwards. For the latter still carried in his transports an
army almost as large as Parma's able to land anywhere on the coast –
in East Anglia, in Catholic Yorkshire, in Scotland, which, with its
dissident Catholic nobles, had always seemed a possible target for the
Armada.

But aboard the great fleet itself, there was no longer any thought
of such adventures. On the evening of the day on which it so miraculously escaped destruction on the Zeeland Banks, a Council of War
was held in the flagship as to what should be done. Medina Sidonia
and his admirals at first spoke of honour and of a return to Calais or
the Channel. But, when it came to the moment of decision, all were
unanimous. No prudent course seemed open to them but to take their
damaged fleet back to Spain to refit and repair. Before them lay more
than two thousand two hundred perilous sea-miles round the rocky
coasts of Scotland and Ireland. But the only alternative was unthinkable. For no one aboard was prepared to face again the terrible English
seamen and their guns. Yet by a strange paradox only one of those
terrible seamen seemed able as yet to grasp the dire nature of the

Spaniards' plight: their old tormentor, Francis Drake. The principal architect of their defeat, he wrote cheerfully on Wednesday July 31st, two days after the battle, 'There was never anything pleased me better than seeing the enemy flying with a southerly wind to the northwards . . . I doubt it not but ere it be long so to handle the matter with the Duke of Sidonia as he shall wish himself at St Mary Port among his orange trees.'

So, with a brisk wind behind it, the Armada continued northwards – past the approaches to the Thames and Harwich, past the great bulge of Norfolk, and far out into the German Ocean. Despite the many thousands of superlative soldiers, trained and ready for invasion, waiting unused in its transports, it turned neither west towards the ports and beaches of northern England nor east towards those of the North German estuaries, Denmark and the Baltic, seeking to find a haven in which, were it tempted to fight again, it could refit, repair and revictual. And, keeping just out of range, the English fleet followed it with no ammunition for its guns and no knowledge that its fleeing enemy had none either. 'We set on a brag countenance,' Howard reported to Walsingham, 'and gave them chase as though we wanted nothing.' Every time that Medina Sidonia in his battered flagship lay to, with a crippled galleon or two in support, to give his demoralized ships time to get away from their dreaded pursuers, the English also lay to and waited and watched until the hasty flight to the north was resumed, when they again followed them.

On Friday, August 2nd, four days after the victory of Gravelines, with the two fleets sixty miles out to sea in the latitude of Newcastle, the wind shifted to the north-east. The English, who had been on short rations ever since they left Calais and were now almost out of food and water, feeling that further pursuit was unnecessary, decided to return home at once with the wind to revictual and re-arm and help defend the country against the threat of Parma's invasion. From the trail of drowned horses, sheep and mules thrown overboard by the flying Spaniards, they knew that the latter must be very short of water and fodder, and that, with a gale shifting now to the north-west, there was no chance of their finding shelter in the Forth should King James of Scotland renege on his alliance with England. Leaving two small fast vessels to shadow the Armada, they turned about and made their way south as fast as possible.

★   ★   ★

Meanwhile all England braced itself for immediate invasion. Wednesday August 7th was the day of highest flood-tide at Dunkirk when ships could enter its harbour and embark the troops Parma had assembled. Had not Howard and Drake broken the Armada's formation with their fireships and defeated it at Gravelines, it could have been the day on which it made its rendezvous with Parma. The wildest rumours were circulating on the Continent: that, in a great battle off Harwich, Drake had been captured with many ships, that he had lost a leg, that, in another fight off Newcastle, the English flagship had been sunk, and 'the great sailor, John Hawkins, had gone to the bottom.'

But in England the only thought now was of the coming battle on land. After it had become known that the Armada had passed the Thames estuary, the panic in the capital subsided, where it had been feared that the fate of Antwerp was about to be visited on London. Here more than 6,000 citizen soldiers,[*] mainly apprentices, officered by merchants and shopkeepers enrolled in the City's Trained Bands, had been drilling twice weekly at Mile End. Now attention passed to the camps at Tilbury and Colchester, where the Militia of Essex had been standing to arms since the beginning of the summer. For in time of war every county raised, through the Justices of the Peace and the Head Constables of the Hundreds, its own local defence force. And as it was in Essex that Parma seemed most likely to land, volunteers and militiamen from other counties had been flocking there in their zeal to defend their Queen, Faith and country. 'It was a pleasant sight,' recalled one eye witness, 'to behold the soldiers as they marched towards Tilbury, their cheerful countenances, courageous words and gestures, dancing and leaping wheresoever they came.'[†] It was, indeed, incredible, Leicester wrote to Walsingham, how many men had been raised in the past six weeks, more than at any time, he believed, since the Norman Conquest. Some put the figure at 20,000, while another 8,000 volunteers were in Kent, guarding the Queen – so far as she permitted it – under her cousin, Lord Hunsdon, who had come down from the North, where he had had a long distinguished military career, to command them. It was while so engaged during the Armada summer that, notwithstanding his advanced age, the old soldier had become the 'protector' of a nineteen-year-old girl –

[*] Michael Lewis, *The Spanish Armada*, 89. John Northouck's *A New History of London, 1772*, 139, which gives the numbers from the different Wards, put them at 10,000.

[†] J. E. Neale, *Queen Elizabeth*, 297.

daughter of an Italian court musician – who later, as 'the dark lady of the sonnets', was to become the mistress of the actor, William Shakespeare,★ of whose licensed company of players Hunsdon, as Lord Chamberlain, was patron.

Yet neither the arms nor the organization of England's amateur military defenders matched their numbers or fervour. Raised for the emergency by the Justices of the Peace and commanded by the Lord Lieutenant and Deputy Lieutenants of the shire, some of the militiamen bore pikes or arquebuses, in the use of which they were being drilled by veterans of the Netherlands and Irish wars, while others were still armed with the bows and arrows of their country's famous, but now remote, military past. Nor did the militiamen from other counties, who flocked so enthusiastically into Lord Leicester's camp at Tilbury, always arrive with commissariat or rations. Four thousand of them, he complained, suddenly appeared after a twenty-mile march without as much as a loaf of bread or barrel of beer between them, though they cheerfully announced that 'they would abide more hunger than this to serve her Majesty and the country'. Though no one doubted they would sell their lives dearly, it was difficult to feel sure how amateur troops so trained and organized would fare if attacked by the massive ranks of the pikesmen and musketeers of Spain's world famous *tercios*. With his not very happy experience against the latter in the Low Countries, Leicester at that moment, was probably a better judge of the matter than any non-seafaring subject of the Queen. 'If her Navy,' he asked, 'had not been strong and abroad . . . what case had herself and her whole realm been in by this time?'

★　★　★

It was at this juncture, on Wednesday August 7th, that Howard's fleet, dispersed by heavy storms on its voyage south, struggled into port at Yarmouth, Harwich and Margate, after its nine days' disappearance and nearly three weeks after it had left Plymouth so suddenly on short rations. 'I pray God,' the Lord Admiral wrote from Margate to Walsingham, 'we may hear of victuals, for we are generally in great want . . . If I hear nothing of my victuals or munitions this night,' he added in a postscript, 'I will gallop to Dover to see what may be got there, or else we shall starve.' Nor was hunger and lack of

★ See A. L. Rowse, *Shakespeare the Man.*

powder and shot the Admiral's only problem. Epidemic typhus, scurvy and malignant disease, caused by putrid food and water and primitive sanitary conditions, were raging in his ships. 'With great grief I must write unto you what state I find your fleet,' he informed the Queen next day from Dover. 'The infection has grown very great and in many ships, and now very dangerous. And those that come in are soonest infected. They sicken one day and die the next.'

But the royal mistress to whom he addressed his letter was no longer at her riverside palace. 'We do instantly beseech Thee of thy gracious goodness,' she had declared in the prayer she had issued to her people when the Armada arrived in the Channel 'to be merciful to the church militant here upon earth, and at this time compassed about with most strong and subtle adversaries. O let Thine enemies know that Thou hast received England into Thine own protection. Set a wall about it, O Lord, and evermore mightily defend it.' On August 6th she had gone down the river by barge to Tilbury, a day's march nearer the enemy, by whom, it was reported, 'she was not a whit dismayed.' Next morning – it was the day of high tide at Dunkirk and of Parma's expected sailing – mounted on a white charger, with Leicester at her side, she rode through the ranks of her army with a marshal's baton in her hand, nine trumpeters in scarlet and Garter King at Arms going before, while her ladies in attendance followed. Then, 'like some Amazonian empress,' she inspected her troops, the pikes, lances and colours of each company being lowered in homage as she passed. Afterwards she addressed them in words which, like Churchill's after Dunkirk, became part of the English heritage.

'My loving people,

We have been persuaded by some that are careful of our safety, to take heed how we commit ourselves to armed multitudes for fear of treachery. But I assure you, I do not desire to live to distrust my faithful and loving people. Let tyrants fear. I have always so behaved myself that, under God, I have placed my chiefest strength and safeguard in the loyal hearts and goodwill of my subjects. And therefore I am come amongst you, as you see, at this time, not for my recreation and disport, but, being resolved in the midst and heat of battle, to live or die amongst you all, to lay down for my God, for my kingdom, and for my people, my honour and my blood, even in the dust. I know I have the body of a weak and feeble woman, but I have the heart and stomach of a king, and of a king of England too, and think foul scorn that Parma or Spain, or any prince of Europe should dare to invade the borders of my realm.'

'This place,' wrote Walsingham who was there, 'breedeth courage.'

Yet no Prince of Parma and his army emerged from Dunkirk. A week earlier, unknown to the waiting English, the great soldier, like Napoleon two centuries later, quick to realize what had happened, had marched his troops away from the invasion coast, knowing that, without command of the sea, no conqueror could any longer hope to put a foot on English soil with impunity. And six hundred miles away to the north, while Elizabeth was speaking, the proud fleet of Spain was flying westwards, with a fair south-easterly wind, between the Orkneys and Shetlands, seeking the quickest way home to Spain and safety. For, in the words of a great naval historian, 'in the running fight off Gravelines on Monday July 29th 1588, . . . the Invincible Armada was thrashed beyond redemption in body and spirit alike.'*

★ Michael Lewis, *The Spanish Armada*, 172.

Chapter Seven

ELIZABETHAN HARVEST

'Our late sovereign, Queen Elizabeth, (whose story hath
no peer among princes of her sex) being a pure virgin,
found it, set foot in it and called it Virginia.'
Sermon preached at Whitechapel April 1609
to the Adventurers and planters of the Virginia Company.

'To seek new worlds for gold, for praise, for glory.'
Sir Walter Ralegh

For nearly thirty years Elizabeth had striven to keep her country out of
war. She had gone on trying almost up to the time the Armada appeared in the Channel. But, by refusing, until it was too late, to allow
Howard and Drake to destroy it in its own harbours, she and her
Council had imperilled the safety of the fleet and all but precipitated
a disaster at the outset of the campaign. Her untimely frugality over
the provisioning of her ships had threatened to rob her seamen of the
fruits of their skill and courage and reduced them to near starvation
in the very hour of victory. 'It would grieve any man's heart,' wrote
the Lord Admiral, when the fleet returned to England after its hungry
and ammunitionless pursuit of the beaten Armada, 'to see them that
have served so valiantly die so miserably.' For what the Spanish heavy
guns and waiting boarding troops – so skilfully thwarted by the
evasive English warships – had failed to achieve, epidemic toxaemia
from putrid rations and typhus from filthy living-quarters struck
down the victors in scores for every man killed in action. 'It is a most
pitiful sight to see,' Lord Howard protested, 'how the men, having no
place to receive them into here, die in the streets. I am driven myself,
of force, to come a-land to see them bestowed in some lodging. And
the best I can get is barns and outhouses.'★

For her seamen having driven the Armada from her shores, the
Queen's chief care was to end the ruinous drain of paying them and
keeping their ships at sea. Only the entreaties of the humane and

★ J. K. Laughton, *The Defeat of the Spanish Armada*, II, 96.

163

honourable Lord Admiral – who offered to advance half the cash needed from his own resources – prevented the Crown from discharging its starving and dysentery-ridden crews with their arrears of wages unpaid. Long before Elizabeth, at the head of her Council and principal officers, with the City Livery Companies following with their banners, drove on November 19th in a gold and jewelled two-horse chariot to St Paul's, to kneel at its west door and give thanks to God for the winds and tempests to which the Armada's defeat was piously attributed, most of the disciplined force which had won England's first great naval victory had ceased as such to exist.

The fate which befell the vanquished proved far more terrible. It fell not only on the humble Spanish and Portuguese seamen who handled the sails and manned the guns of the great fleet which, with the blessing of the Saints and Holy Church, had sailed so confidently from Corunna in July, but on the haughty fighting dons and hidalgos, with their jewelled swords, gold and silver enwrought armour and purses full of treasure, who, under Spain's First Grandee, had led the Armada so triumphantly up the Channel to conquer England. But it was not the force of the winds and tempests, sent by God for their undoing, which had brought them to unthinkable disaster, but the impact and fear of English gunnery and seamanship. On the day after Elizabeth's great speech at Tilbury, the gale which had driven the flying Armada far to the north abated, and the fog which succeeded it, lifted, leaving the sun shining for a brief while almost as brightly on those remote Scandinavian waters as it had done on the Biscay Bay five weeks earlier. But the fleet which had kept such magnificent fighting formation all the way from the Western Approaches to Calais was already breaking into fragments. Faulty navigation and the destruction wrought by the English guns to sails, spars and rigging; abandoned anchors and cables – more than a hundred of which had been lost at Calais; broken pumps and holed water-butts, compelling the jettisoning of thousands of sheep and cattle which, had water been available, could have provided rations for the entire fleet and army for several more weeks; three thousand sick and wounded in crowded airless holds; above all a cumulative and rapid decline in morale and discipline, had all helped to bring the proud fleet of Spain and Portugal to its lamentable pass. Some of its ships had strayed off course almost as far as the Norwegian coast and Iceland; another grounded in Fair Isle; more than one galleon, holed between wind and water at Grave-lines, had sunk under the North Sea waves never to be seen again.

ELIZABETHAN HARVEST

Worse was to follow. For several days, sailing north-about in isolated detachments and then turning west towards the Atlantic, the broken Armada steered a course between the Orkneys and Shetlands, at first in almost halcyon weather, not unwonted in August in those remote waters. On the day after Howard's pursuing but starving fleet had turned back to England, an experienced pilot on Medina Sidonia's command had charted the homeward course over the two thousand and more sea miles which separated the fugitive fleet from its harbours in northern Spain. Sailing-orders were issued by the Admiral under which, after clearing the Northern Isles and Cape Wrath, all ships were to follow the *San Martin* westwards as far as latitude 58 deep in the Atlantic, shunning the shorter and more direct line to Spain south-westwards along the rock-strewn shores of Hebridean islands and the rugged northern and western coasts of Ireland. Only when they reached a point 400 miles west of the mouth of the Shannon were they to make a straight run south for home.

Yet the beaten Armada had to face a foe as deadly as the hidden rocks, shoals and currents and the murderous breakers sweeping out of the Atlantic towards its Celtic eastern coasts. So much of the provision made to feed the fleet and army had been destroyed by the English guns in the four battles fought in the Channel and North Sea that now only the barest rations were available to sustain life during the long voyage home. Sooner than subsist on a daily ration of four ounces of weevily biscuit and half a pint of sour wine per head – all that could be doled out if the fleet was to reach its destination before its stores gave out – many of its captains turned southwards towards home before clearing the perilous inshore waters of western Britain. Nor were the more bellicose among them without hope of avenging their defeat at sea by seizing a military base in Protestant England's restless Catholic dependency.

For on August 24th two despatches reached the Queen's Council in London. One was from Lord Seymour in the Downs confirming that Parma had marched inland and broken up his embarkation camp on the Flemish coast. The other was from Sir William Fitzwilliam, the Queen's Lord Deputy in Ireland, giving warning that the Armada was approaching the north Irish coast and that an invasion of Ulster – the most warlike, turbulent and ungovernable of all the island's half-savage provinces – was imminent. The Spanish threat had shifted from the southern seas and shores of Protestant England to those of the Queen's other and Catholic kingdom.

Yet, though an invasion of Ireland took place, it proved an involuntary one. Instead of choosing where and when they would land, the proud soldiers of Spain, who had conquered half America and driven their European rivals from every disputed foothold in Flanders and Italy, were flung in their unwieldy floating castles on to the Irish rocks and beaches by gigantic waves which drowned them in hundreds and left their ships shattered, holed and helpless. The sodden and half-dazed survivors, laden with treasure – gold chains, rings and jewellery, belt-purses and doubloons sewn into their clothing, velvet and silk cloaks, crucifixes and silver and gold handled daggers and Toledo swords – were set upon, as they lay helpless and famished on those savage, inhospitable strands, by greedy hordes of the poorest peasants in Europe, almost as hungry as themselves and merciless in their search for the fabulous Spanish treasure tossed so providentially onto their shores. For September was wild and gusty with great seas which would have caused little danger to well-found, fully-manned, seaworthy ships, but which threatened to swamp the battered, leaking galleons fighting their way home under Medina Sidonia far in the Atlantic deeps, and drove the little groups of isolated vessels, hopefully edging the Hebridean and Ulster and Connaught cliffs and headlands, inescapably to their fate. All the way south from Fair Isle and Tobermory, Rathlin and Lough Swilly, Sligo Bay and Eris Head, Achill and Clare Island, the lonely Arans in Galway Bay, Loop Head and the Blaskets, to far away Cape Clear and the Kerry and Munster coasts, lay signposts to death for that multitude of broken, storm-tossed sons of Spain.

Yet at least two attempts were made by gallant Spanish officers who, after shipwreck, reformed their men and, still in arms, tried to secure a foothold in Ireland for survival, and, at best, a base for conquest. The most important was that of Alonso de Leyva, the young commander of the Armada's original van and the doyen of Spain's military chivalry whom King Philip, who like everyone else loved him, had secretly appointed to take over supreme command of the expedition should anything happen to Medina Sidonia. Early in September de Leyva's flagship, *La Rata Encoranda*, carrying cadets from almost every Spanish noble family, ran aground in Blacksod Bay on the Mayo coast. With 600 survivors he made a fortified camp round the ruins of an old Celtic castle and tried to establish relations with the mercurial native chieftains. Learning, however, that English forces were moving up to destroy him, and joined by the crew of another stormbound vessel, the *Duquesa Santa Ana*, which had some-how managed to escape shipwreck in the bay, de Leyva with the two ships' companies, now 800 strong, set out once more for Spain, only to be blown north by renewed south-westerly gales and driven ashore on the Ulster coast. Still refusing to accept defeat, he again made a fortified camp and prepared to defy the English, whose Lord Deputy, Fitzwilliam, and the Governor of Connaught, Sir Richard Bingham, had ordered every Spaniard who survived the sea, and the swarm of native plunderers and corpse-robbers, to be hanged or put to the sword. Then, hearing that the galleass, *Gerona*, was lying beached and rudder-less in Donegal Bay some twenty miles away, de Leyva marched his hungry men to join her. After repairing her rudder and chivalrously declining the proffered hospitality of the chief local magnate, the enigmatic Hugh O'Neil, Earl of Tyrone, lest their presence should compromise him with his English overlords, he set out again in mid-October in the patched up *Gerona* for neutral Scotland. After successfully negotiating the entrances to Lough Swilly and Lough Foyle, she struck a rock in the night near the Giant's Causeway and sank with all hands but nine.

Another attempt at military action after shipwreck was made by Don Alonso de Luzon, one of the *tercio* colonels. His ship, the Levan-tine *La Trinidad Valencera*, sprang a leak off the Ulster coast and only just reached it in time, grounding on a reef near the entrance to Lough Foyle. Marching with the combined crews of his own and of another vessel, to whose rescue he had gone before she foundered, he set off inland, but almost immediately ran into a strong English force march-ing north to clear the coast of invaders. A fierce engagement followed in which, though outnumbered, the Spanish commander put up a gallant resistance before surrendering on condition that he and his men should be taken unharmed into the presence of the Queen's Lord Deputy. Yet few in the column of unarmed men who set out next day under escort towards the Irish capital reached their destina-tion save de Luzon himself, who was subsequently ransomed. The rest, officers and men alike, were plundered of their clothes and be-longings, and made to run the gauntlet, many of them being shot or hanged by their escorting guards who, contrary to normal English practice, in the embittered conditions of Irish anarchy and tribal warfare showed little more mercy than that offered by the Spaniards to Protestant seamen captured beyond the oceans and consigned to the dungeons and torture-chambers of the Inquisition.

From the twenty-five or more Spanish ships known to have been wrecked on that cruel coast, only a handful of those who had sailed in them from Spain left Ireland alive. The few who did so, after indescribable sufferings managed, with the help of native Catholic sympathizers, to reach Scotland, where, the richer among them, ransomed by Parma, secured shipment to the continent in Flemish and North German trading vessels. Those, that is, who were not intercepted and slain out of hand by the merciless Dutch sea-beggars who had long been conducting a blockade of terror against Spain and Spaniards off the Netherlands coast. Of the many more who remained in Ireland the English Governor of Connaught, equally set on eradicating every trace of the Spanish presence, wrote to the Lord Deputy, on September 21st, 'I dare assure your Lordship now that in the fifteen or sixteen ships cast away on the coast of this province, which I can on my own knowledge say to be so many, there hath perished at least 6,000 or 7,000 men, of which there hath been put to the sword, first and last, by my brother George, and executed one way and another, about seven or eight hundred or upwards.'

Eleven days before this uncompromising letter was written there had crept into the port of Santander on the Basque Coast twenty-four broken and rotting ships from the outer Atlantic, headed by Medina Sidonia's flagship, the *San Martin*. Their crews were gaunt scarecrows and seemed more like corpses than living men. Many died soon after from their sufferings, among them the fiery, impetuous admiral, Miguel de Oquendo, who, after Gravelines, had challenged his colleagues' decision to fly to the Atlantic, and who now died of shame on the very day his flagship accidentally caught fire and blew up at her moorings. Early in October he was followed to the realms of death and honour by his fellow admiral, Recalde, who, driven by storms onto the southern Irish coast, like the fine seaman he was had anchored his battered galleon, *San Juan*, under the lee of Great Blasket Island in the one position which protected her from every wind but the southerly one that later bore him back to Spain, where he died from his wounds and sufferings. Altogether more than half the Armada's ships and men never returned and, of those who did, probably only half ever recovered from their terrible voyage.

★ ★ ★

Such were the fruits of sixteenth century warfare. The crusade which King Philip had prepared and launched to overwhelm England and which her Queen, with a persistence equal to his own, had tried so hard to avert, had ended for him in bitter and humiliating defeat. It decided that England, and Britain with her, should not be absorbed in Spain's harsh orthodox Atlantic empire, but should remain independent and Protestant. Yet the war continued of its own volition until both principal protagonists were dead, Philip dying in 1598 and Elizabeth in 1603, when her Protestant godson, James VI of Scotland, succeeded peacefully to the English throne, so uniting the British isle under a single crown. England's one positive war-aim – apart from the all-important negative one, secured by the rout of the Armada, of preserving her national independence and religion – was finally achieved in 1609, when Philip III of Spain signed a Twelve Years' Truce with the United Provinces, as the 'rebel' Protestant northern half of the Netherlands had now become, acknowledging their right to trade in Spanish waters and enjoy untramelled political and religious freedom. It was to secure this that Elizabeth had braved the intolerant dynast's wrath and risked open war a quarter of a century before.

For what followed the Armada's defeat was a long-drawn-out war of attrition in which neither side gained anything substantial but, for the sake of which, both paid heavily in human life and material wealth. With the mines of central and southern America and the sea-borne spice trade of the Portuguese East Indies, Spain was still immensely powerful and was able to equip three further Armadas, two against England in 1596 and 1597, and a third in 1601 against the English garrison of Catholic Ireland, then in open rebellion. All failed completely. For, though the Spaniards had learnt much from their maritime foes and had made their warships and the protection of their overseas possessions and trade far more effective than they had been before, all their attempts to overcome their island adversary ended in disaster. For, while they were, historically and geographically, a land and military power, the sea was England's natural element, to which her sons took like ducks to water, while Spain was forced to rely largely on subject and allied countries for the supply equipment of her fleets.★

Nor, with her much smaller population and power-base, was post-Armada England herself any more successful in her attacks on

★ 'To us sea power was natural, based on our own resources, while Philip was wholly dependent on other countries to equip his fleets: timber, spars, pitch, cordage from the Baltic; corn and fish from the Hanse and the Dutch; ordnance and shipping from Italy. Only American silver enabled him to keep his war-effort going, his fleets to sail, his armies to move.' A. L. Rowse, *The Expansion of Elizabethan England*, 290.

Spain and its empire and treasure fleets. Twice, in 1589 and 1596, she launched a major naval and military offensive against the Iberian mainland, the first a fiasco which failed to attract a hoped-for Portuguese patriot rising in Lisbon in its support, the second a brilliant success which reduced the great naval port of Cadiz to a smoking ruin. Yet nothing came of either or of repeated attempts to capture the Plate Fleet or shake Spain's hold on the Azores and Caribbean.

It was England's longest war since her duel with medieval France in the fourteenth and fifteenth centuries. Though, owing to her Queen's reluctance to commit herself to war, never openly declared, it was fought, not only at sea, but on land – in the Netherlands, in France and in Ireland. With the accession of the Huguenot, Henri Quatre, to the throne of France in 1589, King Philip intervened openly in the French wars of religion, sending his armies to the aid of the Catholic League and creating a more or less continuous coastal front against England from the shores of the Bay of Biscay to Zealand, where English troops were still fighting Parma's forces alongside their Dutch allies under Prince Maurice of Orange, the murdered William's able successor. Between 1589 and 1595 England sent five expeditions to Brittany and Normandy, employing 20,000 men, of whom more than half died, mostly, of disease. In their course and in the fighting in the Netherlands, she threw up at least one major military commander, Sir Francie Vere, who, learning both from his ally and chief, Prince Maurice of Orange and his great adversary, Parma, proved a not unworthy predecessor of Marlborough and Wellington, both in battle and diplomacy. His part and that of his English soldiers in the victory of Nieuport in the summer of 1600 was a real step towards the ultimate independence of the United Provinces and the creation of an independent Dutch nation.

All this involved Elizabeth throughout the last fifteen years of her reign in what she most disliked – the uncertainty, violence, and, above all, expense of war. Yet, though she sought every opportunity of ending it, and persistently struggled against the bottomless waste and corruption which attended all sixteenth century warfare, she and her ministers never lost sight of the two aims for which she had always contended and on neither of which was she prepared to compromise – the right of her maritime and mercantile subjects to the freedom of the oceans regardless of Spanish or Papal prohibitions, and the relief of her country's neighbour and ancient trading partner in the Low Countries from religious persecution and military tyranny.

An even worse drain on her military and financial resources faced Elizabeth during the last years of her reign when a Catholic Ulster rose in rebellion under its native princes – Hugh Roe O'Donnell and the great O'Neil, Earl of Tyrone, the one Irishman with the genius to unite and modernize his anarchic country and make it an independent nation. Here the English were forced to fight a guerilla war in which all the natural advantages were on the side of the native insurgents – a wild countryside with primitive communications, a persistently wet, unhealthy and, to strangers, hostile, climate, and a warlike and hardy peasantry nursing savage hatreds and capable of living almost totally without supplies and even clothing. As the Master of the Ordnance, a veteran of the Flemish wars, put it, 'all the soldiers in Christendom must give place in that to the soldier of Ireland.' The wastage of English military manpower and equipment through disease and desertion was appalling. Meanwhile Tyrone proved a magnificent leader, training and equipping his ragged followers with modern arms – most of them stolen from the English – while making the utmost use of terrain and surprise to wear down the disciplined columns vainly trying to control a hostile Celtic countryside.

A succession of humiliating defeats suffered by English columns sent to rescue beleaguered outposts culminated in 1598 in the disaster of the Yellow Ford, when the marshal, Sir Henry Bagenal, lost 2,000 men, half his force and his own life, trying to relieve a small fort on the Blackwater. Thereupon rebellion spread like wildfire to Munster, and all anarchic Ireland was in flames; at one moment it looked as though a victorious O'Neil might march on the English capital, Dublin. But Elizabeth refused to admit even the possibility of defeat, writing how shameful would be 'the Queen of England's fortune (who hath held down the greatest enemy she had) to make a base Irish kerne to be accounted so famous a rebel.' In the spring of 1599, though against her better judgment, she sent to Ireland her impetuous favourite, the young Earl of Essex – her dead Leicester's step-son and popular hero of the storming of Cadiz – as Lord Lieutenant and Lord General with the most powerful army ever employed there. But when, having done little but boast and clamour for reinforcements, he treacherously made a secret truce with the O'Neil, she turned on him with fury and, after he had quitted his post without leave, superseded him by the most systematic and thorough soldier in her army, Charles Blount, Lord Mountjoy. It was he who, after two years' patient campaigning, brought the rebellion to an end when on Christmas Eve 1601, having laid siege for three months to a Spanish army which had landed at Kinsale, he routed the Irish forces attempting to relieve it by a brilliant charge of horse and drove Tyrone, deserted by his discomfited followers, into hiding and ultimate submission in the impenetrable forest of Glenconkein.

It was the chronic shortage of money brought about by this continual warfare, not for the private citizen – whose wealth the Queen's pacific and fructifying policy had done so much to enhance – but to meet the public needs of the Crown, which constituted the chief harm that Spain, sustained by the flow of specie from the Peruvian mines, was able to inflict on Elizabeth's England during the last fifteen years of her reign. The defeat of the Armada had cost her more than half the total war-chest which she and her prudent Lord Treasurer, had built up during the long years of peace. It was soon all spent, leaving the Government for the rest of the long Spanish war with an average annual expenditure of nearly a third of a million, or more than twice the normal revenue of Elizabeth's early years. The Irish rebellion alone had cost a million. For the primitive administrative machinery of the time gave the subject almost unlimited opportunities for cheating the Crown in wartime. Falsified musters, swelling the ranks with imaginary or absentee soldiers, multiplied the numbers the Queen had to pay, clothe and feed; officers and soldiers vied with one another in selling the latter's clothing and even arms, often to those who had originally supplied them, leaving the fighting man half naked and a subject of reproach and public scandal.* As for supplies for the Queen's ships, despite all Hawkins's vigilance and probity and the monarch's own sharp probings and remonstrances, they were sometimes paid for twice over. 'Watch and never look so narrowly', a Justice of the Peace wrote, 'they will steal and pilfer.'

All this tended to nullify the Elizabethan peacetime financial policy of keeping taxation to an indispensable minimum and letting the nation's wealth fructify in the pockets of the industrious and frugal subject. To avoid the unpopular course of repeated requests to Parliament to make good the deficits in the revenue caused by wartime expenditure – so repugnant to a Queen who depended for power on the love of her subjects – the Government was driven to selling off to private purchasers, little by little, almost the whole of the Crown's

* 'Many captains,' reported an honest muster-master writing from Derry in 1601, 'have sold much apparel of this winter's apportion, yet will they not cease to suggest that their soldiers die for want of it. (*Cal. S. P. Ireland 1601–3*, 59–60. Cit. A. L. Rowse, *Expansion of Elizabethan England*, 418.

vast share of the monastic lands that had accrued to it at the Dissolution, leaving a legacy to future sovereigns of royal impecuniosity and need which was to imperil the political balance and unity of the realm. It was also increasingly driven to the easy expedient of using the royal prerogative to lease, to private persons, patents, monopolies and exclusive rights for the sale of essential commodities, many of them indispensible to everyday life, like coal, salt, soap, starch, iron and leather. In the last two Parliaments of the reign, public indignation at these, some of them granted to unpopular Court favourites, boiled over into overt attacks on the Queen herself.

Yet, despite old age, Elizabeth's sense of political realities never failed her. Nor did the touch of her shrewd finger on the public pulse. When in the autumn of 1601 royal monopoly after monopoly had been denounced in an indignant House of Commons, with her perfect sense of timing the Queen yielded without loss of dignity or grace. Letting it be known through the Speaker that 'she herself would take order of reformation' and that no monopoly would henceforth continue unless approved by a court of law, on November 30th 1601 she addressed a delegation of the House of Commons in the Council Chamber at Whitehall in words which epitomized her reign.

'Though God hath raised me high, yet this I count the glory of my crown that I have reigned with your loves. It is not my desire to live or reign longer than my life or reign shall be for your good. And though you have had, and may have, many mightier and wiser princes sitting in this seat, yet you never had, nor shall have, any that will love you better.'

In that noble series of books in which the greatest of all Elizabethan historians, Dr A. L. Rowse, has surveyed her reign, he draws from a contemporary letter a wonderful picture of this invincible Queen in the penultimate year of her life. An old soldier and veteran of the Flemish wars, Sir William Browne, was accorded an interview on an August morning in 1601, as she walked in the garden with her entourage of ladies and courtiers,

'She presently called for me and was pleased to say I was welcome with many good words . . . I had no sooner kissed her sacred hands but that she presently made me stand up and spoke somewhat loud and said, "Come hither, Browne!" and pronounced that she held me for an old faithful servant of hers and said, "I must give content to Browne," or some such speeches. And then, the train following her, said: "Stand, stand back! Will you not let us speak but ye will be hearers?" And then walked a turn or two, protesting of her most gracious opinion of myself. "And before God, Browne;" said she, "they do me wrong that will make so honest a servant jealous that I should mistrust him . . . Having walked a turn or two, she called for a stool, which was set under a tree and I began to kneel, but she would not suffer me; in so much that after two or three denials which I made to kneel, she was pleased to say that she would not speak with me unless I stood up. Whereupon I stood up and . . . she discoursed of many things.'

In the course of his audience the Queen took the opportunity to disabuse the loyal veteran of the prejudice which she suspected his fellow soldiers felt against her politic Secretary of State, Sir Robert Cecil, who had succeeded his dead father, Lord Burghley, in her supreme favour, 'Dost thou see that little fellow that kneels there?' she asked. 'It had been told you that he hath been an enemy to soldiers. On my faith, Browne, he is the best friend that soldiers have.'*

Though in her sixties Elizabeth still presented to the world the same proud, imperious, if unpredictable, front as ever, the years of war, unlike the earlier ones of peace and creative statecraft, were for her inevitably years of loss and decline. One after another those she had loved or worked with dropped away: Leicester only a few weeks after her great speech at Tilbury when, as her Commander-in-Chief, he had ridden by her side through the ranks of her cheering soldiery;† her principal Secretary of State, the Protestant champion, Sir Francis Walsingham, in 1590; the great seamen, Drake and Hawkins, in their last ill-fated West Indian voyage in 1595–6, from which neither returned alive. They were followed by her cousins Lord Hunsdon, the Lord Chamberlain, and his deputy, Sir Francis Knollys. And, in 1598 had gone the closest and most trusted of all, Lord Treasurer Burghley.

Those years of war, too, were checkered by public and social disasters, like the long-drawn-out guerrilla war among the bogs and mountains of northern Ireland; and the one day rebellion and execution for High Treason of the Earl of Essex, which was one of its tragic consequences; the five successive bad harvests at the end of the century which drove up the price of wheat from twenty to nearly sixty shillings a quarter and caused a famine among the urban poor;

* A. L. Rowse, *The Expansion of Elizabethan England*, 406–7.

† A letter to her, written in September from Rycote on his way home from Tilbury to Kenilworth, only reached her after he was dead. 'His last letter,' she endorsed it. A. L. Rowse, *The Expansion of Elizabethan England*, 279.

ELIZABETHAN HARVEST

and the great epidemics of bubonic plague in 1592 and 1593–4, immortalized by Thomas Nashe's haunting threnody, *In Time of Pestilence*.

> 'Brightness falls from the air
> Queens have died young and fair:
> Dust hath closed Helen's eye;
> I am sick, I must die –
> *Lord have mercy on me!*'

A more important literary consequence of these plague-years and their closing of the London theatres, was a sonnet sequence written for his young patron, the Earl of Southampton, by the playwright and actor, William Shakespeare. During his temporary absence from the stage he devoted himself to courtly poetry, writing *Venus and Adonis* and the *Rape of Lucrece* and becoming involved in an unhappy love affair with an Italian court musician's daughter – a former mistress of the old Chamberlain, Lord Hunsdon – Emilia Lanier, 'the dark lady of the sonnets'.

★ ★ ★

Though for Elizabeth herself nearly all the enduring work of her reign had been done before the war, for her subjects the harvest sown in those years was gathered in the years preceding and following her death. The confidence, vitality and sense of common purpose she had given her people inspired and sustained them in every department of life. They were the years of the madrigals and the music of William Byrd – pupil of the great Thomas Tallis – of Tomkins, Weelkes, Morley, Orlando Gibbons and Dowland; of Hilliard's miniatures and Isaac James's sculpture; of Spenser's *Faerie Queene*, Camden's *Britannia* and Hooker's *Ecclesiastical Polity*, of Bacon's *Essays* and *Novum Organum*, and the poems of Walter Ralegh and John Donne; of the building of the great Elizabethan and Jacobean houses that rose out of the ruins of the monasteries – Burghley and Hatfield, Wilton and Knole and Longleat – and the fantastic palace of glass and towers which Bess of Hardwick raised among the Derbyshire hills. Above all, they saw the brief miraculous flowering of the Elizabethan theatre and its supreme product, the genius of Shakespeare; and the publication of the King James or *Authorized Version of the Bible*. Most far-reaching of all in its effects on the future of the world were the colonization by Englishmen of the eastern seaboard of North America and, with it, the genesis of the future United States,

175

and the almost simultaneous foundation of the East India Company and the beginning of English, and presently British, involvement in India and the Orient.

★ ★ ★

The challenge which began in Elizabeth's reign to Spain's and Portugal's monopolist claim to the ownership and use of the outer oceans and of all the unoccupied lands which bordered them, took three forms. One was that of English merchants, trading their wares by land and sea into every country into which they could infiltrate, even at the risk of their lives, from the frozen wastes of Hudson Bay and Greenland to the markets and caravan routes of Bokhara and Samarkand. More spectacular was that of Drake and his fellow privateers and his daring use of his country's hereditary skills in seamanship, shipbuilding and gunnery to win local command of whatever sea he sailed in order to levy a highwayman's toll on the mineral treasure with which the Spanish king financed his wars of conquest and oppression. And a third was that of Drake's fellow West Countrymen, the Devonshire cousins, Humphrey Gilbert, Richard Grenville and Walter Ralegh, whose imaginative minds were more obsessed with the idea of establishing 'plantations' or colonies of English settlers on the other side of the Atlantic than of avenging the oppressions and cruelties★ of imperial Spain and recouping their losses by raiding her ports and capturing her treasure ships. For, though Drake had always cherished the idea of striking at Spain's power by fermenting a rising of her oppressed subject peoples, his essentially practical and matter-of-fact mind, for all its phenomenal daring, never seriously contemplated planting a new England, with English settlers, laws, institutions and language, on the Atlantic shores of the North American wilderness.

Yet, while for nearly a hundred years England, as a nation, had lagged far behind its southern European neighbours in exploiting the

★ A characteristic example of that cruelty, which marred the heroic and chivalrous image of crusading Spain in her imperial heyday, is contained in a report by the Venetian ambassador in December 1604 on the Spaniards' capture of two English trading vessels. 'They cut off the hands, feet, noses and ears of the crew and smeared them with honey, and tied them to trees to be tortured by flies and other beasts.' *Cal. S. P. Venetian, 1603–7, no. 307.* Eight years earlier in 1596, the Venetian ambassador to Spain, reporting on that country's atrocious Spanish cruelty to English prisoners, testified that the English 'most certainly never approached anywhere near such cruel conduct towards the Spanish.' A. L. Rowse, *The Elizabethans and America,* 61.

great ocean discoveries of the latter fifteenth century, there had always been a few English minds which shared the expansive and romantic dreams of the Iberian, Gallic and Italian global navigators and conquerors. As early as the reign of Henry VIII John Rastell, brother-in-law of Sir Thomas More, had expressed a nostalgic wish that

> 'they that be Englishmen
> Might have been the first of all
> That there should have taken possession
> And made first building and habitation
> A memory perpetual!'

Still earlier, in the reign of Henry VII and in the very year in which Vasco da Gama rounded the Cape of Good Hope and before Columbus himself had penetrated beyond the West Indies, a Bristol merchant of Italian origin, John Cabot, coasting the shores of what were to become Newfoundland and Nova Scotia, had been the first known European to discover the North American mainland. His son Sebastian, also sailing from Bristol, claimed to have discovered a north-west passage through the polar ice from the Atlantic into the Pacific.

But it was the Devonshire landowner, dreamer and fire-eater, Sir Richard Grenville, and his fellow West Countryman, Sir Humphrey Gilbert, who, in the second decade of Elizabeth's reign first took practical steps to bring about an English settlement on the coast of North America. Gilbert was an old servant of the Queen's who, with her Welsh ancestry and Renaissance mind and education, was deeply interested in everything pertaining to the New World and its possibilities. Among her Celtic contacts was the Welsh astrologer and clairvoyant, John Dee, at whose home at Mortlake she would sometimes call on her journeys to and from her palace at Richmond. Dee nursed enthusiastic dreams of a 'British' – not English – empire and was the first to use that name in his unpublished 'Atlantical Discourses'. He loved to trace his not unsympathetic sovereign's claim to a global empire based on her descent from the legendary King Arthur. And it was he who produced and submitted to her two rolls of evidence tracing her title to sovereignty in North America. In October 1578, she and her Council granted Letters Patent to Sir Humphrey Gilbert, 'to search, find out and view such remote, heathen and barbarous lands, countries and territories not actually possessed of any Christian prince or people' and settle colonists there under laws 'agreeable to the form of the laws and policies of England'. It was in his Patent that the Queen openly challenged the arrogant claim of the Spanish monopolists who – in the words of Richard Hakluyt, the lifelong historian and chronicler of Elizabethan ocean discovery* – 'account all other nations for pirates, rovers and thieves which visit any heathen coast that they have sailed by or looked on.'

Among those who served in Gilbert's first exploratory voyage to the coast of North America was his half-brother, Walter Ralegh – fifteen years his junior. The expedition achieved nothing, but was followed by others, including one in 1583 in which, after taking nominal possession in the Queen's name of the cod fishermen's island of call, Newfoundland, which thus became England's earliest overseas possession, Gilbert – 'a man noted,' as the Queen put it, 'of not good hap by sea' – lost his flagship in a storm with most of the stores she was carrying to found a transatlantic settlement. Observing that it was as near heaven by sea as by land, he transferred his flag to a ten-ton pinnace, the *Squirrel*, and was last seen calmly reading a book before the tempest swallowed him up.

'The first of our nation that carried people to erect an habitation in those northern countries of America,' as Hakluyt called him in his championship of the cause of American colonization, Gilbert was succeeded by his brilliant and ambitious half-brother, Walter Ralegh, by then the Queen's rising favourite. But though in 1584, at the latter's instance, she invested in a joint stock venture to plant a colony on the North American coast, contributing one of her royal ships, the *Tiger*, as flagship and £400 worth of gunpowder from the Tower, she declined to make the project official, no doubt for fear of offending Spain, with whom war had not yet broken out. This Ralegh's friend and protégé, the 32-year-old Richard Hakluyt, vainly pleaded with her to do in his pamphlet, *A Discourse of Western Planting* – presented to her on his knees in an audience obtained for him by Ralegh – describing it as 'certain reasons to induce Her Majesty and the State to take in hand the western voyage and the planting therein.'

As Elizabeth would not let her new favourite, Ralegh, leave her side, the expedition was commanded in his absence by that even earlier enthusiast for colonization, his cousin, Sir Richard Grenville. But she allowed the infant colony – whose hundred or so settlers, mostly from the West Country, Grenville planted in the summer of

* His first important collection of voyages, *Divers Voyages touching the Discovery of America*, appeared in 1582.

1585 on Roanoke Island – to be named after her, Virginia. When Grenville arrived back in England in the autumn, after leaving his second-in-command, Ralph Lane – a former royal equerry – in charge of the infant colony and promising to return with reinforcements and supplies next year, he was greeted at Plymouth by Ralegh, who reported proudly to the Secretary of State, Walsingham, 'I have possessed and peopled the same to Her Majesty's use, and planted it with such cattle and beasts as are fit and necessary for manuring the country.'

So it came about that for a year, including a hungry winter in which they were forced to live on their stores, a minute colony of Englishmen made what they intended to be a permanent home in the North American wilderness. It was the winter in which Drake captured and ravaged the two capitals of the Spanish Main and Caribbean, returning home to England in triumph in the early summer of 1586. On his way he called at the little settlement on Roanoke Island in the Pamlico Sand. It so happened that the ship bringing provisions and reinforcements, which Grenville and Ralegh had promised should reach the colony in the spring, had not yet arrived, and, a sudden storm arising, the settlers, thinking themselves abandoned, lost heart and at the last moment decided to accept Drake's offer to take them home in his fleet. Hardly had they gone when a supply ship sent by Ralegh appeared, 'freighted with all manner of things in most plentiful manner for the supply and relief of his colony',* followed soon after by Grenville himself, only to find the settlers gone.

It seemed a great opportunity lost, all the more so as the first reports from the young colony had been so hopeful. 'We have discovered the [main] land', Lane had written to the enthusiastic Hakluyt in England, 'to be the goodliest soil under the cope of heaven, so abounding with sweet trees that bring such sundry and pleasant gums, grapes of such greatness yet wild, . . . so many sorts of apothecary drugs, such several kinds of flax, and one kind like silk, the same gathered of a grass as common there as grass is here . . . It is the goodliest and most pleasing territory of the world, for the continent is of a huge and unknown greatness, and very well peopled and towned, though savagely, and the climate so wholesome that we had not one sick since we touched the land here. If Virginia had but horses and kine in some reasonable proportion, I dare assure myself, being

* R. Hakluyt, *The Principal Navigations, Traffics and Discoveries of the English Nation*, (Everyman edition), VI, 162.

inhabited with English, no realm in Christendom were comparable to it.'*

Because of this, Ralegh and Grenville were not deterred. 'Unwilling' as Hakluyt put it, 'to lose the possession of the country which Englishmen had so long held', before returning to England Grenville left fifteen men on the island with two years' provisions. Meanwhile Ralegh fitted out another colonizing expedition of a hundred men and seventeen women, which sailed for Virginia in the following year with a charter to found a city on the Chesapeake estuary to the north. But when in the summer of 1587 they landed on Roanoke, they found the bones of only one of the fifteen men left behind by Grenville, and the little fort built by their predecessors razed to the ground by hostile Indians, with whom the English, unlike the conquering Spaniards in Central and South America, had tried to live in utopian peace and amity.

But though, in a Latin dedication to Ralegh, Hakluyt wrote that 'no terrors, no personal losses or misfortunes could or ever would tear you from the sweet embracements of your own Virginia, that fairest of nymphs . . . whom our Sovereign has given you to be your bride', two small pinnaces despatched by Ralegh in the spring of 1588 to make contact with the Virginia settlers never managed to weather the Atlantic storms of that summer, while the expedition of seven ships – the largest yet planned for a trans-Atlantic plantation – which he and Grenville were fitting out at Bideford, never sailed. Instead it was ordered to join the fleet Drake was assembling at Plymouth against invasion, while he and Ralegh, as Lords Lieutenant of Devon and Cornwall, took command of the levies raised to resist a Spanish landing. And in the following year, after the Armada's defeat, when all the country's resources were mobilized for the amphibious attack on Lisbon under Drake and Sir John Norris, no one could spare time for colonizing America. Meanwhile, busied in the Queen's business in Ireland, Ralegh assigned his rights in the city to be named after him on the Chesapeake to a syndicate of London merchants, who, reinforcing his own efforts to contact the lost planters, sent out in 1590 a relief expedition, only to find that the entire colony had disappeared without trace.

Yet, though as a result of its disappearance, the continuance of the war, Grenville's death in the last fight of the *Revenge* in 1591 and Ralegh's fall from royal favour in the following year, the Virginian

* A. L. Rowse, *The Elizabethans and America*, 49–50.

project lapsed, England's maritime and commercial activities in the world's oceans and furthest shores continued. Frobisher's earlier attempts 'to ship a course for China' by finding new trading routes to the Pacific round the northern extremities of America and its encircling ice, were succeeded by those of three great navigators, John Davis – author of *The Seaman's Secrets*, the first practical work on navigation published by an Englishman – Henry Hudson and William Baffin. Living at Sandridge on the Dart, a close friend of Humphrey Gilbert and his family, between 1583 and 1587 Davis made three attempts to penetrate that steely corridor of dreams, the North West Passage, greatly enlarging knowledge of the mysterious and baffling waters between Greenland, the Pacific and the North Pole. About the same time, a 26-year-old East Anglian from Trimley in Suffolk, Thomas Cavendish, emulated Drake's voyage round the world by sailing in 1586 through the Magellan Straits into the Pacific, where he captured a rich Manila galleon, and, subsequently rounding the Cape of Good Hope, was the first Englishman ever to land at St Helena, returning victorious to England in the autumn of 1588 when he crossed the shattered Armada's homeward course.

All this, and much more, Richard Hakluyt recorded in his great book, *The Principal Navigations, Traffics and Discoveries of the English Nation*, which he had been preparing for press throughout the Armada year and published in 1589, proudly claiming that the English 'in searching the most opposite corners and quarters of the world and, to speak plainly, in compassing the vast globe of the earth more than once, have excelled all the nations and peoples of the earth. For which of the kings of this land before her Majesty,' he asked in his Epistle Dedicatory to Walsingham, 'had their banners ever seen in the Caspian Sea? Which of them hath ever dealt with the Emperor of Persia, as her Majesty hath done, and obtained for her merchants large and loving privileges? Who ever saw before this regimen an English lieger in the stately porch of the Grand Signior at Constantinople? Who ever found English consuls and agents at Tripolis in Syria, at Aleppo, at Babylon, at Basra and, which is more, who ever heard of Englishman at Goa before now? What English ships did heretofore ever anchor in the mighty river of Plate? pass and repass the unpassable (in former opinion) strait of Magellan, range along the coast of Chile, Peru and all the backside of Nova Hispania, farther than any Christian ever passed, traverse the mighty breadth of the South Sea, land upon the Locones "(Philippines)" in despite of the enemy, enter into alliance, amity and traffic with the princes of the Moluccas and the Isle of Java, double the famous Cape of Bona Speranza, arrive at the Isle of St Helena, and last of all return home most richly laden with the commodities of China, as the subjects of this now flourishing monarchy have done?'*

★   ★   ★

Over one route, the passage round the Cape to the Indian Ocean to break into the Portuguese monopoly of the seaborne spice and silk trade, the English were at first far less successful than in their forays into the Spanish Caribbean and Pacific a generation earlier. For the great Portuguese carracks of over a thousand tons were more than a match in those remote waters for the smaller English armed merchantmen, superior in gunnery and seamanship though the latter were. And before the end of Elizabeth's reign the enterprising merchants and seamen of the United Provinces, to preserve whose independence she had gone to war with King Philip, had themselves begun, not only to challenge, but to usurp for themselves the Portuguese monopoly, sending out powerful trading ships of their own built and equipped for long voyages in eastern waters. The first two English ventures to break into the Indian Ocean met with total disaster; of the three armed merchantmen which sailed in 1591 only one successfully rounded the Cape of Good Hope, and, though it ultimately reached Cape Cormorin, all it brought back to England, after a two years' voyage of indescribable hardships, was a cargo of sick sailors, victims of scurvy, starvation and their own mutinies. A second expedition in 1596 fared no better, not a single survivor of its three ships returning to England.

It was the success of the Dutch, and the ageing Queen's determination that her own subjects should not be outdone by them, that led to the successful entry into the luxury trade of the Orient of the English East India Company. Founded by a consortium of London merchants under the title of 'the Governor and Company of the Merchants of London trading into the East Indies', and granted by a royal charter of December 31st 1599 a monopoly for fifteen years of all trade with lands beyond the Cape of Good Hope or Magellan Straits, it sent out its first fleet from Torbay in the spring of 1600. Its moving spirit, and for many years its chairman, as also of the Levant Company, was Sir

* Cit. A. L. Rowse, *The Expansion of Elizabethan England*, 161–2.

Thomas Smythe, one of the rich sons of 'Customer' Smythe – the immensely able and shrewd financier who from 1570 to 1588 had farmed the royal Customs to the benefit, thanks to his remarkable efficiency, both of the Crown and, even more, of himself.*

Though in the more distant spice islands the Dutch, superseding the easier-going Portuguese, had gained a long march on their former protectors and allies, who, at the time of the Queen's death, had established only a single trading 'factory' at Bantam in Java,† the English directed their efforts instead towards India, where one or two daring Elizabethan merchants had already penetrated by land. Through Smythe's initiative the Company, early in the reign of James I, established a permanent representative at the court of the Mogul emperors at Agra – at that time virtual rulers of the peninsula. Within six years of Elizabeth's death, when her successor renewed the company's fifteen years' monopoly 'for ever', it was sending out regular voyages to the Indian Ocean every year, establishing 'factories' on both India's eastern and western coasts, and penetrating far beyond, to Siam in 1612 and Japan in the following year. The £72,000 of capital initially invested in the Company earned in the course of a few decades a return far greater than that of the most spectacular of Drake's plundering voyages of the past.

Almost simultaneously this far-sighted Elizabethan merchant prince, operating from the City of London, sent out his country's tentacles across the North Atlantic to refound the lapsed Virginian settlement which Ralegh and Grenville had planted before the Armada and the long Spanish war. Here there were no hopes of rich trading argosies or quick – or even, at first, any – returns on the capital required to recruit, ship and maintain emigrants and establish homes and farms in a wilderness as yet only inhabited by savages. Even Ralegh, who in his darkest hour was still to write of Virginia that 'he would yet live to see it an English nation', had hitched his dreams to a new star – that of the legendary golden kingdom of El Dorado which he persisted in believing existed in the mountains of that vast and still

* There is a portrait of this shrewd, pious and acquisitive Elizabethan in the possession of his direct descendant, my neighbour, Lord Teynham.

† On November 5th 1601 the East India Company, then nearly two years old, received a sharp rebuke from the impatient Queen, calling attention to 'Her Majesty's mislike of the slackness of the Company in the seconding of their former voyage to the East Indies by the Cape of Bona Speranza, propounding unto them the example of the Dutch as prosecuting their voyages with a more honourable resolution.' A. L. Rowse, *The Expansion of Elizabethan England*, 197.

unexplored tract of tropical South America which lay beyond the Spanish Main between the mouths of the Orinoco and Amazon. In 1595, in the desperate hope of winning back the Queen's lost favour by presenting her with a fabulously rich dominion surpassing even Spain's Peru, he fitted out and led an expedition to this elusive land, subsequently publishing a book about it entitled *The Discovery of the Large and Beautiful Empire of Guiana*. Thrown after Elizabeth's death into the Tower and sentenced to death for treason on dubious charges of plotting against the new King, he was to spend the rest of his life as a prisoner, the last great Elizabethan, writing his noble *History of the World* and only released on sufferance in 1616 – the year of Hakluyt's death – to prepare for a last and fatal voyage to Guiana to seek his illusory El Dorado, paying for it two years later with his head, at the instance and demand of his unrelenting enemies, the Spaniards, who, like King James, hated him and all he stood for.

It had been men of such soaring vision and imagination as Ralegh and Hakluyt who had first conceived the idea of making new Englands beyond the oceans. By their propagation of it, the one in the Council chamber and at sea, the other by his pen, they had caused it to germinate in the minds of their countrymen. But it required qualities of a different kind to turn their vision into everyday reality. Such were those of Sir Thomas Smythe and his fellow merchants in their city counting-houses who, pooling their knowledge and resources and sharing their risks, laid out their money, prudently but boldly, on a long-term investment in their country's future, with the patience, persistence and resolution to see the thing through. Calling all prepared to join them Adventurers, they used the capital raised from them to recuit planters and maintain plantations until these were able to support themselves.

As soon as Elizabeth's pacific successor had brought the long wasting war with Spain to a conclusion in 1604, two joint-stock companies were formed, one in London presided over by Smythe, and the other by West Country merchants and gentry at Plymouth, Exeter and Bristol. The London company, by far the richer of the two, sent out three ships – the *Susan Constant, Godspeed* and *Discovery* – in December 1606 with a hundred settlers to take the place of those who had vanished twenty years earlier. In the spring of 1607, landing on the shores of Chesapeake Bay, they built a fort and a little timber settlement which they named Jamestown after the new King. Though only thirty-eight of them remained alive at the end of the first winter, successive batches of settlers were sent out by Smythe and his partners every summer. At first their losses were enormous. Six years after the original landing Smythe told the Spanish ambassador that, of the thousand men and women sent out in the previous summer, eight hundred had already died. By 1622 of more than ten thousand who had landed in Virginia, fewer than two thousand survived.

Yet the colony itself survived. Two things enabled it to do so. One was the resolution and persistence of its promoters in London. 'With such very great losses as they have suffered,' the Spanish ambassador, who hoped the venture would fail, reported to his master, 'they still show so much courage.' For of the £80,000 which Smythe and his partners put into the colony in its first years, not one penny had been provided by King James and his government. It was their Elizabethan faith in the English future which sustained them and the colony. Building on the growing enthusiasm for the idea of American plantation which successive editions of Hakluyt's great work was generating, the Virginia Company sent supply ship after ship across the Atlantic to give the colonists the chance to establish themselves. 'Divine Providence,' it was claimed, 'having reserved for us this magnificent region and the discovery of this great world, which it now offers to us; and, since we have arms to embrace it, there is no reason why we should let it escape us.'[*]

The other factor which enabled the colony to survive was the spirit of self-help and self-survival, replacing the first settlers' sanguine and idle dreams of utopia, with which the colonists themselves, under the spur of necessity, set to work to cultivate the ground. 'If any would not work neither should he eat,' was the rule which their self-appointed leader, Captain John Smith, a typical younger Elizabethan, had by the second winter established in the little colony, where every man was given an initial allotment of three acres to cultivate. 'When our people were fed out of the common store and laboured jointly together,' he reported, 'glad was he who could slip from his labour or slumber over his task, he cared not how; nay the most honest among them would hardly take so much true pains in a week as now for themselves will do in a day. Neither cared they for the increase, presuming that howsoever the harvest prospered, the general store must maintain them, so that we reaped not so much corn from the labour of thirty as now three or four do provide for themselves.'

[*] Cit. A. L. Rowse, *The Elizabethans and America,* 83.

Instead, from then onwards, self-help became the rule among the English pioneers in America. At their back was the ocean, and before them the forest. Every man had to 'root, hog or die'. 'I live a simple life,' one of them wrote a few years later, 'and hath builded a shop, and doth follow the weaving of linen cloth, and I have bought 450 acres of land in the woods.'

Untamed, encroaching forests, feverish swamp and unfordable rivers, wild beasts and wilder red man, cold, famine and disease were the realities which faced the early colonists in their new homeland. During the Indian massacre of 1622 more than three hundred and fifty of them perished, and a further five hundred in the year that followed. Yet in England determination to make the Virginian plantation succeed had now become a point of national pride. Among those who lent support to the London Virginia Company after the royal grant in 1609 of the colony's second Charter, were the Archbishop of Canterbury, the Earls of Pembroke, Montgomery and Southampton – Shakespeare's friend and patron – eighteen other peers, ninety-eight knights, including Sir Oliver Cromwell – uncle of the future Protector – and Fulke Greville, Sir Philip Sidney's friend and biographer, and fifty-six of the City Livery Companies. And the Poet Laureate, Michael Drayton, in his *Ode to the Virginian Voyage*, hailed the Adventurers and planters now streaming across the Atlantic to take possession of the new transatlantic England – the right to which the Elizabethans and their dead Queen had won through their long struggle with Spain.

> 'You brave heroic minds,
> Worthy your country's name,
>   That honour still pursue,
>   Go and subdue,
> Whilst loitering hinds
> Lurk here at home with shame.
>
> 'Britons, you stay too long,
> Quickly aboard bestow you,
>   And with a merry gale
>   Swell your stretched sail
> With bows as strong
> As the winds that blow you.
>
> 'And cheerfully at sea,
> Success you still entice,
>   To get the pearl and gold

ELIZABETHAN HARVEST

And ours to hold,
Virginia,
Earth's only paradise.'

While the attention of England was focused on the activities of the London Virginia Company, those of the West Country or Plymouth company, with its smaller financial resources, had passed largely unnoticed. In the opening years of the century some exploratory voyages south from the Newfoundland fisheries had been made along the northern part of the Atlantic littoral which was the Plymouth company's plantation area. These had roughly mapped out the future Maine and Massachusetts coastline and given names to some of its geographical features such as Cape Cod and Martha's Vineyard. Early in 1607, following the lead of the London company, the West Country company's two chief promoters, Sir Ferdinando Gorges, governor of the fort at Plymouth, and Lord Chief Justice Popham, a former Recorder of Bristol, had sent out a hundred colonists in two ships, the *Gift of God* and *Mary and John*, the latter commanded by Ralegh Gilbert, a son of Sir Humphrey. They made a landing at Sagadahoc on the Kennebec River where they survived the winter. But when the supply ship arrived in the summer of 1608, the colonists had had enough and decided to return home. In the meantime Popham had died and, the Company's finances being temporarily exhausted, colonization of the eight hundred or so miles of coastline of what was still thought of as northern Virginia lapsed for another twelve years.

It was the enthusiasm of John Smith, whose vigour and common sense had done so much to save and establish the pioneer colony on the Chesapeake, that kept interest in this unexploited northern area of colonization alive. It was he who, cruising its coasts every summer, published in 1616 a *Description of New England*, which gave it its name. 'New England,' he wrote, 'is great enough to make many kingdoms and countries, were it all inhabited . . . As for the goodness and fine substance of the land, we are for the most part yet altogether ignorant of them, but only here and there where we have touched or seen a little, the edges of those large dominions which do stretch themselves into the main, God doth know how many thousand miles.'*

Four years later in 1620, partly through the continued efforts of Sir Ferdinando Gorges – a simple soldier who had begun life fighting in Elizabeth's Netherlands wars and who devoted his modest fortunes

* cit. A. L. Rowse, *Expansion of Elizabethan England*, 231.

and the portions of his two wives to the cause of colonization – two expeditions went out from the West Country for what was still thought of as northern Virginia. The nucleus of one was a small group of Nottinghamshire separatists, calling themselves the Pilgrims, who had earlier migrated to Holland in order to practise their own peculiar kind of worship. Sailing from Plymouth that September with other emigrants in a 130 ton ship, the *Mayflower*, they were driven by storms as far north as Cape Cod, where after a month's voyage they landed at what became known as New Plymouth. Though half of them died during that first terrible New England winter, the colony itself survived. In the next two decades they were followed by thousands of other emigrants who settled in ever-growing numbers round the shores of Massachusetts Bay and in the town they had founded and named after Boston in Lincolnshire. They were mostly of a strong Puritanical bent, born of the growing conflict between the Laudian Anglican church establishment at home, supported by the Stuart kings, and its Puritan critics backed by an increasingly intransigent Parliament. Elizabethans by birth though the founding fathers of New England were, they derived their ideology from those who had opposed the dead Queen's unifying efforts and refused to conform to her cherished Anglican settlement. They can therefore hardly be regarded, like the colonizers of Virginia, as part of the Elizabethan harvest. Theirs, as they proudly insisted, was 'a Bible Commonwealth', where, as one of them put it, 'the righteous are in authority'.

* * *

Yet the Bible to which these authoritarian fanatics appealed as the justification of their beliefs, and on the literal interpretation of which they founded their commonwealth, was itself an essential part of the Elizabethan harvest. It was a measure of that harvest, reaped from the seed of national unity sown by Elizabeth in the germinative first years of her reign, that at the very moment when England's merchants and seamen were carrying her life and influence into every ocean and continent, her writers were creating, out of a formerly rude vernacular a literature, not only potentially, but already in achievement, as great as any known to history, even that of ancient Greece. Three contributions of supreme literary genius – two of them, as befitted an intensely religious age, sacred in character and, the other secular – took their place at that moment in the continuing national consciousness and in that of all the lands overseas in which the writ of England ran or was to run. One was the liturgy of the Anglican Church, the other the Authorized Version of the Bible published under James I in 1611, following the Hampton Court Conference of divines called in the year after Elizabeth's death. The third contribution were the plays of William Shakespeare.

The Anglican or Elizabethan Book of Common Prayer was originally conceived in the deeply receptive mind of Queen Elizabeth's godfather, the martyred Archbishop Cranmer, and was based on the traditional Catholic liturgical rite, purged of what to Protestants seemed idolatrous accretions. Never used by the whole nation like the James I Bible – for the extreme Puritans and their Nonconformist successors could never bring themselves to accept it as did the more conservative elements in the nation – the Anglican Prayer Book nevertheless helped to shape and ennoble the thoughts and minds of generations of English folk, gentle and humble alike. For its resounding passages and phrases, and its translations from the lovely Psalms of David, sank deep into the national consciousness.

> 'We have erred and strayed from thy ways like lost sheep;
> we have followed too much the devices and desires of our own
> hearts; we have left undone those things which we ought to
> have done, and we have done those things which we ought not
> to have done, and there is no health in us.'

> 'Lord, who shall dwell in thy tabernacle, or who shall
> rest upon thy holy hill? Even he that leadeth an uncorrupt
> life, and doeth the thing which is right, and speaketh the
> truth from his heart . . . He that setteth not by himself, but
> is lowly in his own eyes, and maketh much of them that fear
> the Lord. He that sweareth unto his neighbour and disappointeth
> him not, though it were to his own hinderance.'

> 'The Lord is my shepherd; therefore can I lack nothing.
> He shall feed me in a green pasture, and lead me forth beside
> the waters of comfort. He shall convert my soul, and bring me
> forth in the paths of righteousness, for his name's sake. Yea,
> though I walk through the valley of the shadow of death, I will
> fear no evil; for thou art with me; thy rod and thy staff
> comfort me.'

One passage from the Psalms illustrates more perfectly what the

Elizabethan ideal of national unity meant, and was long to mean, for the English people.

> 'O pray for the peace of Jerusalem; they shall prosper
> that love thee. Peace be within thy walls and plenteousness
> within thy palaces. For my brethren and companions' sake I
> will wish thee prosperity.'

So, shaping the thoughts, feelings and speech of future generations, were the sayings, injunctions and definitions of the Elizabethan liturgy, as finalized in the great post-Restoration Anglican Prayer Book of 1662, re-issued after the Civil War and Interregnum during which it had been temporarily interdicted. 'We have heard with our ears, and our fathers have declared unto us, the noble works that thou didst in their days, and in the old time before them.' 'The fear of the Lord is the beginning of wisdom.' 'To strengthen such as do stand; and to comfort and help the weak-hearted and to raise up them that fall; and, finally, to beat down Satan under our feet.' 'The author of peace and lover of concord, in knowledge of whom standeth our eternal life, whose service is perfect freedom.' 'Those whom God hath joined together let no man put asunder.' 'All sorts and conditions of men.' 'That peace which the world cannot give.'

What was true of the Anglican liturgy was even more true of the Authorised Version of the Bible, the supreme popular literary legacy of the Tudor age. As has been said, it made the English throughout the world the people of one book and that book the Bible, as distilled by English scholars and divines from the successive translations and versions of the seventy years of Elizabeth's lifetime and the decade immediately preceding it. For generations it became natural for English men and women of all classes – and most of all the humblest and least educated – to lard their speech and thought with phrases and analogies based on the Bible. Even when, as sometimes happened, they got it wrong. So Dickens put into the mouth of his immortal creation, Sairey Gamp, as she anathemized the 'Ankworths Package' boat, the indignant words, 'I wish it was in Jonadge's belly, I do,' so appearing, as her creator observed, 'to confound the prophet with the whale in this miraculous aspiration.'

The spiritual history, beliefs, traditions and legends of an ancient Christian people on the threshold of a new age were set out by the great post-Elizabethan revisers and editors in language as simple as it was profound and in a rhythm as moving as the greatest music. 'In the beginning was the Word and the Word was with God . . . All things were made by him, and without him was not anything made.' 'And the light shined in the darkness, and the darkness comprehended it not.' 'We never thought,' wrote Dr Miles Smith – later Bishop of Gloucester – in his modest Preface to the King James Bible, 'that we should need to make a new translation, nor yet to make a bad one a good one, . . . but to make a good one better, or, out of many good ones, one principal good one.'

No work of literary intent and endeavour was ever more successfully performed. For nowhere in the compass of a single volume have the great truths and mysteries of human existence been made more clear and comprehensible to simple minds – or, for that matter, to sophisticated and complex ones – than in the inspired language of great poetry and prophecy contained in this marvellous communal work of revision and recapitulation. 'The Kingdom of God is within you.' 'God is a spirit and they that worship him must worship him in spirit and in truth.' 'All things work together for good to them that love God.' 'For I am persuaded that neither death, nor life, nor angels, nor principalities, nor powers, nor things present, nor things to come, nor height, nor depth, nor any other creature shall be able to separate us from the love of God which is in Jesus Christ our Lord.' In what other book in any language has more inspired truth and wisdom been set out more effectively than in the Authorised Version of the scriptures which our Elizabethan and Jacobean forbears transmitted to the men and women of their race and polity? 'Not of the letter but the spirit;' for, as St Paul said, 'the letter killeth, but the spirit giveth life.'

★   ★   ★

The other supreme legacy of the Elizabethan harvest were the plays of William Shakespeare. They were not the only works of great English secular literature evoked by the age which the Queen had inaugurated; the prose of Hooker, Ralegh and Francis Bacon were all, in their different ways, masterpieces of the art of verbal communication. So, was the arcadian, and in part archaic, poetry of Philip Sidney and of Edmund Spenser and the anything but archaic poetry of the great late Elizabethan amorist, metaphysic and divine, John Donne, Dean of St Paul's. Yet these, unlike the Prayer Book and Bible, were written only for a very small literary, scholarly and, virtually private, readership. For at that time no general reading public existed for any but religious and theological works.

But the plays of William Shakespeare were composed for acting before audiences drawn from every class, were immensely popular in their day, and, as no other secular literature of the time, represented the thoughts and feelings of the nation as a whole. And, as their posthumous fame was to prove, their appeal was not limited to their own time. Yet though, as Matthew Arnold was to write, Shakespeare was not for an age but for all time, he was by birth and environment an Elizabethan of Elizabethans. Born in 1564 in the little Warwickshire market town of Stratford-upon-Avon, just over seven years after Elizabeth's accession, and, outliving her by little more than a decade, the bulk of his work – though not all the greatest – was written during her reign. Son of a glover and wool-dealer who became an alderman, and, in the crisis year of 1569, bailiff or mayor of his native Stratford, in his fifty-two years Shakespeare experienced and shared in the social and cultural life of all three main classes into which contemporary England – at that time more homogeneous than at any period in her history – was divided. For growing up in the ranks of the rural trading middle class, with a good Latin education at the local Grammar school, owing to his father's failing fortunes and debts, and his own improvidence at the age of eighteen in getting a neighbour's daughter into trouble and having to marry her, he missed the chance of a university education and had to seek his fortunes in the rough and tumble tavern and slum life of the English capital. Here, as his plays reveal, he acquired a wonderful knowledge and understanding of the life and familiar speech of the poor and uneducated. Here, too, at first in some subordinate capacity, he became attached to one of the licensed companies of players competing for the favours of the theatre-loving London populace and, in his late twenties, while serving it as an actor, made a name for himself by writing for it three successful chronicle plays on the reign and civil wars of Henry VI, as well as two modish Italian comedies, *The Two Gentlemen of Verona* and *The Comedy of Errors*.

At this point he seems to have won the affectionate friendship and patronage of the eighteen-year-old Earl of Southampton, ten years his junior, a wealthy young nobleman of the highest fashion in whose household he lived, possibly as some kind of tutor, during the plague years of 1592–93 when the London theatres were shut. During this time, in addition to a long intimate sonnet sequence for his patron, he wrote two much admired courtly poems dedicated to him, *Venus and Adonis* and *The Rape of Lucrece*. All this, as well as his growing fame as a maker of plays, brought him before he was thirty to the notice and into the society of the royal Court and aristocracy.

By his early success as a playwright Shakespeare, a journeyman actor, incurred the jealousy of the university-educated poets and wits who at that time enjoyed a virtual monopoly of writing blank-verse dramas for the new London theatres. For during the first half of Elizabeth's reign a professional class of licensed actors, presenting plays with an immense popular appeal, had come into being. It had grown originally out of the universal English love of acting and drama – itself a legacy of the medieval Church which had familiarized the Christian story and its legends through the dramatized ritual of its services, and by the Christmas, Resurrection and other seasonal plays acted in church and churchyard. Supplemented by the 'mystery' plays and 'storial cycles' given by the trade and religious gilds of the cities and chartered towns, in an age without newspapers and popular books, when very few could read, everyone had taken part in these, both as actors and spectators. When after the Reformation a Protestant Church discarded them in favour of sermons and extemporare prayers and readings from the translated scriptures, they survived in the popular heart and habit in the shape of performances by troupes of strolling players, given in inn-courtyards, stage-wagons and barns in the towns, and by traditional mumming-plays, 'disguisings' and morris and country dances in the villages.

Frowned on by puritanical precisians addicted to long sermons and prayer-meetings and who, being themselves virtuous, wished there to be 'no more cakes and ale', attempts were made by the civic authorities in London and the larger towns to suppress the strolling players as 'sturdy rogues and vagabonds'. But the acting fraternity was supported, not only by the unpoliced urban populace of pleasure-loving artisans and apprentices, but by the Queen and Court, whose favourite entertainments were the seasonal dramatic performances enacted by the boys and choristers of the Chapel Royal and St Paul's at Christmas, Shrovetide and other holidays. For it was part of Elizabeth's unifying policy that England, despite the wish of Puritan extremists, should remain 'merry England'; and pageants, plays, masques, processions and royal ceremonies were all manifestations of her resolve to keep it so. So were the Latin plays of universities and schools indications of her educated subjects delight in drama and acting.

One feature of the reign was the patronage by drama-loving nobles of troupes or companies of actors who, in return for bearing the name and wearing the badge of their patron, were protected by royal licence from the enactments of puritanical Parliaments and civic authorities. Their earliest patron was Elizabeth's first favourite and suitor, Lord Robert Dudley, who, it was said, 'loved a play and players'. In the opening year of her reign he formed his own company which, after his elevation to an earldom, became known as Leicester's Men. In 1574, faced by attempted restrictions on their freedom by the City, he helped to secure them Letters Patent under the great seal, giving them the right to act in London and all towns throughout England, 'any act, statute, proclamation to the contrary notwithstanding'. Two years later, the leading member of his company, James Burbage, previously a joiner, built the first London theatre in the precincts of the former priory of Holywell in Shoreditch, just outside the City bounds; a second theatre, the Curtain, rose in the same year. Other licensed companies of players under aristocratic patronage were Lord Strange's, later the Earl of Derby's, the Earl of Warwick's, the Earl of Sussex's, Lord Chandos's, Lord Worcester's, the Lord Admiral's and the Earl of Pembroke's, the company for which Shakespeare probably wrote his earliest plays. In 1583 five years before the Armada, the Queen's own company was formed, with the greatest clown in England, Richard Tarleton, the favourite alike of the London mob and of Elizabeth herself, who, it was recorded, once bade them 'take away the knave for making her laugh so excessively as he fought against her little dog, Perrico de Faldas, with his sword and long staff'.

The fare provided by such actors was declamatory, rhetorical and accompanied by highly dramatic action. Played on platforms closely surrounded by a jostling excited audience, the more important of whom sat not only in boxes above, but sometimes, on the stage itself, their appeal was even more to the ear than the eye. The contact between actor and audience was exceedingly close, the whole auditorium often rising and shouting in excited response to the words or actions of the leading players. As their art developed with practice, many of them acquired an extraordinary skill in arousing the emotions of their auditors. The plays they performed also evolved rapidly, from crude melodrama or rough and tumble, into a fine art, the best written by university graduates in declamatory blank verse from familiar Italian or classical tales. Among these were George Peele and

John Lyly from Oxford, and Robert Greene, Thomas Nashe and Christopher Marlowe from Cambridge, the last, though short-lived, a poet of the highest promise, whose resounding lines in his *Tamburlane*, *Faustus* and *The Jew of Malta* aroused passionate excitement and admiration in his audiences.

Playing in the crowded London theatres in the winter and in the summer touring the provincial towns of southern and central England, the actors of the licenced companies were peculiarly well-fitted to reflect and interpret the life and feeling of contemporary society. As Stratford was visited almost every summer by one or more of these companies – in 1587 there were no fewer than five – it was probably through such visits that the young Shakespeare was first drawn to the stage.

After the plague years of 1592 and 1593, which broke up several of the old licensed companies and wrought havoc in the ranks of the university playwrights, Shakespeare, at the age of thirty, found himself, for the next decade, without a serious rival as a popular dramatist. In 1594, possibly with the help of his patron, Southampton, he bought a proprietary share in a new licensed company, the Lord Chamberlain's, formed under the patronage of the Queen's elderly cousin, Lord Hunsdon, who a few years earlier had been the 'protector' of Shakespeare's 'dark lady of the sonnets'. This company quickly outdistanced all rivals in the favour of both London audiences and the Court, its members including both James Burbage's son, the great tragedian, Richard Burbage – who made his name, like Garrick after him, playing the character part in Shakespeare's *Richard III* – William Kemp, Thomas Pope, and John Hemmings who, with Henry Condell, collected and edited Shakespeare's plays for the folio edition published seven years after his death. On James I's accession, the company became the King's Company, its members wearing royal livery and becoming officers of the Household as grooms of the chamber-in-ordinary, while the fees for its performances at Court were doubled.

Shakespeare did not write his plays to be read or published; he wrote them to be acted. And since the effectiveness of speech in the densely packed proscenium theatres of the Elizabethan stage depended on declamation and sound, being a poet he used the language of poetry to mould and sway his auditors' feelings. Nurtured, like every Elizabethan through compulsory church attendance, on the noble rhythms and music of the Anglican Liturgy and the English translations of the Bible, he employed his natural sense of music – for no greater musician of words ever lived – to carry his audience with him into whatever mood the course of his play demanded.

He had a marvellous facility with words and the English language, which he naturalized, so that in his hands it ceased to be stilted. His was a genius for coining casual phrases whose use became universal. 'One touch of nature makes the whole world kin.' 'The Devil can cite Scripture for his purpose.' 'The slings and arrows of outrageous fortune.' 'The course of true love never did run smooth'. 'There is a tide in the affairs of men which, taken at the flood, leads on to fortune.' 'There's a divinity that shapes our ends, rough-hew them as we will.' All these, and many more, rose naturally out of the plays he put together with such prolific industry during the next fifteen years.

Having to make money for the company for which he worked and of which he was a shareholder, Shakespeare sought to give the public what it wanted, though, in doing so, he shaped his material as his artist's instinct dictated. His first success, while still working for Lord Pembroke's company in the years after the defeat of the Armada, had been based on the patriotic fervour aroused by Spanish intervention in France in 1591, when, to aid the Huguenot king, Henri Quatre, English expeditions were sent to Britanny and Normandy under Sir John Norris and the dashing young Earl of Essex, the popular hero both of the London mob and of Shakespeare's youthful patron, Southampton. His three chronicle plays about the reign of Henry VI and the Wars of the Roses, with their memories of 'brave Talbot' and his heroic defence of England's lost French dominions, were all appeals to the patriotism which Elizabeth's unifying reign had fostered. So were his later historical plays – founded on Holinshed's chronicle history of England – *King John* staged in 1596, the year of Essex's gallant exploits at Cadiz, *Richard II* and *Richard III*, the two parts of *Henry IV*, and *Henry V* in 1599, when amid scenes of tumultuous enthusiasm, as the Queen's Lord General and Viceroy of Ireland, the popular hero earl rode out of London, 'the people pressing exceedingly to behold him for more than four miles space, crying out "God save your Lordship" "God preserve your Honour." ' Shakespeare's hope of his victorious return:

'Were now the General of our gracious Empress,
As in good time he may, from Ireland coming,
Bringing rebellion broached on his sword,

196

> How many would the peaceful City quit
> To welcome him.'

was to be tragically dashed. For it was the spoilt and neurotic favourite's reliance on his fatal popularity with the London mob that was
to cause him, after his ignominious return from Ireland, to raise what
the Queen contemptuously called his 'rebellion of one day', leading
in February 1601 to his execution for High Treason, and his lieutenant,
Southampton's two years' incarceration in the Tower.

Two features of Shakespeare's historical plays distinguished them
from those of his contemporaries. One was his genius, anticipating
that of Walter Scott in the Waverley novels, of peopling them, not
only with historic characters, but with imaginary ordinary men and
women who figure in no history books but are the real stuff of
contemporary life in any age. With these he created those wonderful
scenes in Justice Shallow's Cotswold garden and Falstaff's haunts in
the Boars Head tavern and Mistress Quickly's Dolphin chamber,
which, contrasted with the great scenes of state, follow one another
in quick succession, and with exquisite artistic mastery, give a sense
of instant reality to Shakespeare's re-enactment of his country's past,
making his pride in it a living irresistible thing, as when he himself
as Chorus introduced his *Henry V* to the excited audience at his
company's new theatre, the Globe, on Bankside.

> 'Can this cockpit hold
> The vasty fields of France? or may we cram
> Within this wooden O the very casques
> That did affright the air at Agincourt?'

Or when, at the end, he spoke its epilogue:

> 'Thus far, with rough and all-unable pen,
> Our bending author hath pursued the story,
> In little room confining mighty men,
> Mangling by starts the full course of their glory.
> Small time, but, in that small, most greatly lived
> This star of England.'

The other distinguishing feature of Shakespeare's historical plays
was his political realism, rare in writers and intellectuals who in all
ages tend to lack it in their obsession with ideals and abstractions. Like
the Queen, he never forgot the fallibility which underlay the relations
of human beings in society. For all his keen perception of the injustices

and corruptions of the world, he was, therefore, a conformist and never a rebel or destroyer. With Dr Johnson he saw how precarious were the assumptions on which civilization rests, and how easily they can be undermined. So in the great speech on degree in *Troilus and Cressida* – written just before Elizabeth's death with its renewed fears of a disputed succession – Ulysses asks

> 'How could communities,
> Degrees in schools and brotherhoods in cities,
> Peaceful commerce from dividable shores,
> The primogenetive and due of birth,
> Prerogative of age, crowns, sceptres, laurels
> But by degree, stand in authentic place?
> Take but degree away, untune that string
> and hark what discord follows! . . .'

Not all Shakespeare's plays were written for the London theatre and its tough masculine audiences. Several were intended for performances at Court, where he was a favourite playwright of both Elizabeth and James I, or in some great country house. An early example was his *A Midsummer Night's Dream*, produced in May 1594 to grace the nuptials of Southampton's mother to Sir Thomas Heneage, Vice Chamberlain of the royal household. In this enchanting play, moonlit with exquisite poetry, Shakespeare let his fancy loose, peopling the great hall where his fantasy was probably played, with the creatures, real and imaginary, of his Warwickshire childhood: Snug the joiner, Snout the tinker, and Bottom the weaver, with whom, so unaccountably, Titania, Queen of the Fairies, fell in love. Her king, Oberon, and her attendant fairies-in-waiting, Peasblossom, Cobweb, Moth and Mustardseed share the stage with the humans.

> 'Through the house give glimmering light,
> By the dead and drowsy fire,
> Every elf and fairy sprite
> Hop as light from bird to briar.'

The same happy intrusion of the scenes and fauna of his native countryside occurs in half a dozen of his plays, though intended for the rough London theatre. Even in one of his earliest comedies, the audience is suddenly transported from a royal palace in Navarre to an English village, first in summer, then in winter.

'When shepherds pipe on oaten straws
  and merry larks are ploughmen's clocks.
When turtles tread and rooks and daws,
  and maidens bleach their summer smocks . . .'

'When icicles hang by the wall,
  And Dick the shepherd blows his nail,
And Tom bears logs into the hall
  And milk comes frozen home in pail . . .'

So, too, into play after play, whether comedy or tragedy, the most
exquisite lyric poetry finds its way without the least seeming in-
congruity, so much master was this greatest of all Elizabethans of his
dramatist's craft.

'Take, O take those lips away
That so sweetly were forsworn
And those eyes, the break of day,
Lights that do mislead the morn.'

For he was the poet of nature and natural feeling; 'sweetest Shakespeare, Fancy's child' as his great Puritan successor, Milton, put it,
'warbling his native woodnotes wild.'

Drama being constructed out of the clash and contact of human
beings with one another, the basic work of an Elizabethan playwright
was to use the spoken word to delineate character. Where Shakespeare
differed from nearly all his predecessors and contemporaries was
that, instead of using stock types as the *personae* of his plays, he made
them real human beings with all the differences and idiosyncrasies of
individual human nature and character. In this he was aided by the
extraordinary range of his sympathies which enabled him to enter
into the inner feelings of every character he delineated. So, instead
of making his Shylock, the merciless Jew moneylender, the type of
total evil his contemporary and fellow poet, Marlowe, made Barabas
in *The Jew of Malta,* he put into his mouth words that showed he was
a human being like everyone else. 'Hath not a Jew eyes? hath not a
Jew hands, organs, dimensions, senses, affections, passions? fed with
the same food, hurt with the same weapons, subject to the same
diseases, healed by the same means, warmed and cooled by the same
winter and summer as a Christian is? If you prick us, do we not bleed?
if you tickle us, do we not laugh? if you poison us, do we not die? and,
if you wrong us, shall we not revenge?'

Shakespeare had a natural compassion and instinctive sympathy for all sorts and conditions of men. It is this quality that informs his tragedies and raises them to a level unattained by even the great Greek dramatists. The essence of classic pagan tragedy was the fall, from the height of power and fortune, of a great man, struck down by the inexorable workings of Fate or Nemesis. But in the Christian drama of Shakespeare the tragedy which befalls a great man arises primarily out of some flaw or weakness in an otherwise noble character which exposes him and others dependent on him to the buffets of Fate and misfortune – ambition, jealousy, passion, arrogance, indecision. The element of free will which lies at the heart of the Christian concept enters into and dominates the dramatic story. So Othello, speaking of Desdemona, recalls,

> 'She loved me for the dangers I had pass'd,
> And I loved her that she did pity them.'

and, in his last terrible realization of what, through jealousy, he had done to her, cries out,

> 'Speak of me as I am; nothing extenuate,
> Nor set down aught in malice; then must you speak
> Of one that lov'd not wisely, but too well;
> Of one not easily jealous, but, being wrought,
> Perplex'd in the extreme; of one whose hand,
> Like the base Indian, threw a pearl away
> Richer than all his tribe. . .'

For, as Shakespeare put it in his *Julius Caesar*, 'the fault, dear Brutus, lies not in our stars, but in ourselves that we are underlings.'

After the great sequence of tragedies which Shakespeare wrote between his thirty-sixth and forty-fifth year – *Julius Caesar, Hamlet, Othello, King Lear, Macbeth, Anthony and Cleopatra, Coriolanus, Timon of Athens* – in his last plays he turned, like the great artist he was, to something new: to a theme which was neither comedy nor tragedy, but that of human repentance and forgiveness. All three involved bringing in a new generation to redress the failure and folly of an old. And all three – *Cymbeline, The Winter's Tale* and *The Tempest* – are transfused with a gentle and elegiac music:

> 'Daffodils
> That come before the swallow dares,
> And take the winds of March with beauty.'

ELIZABETHAN HARVEST

'Some say that ever 'gainst the season comes
Wherein our Saviour's birth is celebrated,
The bird of dawning singeth all night long.'

'Be not afraid; the isle is full of noises,
Sounds and sweet airs, that give delight and hurt not.'

The last and greatest of these pastoral romances, *The Tempest*, was inspired by the account of a hurricane which shipwrecked, on the then still unexplored island of Bermuda, the flagship of the expedition sent by the London Virginia Company in the spring of 1609 to put the infant American colony, as was hoped, on its feet. The account of the storm and shipwreck, in which everyone was miraculously saved, reached England in a news letter sent home by one of the survivors, William Strachey, Secretary designate to the Virginia colony.* From it, and his description of the island, Shakespeare reconstructed the story in this magical play, first produced on Hallowe'n night 1611 at Whitehall before the King. It was one of the fourteen plays, six of them by Shakespeare, played two years later to celebrate the nuptials in 1613 of the Princess Elizabeth – Wotton's 'Queen of Hearts' and ancestress of the present Queen – to the Elector Palatine of the Rhine.

In its course, Shakespeare himself, in the person of the magician, Prospero, bade farewell to his art:

'Our revels now are ended. These our actors
As I foretold you, were all spirits, and
Are melted into air, into thin air:
And like the baseless fabric of this vision
The cloud-capp'd towers, the gorgeous palaces,
The solemn temples, the great globe itself,
Yea, all which it inherit, shall dissolve
And, like this insubstantial pageant faded,
Leave not a rack behind. We are such stuff
As dreams are made on, and our little life
Is rounded with a sleep.'

It was not, however, quite Shakespeare's last word. In 1612, when he was forty-eight and four years before his death in April 1616, he contributed a final historical play on the reign of Henry VIII. In it, describing the christening of Henry's daughter, the Princess Elizabeth, he paid his tribute to the great Queen and her reign, of which he and

* An ancestor of Lytton Strachey.

his work had been part.

> 'This royal infant – Heaven still move about her –
> Though in her cradle, yet now promises
> Upon this land a thousand thousand blessings,
> Which time shall bring to ripeness: She shall be . . .
> A pattern to all princes living with her,
> And all that shall succeed . . .
> She shall be loved and feared; her own shall bless her;
> Her foes shake like a field of beaten corn,
> . . . and hang their heads with sorrow . . .
> In her days every man shall eat in safety
> Under his own vine what he plants, and sing
> The merry songs of peace to all his neighbours . . .
>
> She shall be to the happiness of England
> An aged princess; many days shall see her
> And yet no day without a deed to crown it.'

Epilogue

SHAKESPEARE'S LONDON

'At length they all to merry London came . . .
. . . Sweet Thames, run softly till I end my song'

Edmund Spenser

The Shakespearian capital from which, in the opening decades of the seventeenth century, the first American colonies sprang, was no old-fashioned town inhabited by unadventurous backward-looking folk. It was a fast expanding and intensely energetic, aggressive and excitable community with only one foot in the rustic England out of which it had sprung and the other in the trading oceans. 'The most scoffing, respectless and unthankful city that ever was,' a contemporary lover of the half clerical and monastic medieval London of the past called it. It was peopled and ruled by men who were the architects of their own fortunes and lived by taking risks. They or their forefathers had taken a very big one when they first migrated from the country to the city to make their fortunes. For, out of every three or four who came to London, at least two died of plague or fever in its noisome, pestilential courts and alleys. Their prototype was the fabulous Dick Whittington, who according to popular legend had tramped to London as a boy two centuries before with his worldly goods tied in a handkerchief on his back, and who, in real life, had lived to become Lord Mayor and the equivalent of a modern millionaire. It was such men, who, in the years following the defeat of the Armada, when Shakespeare was writing his first plays, set the pace and found the finance for the feverish pioneering – the 'root, hog or die' courage – of the founding fathers of the United States.

Though in the Middle Ages England had been an island kingdom on the road to nowhere – the last outpost of civilized Christendom, save for wild Scotland and still wilder Ireland beyond it – during the reign of the Tudors, with the discovery of a new World beyond the Atlantic and of an ocean route round Africa to the golden East of silks and spices, she had gradually found herself in the commercial centre of the world instead of on its outer fringe. It had taken Londoners several generations to realize the full implications of this momentous change. But by the closing decades of Elizabeth's germinative reign, with the awareness of their national unity which she had awoken in them, its consciousness had given to the life of England's capital an immense vitality. When country lads – the Dick Whittingtons of the age – travelled to it, as thousands did every year, like young Will Shakespeare from Warwickshire Stratford-upon-Avon, hoping to make their fortunes in its crowded, narrow, evil-smelling but intensely exciting streets, they felt that they were coming not only to by far the largest city in their own island, but to the doorway to a greater and wider world.

It is this sense which pervaded the new plays of the Elizabethan and Jacobean dramatists, with their international settings and their plots taken from Athens and Rome, Sicily and Illyria, Denmark and Egypt and the cities of Lombardy and Bohemia. It is a measure of Shakespeare's all-embracing genius that, while he peopled even the glades of Greece with Warwickshire rustics and first made his name as a dramatist by writing three chronicle plays immortalizing the changing fortunes of the Lancastrian and Yorkist princes in the century before he was born, the themes and leading characters of his more ambitious comedies were scarcely ever taken from England, or if they were, were drawn from an England so remote in time as to be part of a foreign world. Even those of the great tragedies of his later years – the years when the first English settlers were about to make a lodgment beyond the Atlantic – Anthony and great Caesar, Othello the Moor and Coriolanus, Timon of Athens and Hamlet the Dane, were not born within sound of Bow Bells or even those of Stratford-on-Avon.

This was the real significance of Shakespeare's London. It was English, but its face and bright eyes were turned toward the new lands of fable and romance beyond the seas. The Londoners of his day were as obsessed with the thought of those lands, of foreign princes and foreign courts and voyages to remote parts, as little American and English boys today are with tales of space ships and flights to the moon. The rough mob which flocked to the new bear gardens, stews and playhouses of Shoreditch and the South Bank were given dramas about merchants of Venice and gentlemen of Verona and Roman Caesars and senators because that was what they wanted to hear about. They might have burnt down the theatres – for they were not a patient or polite audience – had they been offered anything else.

One can see that vibrant city in John Stow's great *Survey of London*, written in the latter part of Elizabeth's reign and published in 1598 – a metropolis crowded and almost bursting at the seams with its fast-growing population: a proud, turbulent, beautiful and dangerous city, with its filthy open ditches and rat-haunted laystalls and its crowded overhanging gabled houses almost touching one another across the narrow streets and inviting fire at the first spark. Such houses were framed in oak, with walls of lath and plaster, and their piled soaring stories painted and heavily carved. Because of the ever-present risk of fire, every substantial one had by law to keep a supply of leather fire-buckets, and every parish had its great iron hooks with ropes and pulleys for pulling down burning buildings.

Above the city towered the immense, five hundred-year-old St Paul's Cathedral, the second largest in the world crowned, until a few years after Elizabeth's accession, when it was struck in 1561 by lightning, by an enormous spire – 150 feet higher than the dome and cross of its present successor. From the river, Tudor London, with its forest of Gothic church spires and towers soaring above the little three-storied houses, must have made much the same impression on contemporaries as modern New York with its skyscrapers seen from the sea. The city, among the largest in Europe, glimpsed from northern height or Kentish heath, gave the approaching traveller a breathtaking sense of size and urban sophistication, for it was far larger in proportion to all the other towns of the kingdom than it is today. Its population, 100,000 at the time of Elizabeth's accession in 1558 and a quarter of a million by the middle of the seventeenth century, was something like twenty times that of the next largest English city, Norwich. The noise and uproar – of hoofs and wheels on the cobbles, of apprentices and hawkers bawling their wares, of the constantly creaking painted and gilded signs which hung and swung over the narrow streets from every shop, inn and alehouse – was like a cannonade.

Around the older and inner London of the Middle Ages the ancient walls still stood, thirty feet high in places, with bastions and gates such as King Hal had ridden through as he went out to Agincourt two centuries before. But the suburbs, or 'liberties' as they were called, with their rich merchants' pleasances and squalid squatters' hovels and shacks, were spreading their untidy tentacles in every direction over the fields. Within a lifetime of Shakespeare's death in 1616, despite the constant inroads of typhus and smallpox, and the horrifying epidemics of bubonic plague, which, until the last great pestilence in 1665, swept the city in almost every decade, 'this great and monstrous thing called London' stretched almost from Blackwell to Chelsea, as the twin cities of London and Westminster drew ever closer to one another. It was hard to say exactly where one entered it, but the traveller knew by the old formula, 'so soon as the coach was got upon the stones.'

For it was then that the rattle began – of wooden and iron wheels rumbling on cobbles – of apprentices standing before every shop bawling, 'What d'ye lack?' – of hawkers crying, 'Hot fine oatcake,' 'Lily-white vinegar,' 'White-hearted cabbages,' and 'Kitchen stuff, ha' you maids;' and, as the warm months drew on and rich folk wished themselves on their country estates, 'Cherry Ripe,' 'Peas' and 'Fine strawberries.' There were costard mongers – the forerunners of the Victorian and Edwardian costers – hawking apples; old-clothes men and small-coals men with sacks of Newcastle cobbles on their backs; milkmaids intoning 'Any milk here?' as they rattled their pails; tinkers with loud 'Have you any brass pots, iron pots, skillets or frying pans to mend?' and mousetrap men with 'Buy a mousetrap, a mousetrap, or a tormentor for your fleas?' One sensed the context of these incitements to commerce by their music rather than their words; by the lilt and rhythm of: 'Here's fine herrings, eight a groat!' 'Come buy my Wellsfleet oysters, ho!' 'Come buy my whitings fine and new!' For the art of advertising was then vocal, not visual.

One not only heard London, one smelt it. The sanitation of the age was oriental in its simple grandeur, and its effects, comparatively innocuous in a country village, were appalling in a metropolis. Rivers of filth coursed down the centre of every street, and at the time of the emptying of slop pails, the passer-by nearest the wall had cause to be grateful for the overhanging stories. Around the city stretched a halo of stinking, steaming laystalls, haunted by flies and kites, while in its denser quarters the graveyards, piled high above the surrounding ground, constantly repeopled themselves. The most cultured, however nice in their own tastes, were utterly innocent of public sanitary sense: one great lord in Stuart times installed a pump to drive the piled ordure from his cellar into the street. Drinking water, though a few of the larger houses enjoyed a piped supply, was hawked from door to door in large wooden vessels, broad at the bottom and narrow at the top, and filled from the conduits at the principal street corners.

The streets between the crowded buildings were narrow, cobbled with egg-shaped stones, with posts at the sides of the broader thoroughfares to protect pedestrians, and rendered fantastically crooked by the uneven frontage of the houses. Above them painted signs indicated to an illiterate age the addresses of their occupants – the 'Three Pigeons' in Great Queen's Street, or the 'Crooked Billet' 'over against Hill, the Quaker cook's, upon the Mall Bank, Westminster.' Behind the streets were courtyards and lanes giving access to others still narrower, and to the stables which housed the countless riding and draught-horses of the metropolis.

Carts, coaches and sledges jammed the narrow streets, and traffic control tended to be a matter of vocal adjustment 'till the quarrel be decided whether six of your nobles sitting together shall stop and give way to as many barrels of beer.' Every nobleman's coach was preceded by footmen calling on the groundlings to make way for their master, a demand which draymen and drivers of hackney coaches had no hesitation in disputing. These last, which waited for their fares in ranks at street corners, were a post-Elizabethan innovation, and, despite the attempts of the Thames watermen to get them prohibited, multiplied rapidly throughout the seventeenth century. By its second half they had firmly established themselves as one of the principal institutions of London. To travel in them was to be involved in frequent turmoil. There were traffic blocks which lasted half an hour and set whole streets swearing and shouting; accidents when wheels came off or bolts broke, so that the horses went on while the unfortunate passengers remained stationary; Jehu-like incidents which left splashed and endangered pedestrians screaming with rage, or in narrow thoroughfares brought down the hanging wares from the hooks outside the shops. Even at night, while the city slept, the clamour of London persisted, the constable and his watch brawling with midnight revellers, the watchman's cry of 'Past one of the clock and a cold frosty windy morning!' and the sounds of cattle, pigs and poultry which bespoke the agricultural undertakings hidden behind London's urban exterior.

In winter the principal streets were lit until ten or eleven at night by lanterns placed at regular intervals, and, less certainly, by householders who were expected, between the feasts of All Saints and Candlemas, to expose their light to the roadway. In summer a frugal age dispensed with artificial illumination altogether. More reliable were the linkboys who waited at every corner with torch and lantern to light travellers home. These poor urchins, recruited from the ragged

homeless strays who lodged in doorways and disused penthouses –
assailed the passer-by with cries of, 'Do you want light?' Grander
citizens went out to supper with a servant carrying a lanthorn before
them and so provided their own street lighting.

If there was not much light by night, there was plenty of smoke by
day, particularly in the winter when the thousands of wood or sea-coal
fires rose into the damp air. Above the city hung a permanent pall of
vapour from the furnaces of brewers, soap boilers and dyers. This
phenomenon, already a minor nuisance at the end of Elizabeth's
reign, had become a major one half a century later. Evelyn, the most
fastidious observer of his day, wrote indignantly of the 'horrid smoke
which obscures our churches and makes our palaces look old, which
fouls our clothes and corrupts the waters.' In winter this coal vapour
sometimes descended on the streets in a blanket of fog so thick that
'horses ran against each other, carts against carts, coaches against
coaches.'

Trade and manufactures were expanding fast; London was above
all a city of merchants, shopkeepers, artisans and turbulent apprentices.
Traders still congregated in particular districts; the goldsmiths in
Cheapside – the city's broadest street and most fashionable shopping
centre – the fishmongers in Bridge Street, mercers and haberdashers
on London Bridge, pepperers and grocers in Bucklersbury, book-
sellers and stationers in St Paul's churchyard where they set up their
stalls against the walls of the ancient cathedral and stocked their books
in its vaults. The raw materials of trade reached Londoners through the
great provision markets – meat from Hungerford and Queenhithe,
fish and coal from Billingsgate, cloth from Blackwell Hall, herbs
from Covent Garden and the Stocks Market, horses and livestock from
Smithfield, and fish, butter, poultry, bacon, hides and leather from
Leadenhall.

The shops were small, consisting generally of the front downstairs
room of the house in which the shopkeeper's family and apprentices
lived and worked. But though the multiple shop was unknown, the
bazaar was already flourishing by the time of Shakespeare's death.
Great ladies with their husbands and 'servants' – as their cavaliers
were called – flocked to the New Exchange in the Strand, which, with
its row of shops along double galleries of black stone, conveniently
adjacent to the new fashionable quarter of the town round Covent
Garden, which during the reigns of the first two Stuarts had begun to
outdistance the nave of St Paul's and the old Royal Exchange in

Cornhill as popular marts. And in the latter were those elegant young women, the semptresses and milliners of the Exchange, who, with their ogling eyes and pretty chirpings of 'Fine linens, sir, gloves or ribbons,' made gentlemen customers buy more than they had intended, and, unless they have been maligned by their contemporaries, were sometimes not averse to selling their persons as well.

All this business required refreshment, and it was easily to be had by those with well-lined purses. Eating houses ranged from famous taverns like the 'Boar's Head' in Eastcheap, the 'Mermaid' and 'Mitre' in Bread Street and Mitre Court, and the 'Sun' in Fish Street, to little cookshops where one could feast on a chop of veal, bread and cheese and beer for a shilling, or buy a joint or sirloin of roast ready cooked for consumption at home.

> 'The gentry to the "King's Head",
> The nobles to the "Crown",
> The knight unto the "Golden Fleece",
> And to the "Plough" the clown.'

A common mode of dining in a tavern was to take the 'ordinary' at the long table, each man contributing to the conversation and paying his 'club' or share. Places of purely liquid refreshment were innumerable; had one tried to count all the alehouses between the 'Hercules Pillars' by Hyde Park Gate and the 'Boatswain' in Wapping, one might have counted for ever. In these, with their red or green painted lattices, men of all classes congregated to drink and talk, as often as not about the political doings of their betters – much to the astonishment of foreigners, who could not accustom themselves to the way the English left their work at all hours of the day for this purpose.

For London was not only a trading but an intensely libertarian city. It had been so from time immemorial: a refuge from and a counterweight to the feudal order of the English countryside. From its rich aldermen and livery men to its rowdy apprentices all its people claimed a large measure of liberty and what to foreigners seemed outrageous political license. The traditional cry of 'clubs' could quickly fill a street with 'truncheoners', as the growing hatred and fear of 'popery' intensified after the massacre of St Bartholomew in 1572, the atrocious cruelty of the Spanish Inquisition to English seamen captured beyond the 'Line', and the Gunpowder Plot of 1605. Ready to mob anyone who outraged popular beliefs and prejudices by the least suspicion or appearance of popery, if anyone interfered in the name of authority, the City's 'brisk Protestant boys' would beat up with impunity the constables and aged infirm watchmen who formed the bulk of its only police force.

Yet, for all its noise and turbulence, London was still half rustic. The fields were never far away, and most of the main streets filled at least once a day with herds of cattle and flocks of sheep, making their dolorous way to the markets which kept London's swarming population fed. Milkmaids vending their wares, and scavenging pigs were among the common sights of the town. And there were gardens and trees in every part of it, and farms and byres among the densely packed surburban houses. Stow, its Elizabethan chronicler, used as a boy to fetch home from the nunnery farm in Goodman's field 'many a half-penny worth of milk, and never had less than three ale-pints for a half-penny in the summer, nor less than one ale-quart for a half-penny in the winter, always hot from the kine as the same was milked and strained. And on May Day, he recalled, 'in the morning, every man, except impediment, would walk into the sweet meadows and green woods, there to rejoice their spirits with the beauty and savour of sweet flowers and with the harmony of birds.' After the stench and racket of the narrow streets and alleys they must have seemed sweet indeed. The Puritans, however, a fast growing class even in Shakespeare's lifetime, took a far less kindly view of these outings; 'all the young men and maids, old men and wives,' one of them complained, 'run gadding overnight to the woods, groves, hills and mountains, where they spend all night in pleasant pastime' and, he added, in every sort of immorality.

If fields, farms and woods – never more than a mile away to the north – were within the Londoner's easy reach, and the wooded heights of Hampstead and Highgate crowned his northern horizon, to the south lay the steep streets and alleys which sloped down to the river and its countless ships, boats and wherries. Beyond it, except where the borough of Southwark crowded round the southern end of London Bridge, stretched marshes and green water meadows, and beyond them the hanging woods of Penge and Norwood. The river was both London's southern boundary and principal highway and its link with the world, 'brimming with craft and commerce.'

No other city in Europe had a larger waterfront and none so famous a bridge. There was only one, but with its gabled houses and shops making a continuous street across it, its spired chapel, and gateway crowned with traitors' heads, its two cornmills and water works, its nineteen arches, with the rapids roaring under them, it was one of the wonders of the world.

Below the Bridge and guarding the Pool of London, where tall-masted ships unloaded and loaded before their ocean voyages, was the grim Norman Tower whose guns looked down on the swarming, unpoliced, libertarian city at its feet. Though no longer a place of royal residence, it served the purposes of a prison for State offenders, an armoury, a national mint, a public-record office, a menagerie, where some rather mangy lions and a few other beasts from Africa were kept for Londoners to gape at, and the treasury for the crown jewels. Stow described it as 'a citadel to defende or command the citie; a royall place for assemblies and treaties; a prison of Estate for the most dangerous offenders; the onely place of coynage for all England at this time; the armories for warlike provision; the Treasurie of the ornaments and jewels of the Crowne, and general conserver of the most recordes of the King's Courts of Justice at Westminster.' In his day, with its dungeons and torture chambers, its block and tall scaffold on Tower Hill, its sentinel warders in their scarlet-and-gold royal liveries, it was still a very real reminder to the ambitious and great that the Crown would brook no rival.

The rough mob of the city loved the strong-nerved, sensible and not-too-scrupulous Tudor sovereigns who kept the old feudal nobility in order, encouraged trade and, respecting popular liberties, enforced peace. So did the lawyers in their gated and gardened Inns of Court and the country squires and yeomen in the shires who together made up the faithful, but by no means uncritical or sub-servient, Commons. The latter met periodically in the Parliament House at Westminster to vote reluctant supplies for the Queen or her indignant, bumbling Scottish successor, King James. Here they discussed business of State, and wrestled for their interests and beliefs with the royal Ministers and the hereditary nobles and lawn-sleeved prelates of the Church, assembled in Parliament's Upper House. By the time of the Stuart succession the 'faithful Commons' were already a major power in the land and were soon to become a greater, and they were stoutly supported by the magistracy, populace and rowdy apprentices of the City.

During Shakespeare's lifetime there were still a number of the great walled medieval palaces of the nobility – which figured so often in his historical plays – left in London, with their parks, gardens and gatehouses. The traditional site for them was on the south side of the

Strand – the highway which linked the City to royal Westminster. In summer their shady gardens, full of roses and fruit trees running down to the water's edge, and their owners' stately gilded and coloured barges moored before them, impressed the eye of travellers on the River.

The most splendid of all the buildings on the Thames belonged to the Crown. Five miles below London Bridge, among the Kentish meadows, was Greenwich where Queen Elizabeth had been born, where Shakespeare sometimes acted before her and her successor, King James, and from whose windows she had often watched her seamen setting forth on their exploring and trading voyages, 'Her Majesty beholding the same with shaking her hand out of the window,' as she did when Frobisher sailed past her riverside palace on his first voyage to find a north-west passage through the ice to the golden illusory East. Nearby, at Deptford, lay the famous ship in which Drake had circumnavigated the globe and on whose deck he had been knighted by his delighted sovereign. It became in the next age a popular resort for dinner and supper parties. Its natural decay was hastened by souvenir hunters who chipped so many pieces off its timbers that it gradually fell to pieces.

At the other end of London, a mile to the west of Temple Bar and close to Westminster Hall, St Stephen's Chapel, where the Commons sat, and the Abbey – then without the towers which Wren was to add in the reign of Charles II – was the palace of Whitehall, the chief residence of the monarch and the seat of government. Here was a little city of its own, with walls, gates, chapels, halls, courtyards, lawns and numerous apartments, and by the river an embankment planted with trees, and stairs for taking barge and boat. And here, begun a quarter of a century after Shakespeare's death, the Great Rebellion was to culminate in an English King stepping out of a window of his own Banqueting Hall to die at his subject's hands for having claimed that the royal prerogative could still override Parliament and the laws it made.

At no point did London stray far from the river. Except where the gardens of the greater houses were embanked, the houses came down to the waterside, where a succession of slippery stairs linked the city lanes to the life of the river. Here, as one approached the waterside, there started up from the wooden benches by the stairs a multitude of grizzly Tritons in sweaty shirts and short-backed doublets with badges on their arms, hallooing and hooting, 'Next oars!' and 'Eastward Ho!' and 'Westward Ho!' according to the direction in which they plied. The thousands of licensed watermen on the rolls of the City's Watermen's Company were ruled and licensed by the Lord Mayor and his Water Bailiff, whose jurisdiction as Thames Conservator stretched from Staines bridge to the Medway. Their boats were of two kinds – sculls with one rower, and the faster 'oars' with two, in which one could travel with a favourable tide from the heart of London to Westminster in a quarter of an hour. Passengers sat on cushions and had a board to lean upon. But there was no covering except for a cloth spread over a few rough hoops in the stern, and, if a rainstorm came, one was usually soaked before there was time to raise it. The rich and great had barges with cabins, painted panels and, by the middle of the seventeenth century, windows that slid up and down in sashes like those of coaches.

The great obstacle to travel on the river was London Bridge. Nervous passengers, frightened by the foam and roar of its cataracts, were wont to land at the Old Swan on the north bank and rejoin the boat 'below Bridge'. Save that one was apt to get 'soundly washed', shooting the rapids was not so bad as it looked; in flood time one could take up fish with one's hands as they lay blinded by the thickness of the stream.

The language of the watermen was almost as great a wonder as the Bridge itself. It was a point of honour among them to exchange badinage of the coarsest kind with every passer-by; those acquainted with the adventures of Sir Roger de Coverly in the reign of the last Stuart will remember how this worthy gentleman, crossing to Vauxhall Gardens, was hailed as an 'old put', and asked if he was not ashamed to go awenching at his years. And this was mild abuse from a Thames Waterman. Sometimes they met their match: a boatload of Lambeth gardeners, it was held, could return them as good as they gave and better. Knowing clients took a hand in the game themselves, and flung back gibes at the passing boats, almost as though this sort of thing were a requirement of river travel.

To those who took the foul language and rough humour of the watermen as part of the game, the river was full of delight. There were the gilded barges of the Sovereign and the great lords, and of the Lord Mayor and City Companies, with gorgeous liveried boatmen; the long, shallow lighters which carried malt and meat to feed London; the picturesque and very dirty vendors of fruit and strong waters, who with wheedling shouts brought their unlicensed skiffs

213

alongside. When the weather was hot, one might pull off one's shoes and stockings and trail feet and fingers in the stream; at flood tide see the water coursing over the mill banks opposite Vauxhall and boats rowing in the streets of Westminster, or at low tide watch a daring boy wading through mud and pebbles from Whitehall to Lambeth. For the river served for pastime as well as business. Young Mr Pepys, born in London seventeen years after Shakespeare's death, would 'on a sudden motion' take up his wife and maids in a frolic and with cold victuals and bottled ale sail down to Gravesend to see the King's ships, or take the evening air as far as Greenwich or the Chelsea Neat House. At Barn Elms in his time ladies and courtiers came on June afternoons with bottles and baskets and chairs to sup under the trees by the waterside. And on moonlit nights the river took on a peculiar enchantment as parties of pleasure seekers, in an age when the English were still a nation of music makers, sang and accompanied themselves upon the water. Small wonder that the Londoner loved his river and went abroad on it whenever he could to look on 'the sun, the waters and the gardens of this fair city.'

Some time in the second decade of the seventeenth century – that great watershed of English history, when Shakespeare was living in retirement at Stratford-upon-Avon, when the first American settlers were struggling to secure their frail bridgehead in the transatlantic wilderness, when the child Milton was first feeling his way to beauty in the Bread Street house of his father, the music-loving Cheapside scrivener, and the men who were to make the Great Rebellion were growing up – Beaumont and Fletcher in their comedy, *The Knight of the Burning Pestle*, put into the mouth of a London apprentice, summoning his fellows to their traditional May Day rites, the spirit, pride and vigour of the late-Elizabethan and early Stuart capital.

'London, to thee I do present the merry month of May;
Let each true subject be content to hear me what I say . . .
Rejoice, oh, English hearts, rejoice! Rejoice, oh, lovers dear!
Rejoice, oh, city, town, and country! Rejoice, eke every shire . . .
With bells on legs, and napkins clean unto your shoulders tied,
With scarfs and garters as you please, and "Hey for our town!" cried,
March out, and show your willing minds, by twenty and by twenty,
To Hogsdon or to Newington, where ale and cakes are plenty;
And let it ne'er be said for shame, that we the youths of London
Lay thrumming of our caps at home, and left our custom undone,
Up, then, I say, both young and old, both man and maid a-maying,

With drums, and guns that bounce aloud, and merry tabor playing!
Which to prolong, God save our King, and send his country peace,
And root out treason from the land! And so, my friends, I cease.'

As one listens, one can see the colour and pageantry, the crowded
streets and bright garments, the painted, gabled houses and spires
and towers, the swift gravel streams sparkling in the meadows on their
way towards Holborn and the Thames, and the concourse of revelling
Londoners setting out to the green-wood, as their fathers had done
before them and as their sons, in a sadder and drabber age, were to do
no longer.

INDEX

INDEX

INDEX

Carey, Henry see Hunsdon, Lord of
Carey, John (later 3rd Baron
  Hunsdon), 100
Caribbean, 13, 16, 25, 48–50, 71–8,
  108–9, 170
Carleill, Christopher, 108
Carlos, Don, 41
Cartagena, 75, 77, 108–9
Caspian Sea, 72, 181
Cateau-Cambresis, Treaty of, 30
Cathay, 72–3
Catherine of Aragon, 1st Queen of
  Henry VIII, 15, 20
Catherine Howard, 5th Queen of
  Henry VIII, 16
Catherine de Medici, 66
Catherine Parr, 6th Queen of
  Henry VIII, 23
Catholicism and Reformation, 14, 18;
  Henry VIII repudiates Roman
  supremacy, 15–16; Mary re-imposes
  it, 20–1; Elizabeth breaks with
  Rome, 26–8; fugitive Mary a focus
  for Catholic plots, 43, 51–5, 100–3,
  110–12; Jesuits' and Catholic
  priests' crusade to win back England
  to the Faith, 101–3; priests forbidden
  and persecuted in England, 102–3,
  112–13, 113n; growing English
  hatred of Popery, 21, 50, 55, 66–7,
  68, 73, 102–3, 113; see also
  Counter-Reformation, Inquisition
Catholic League (France), 112, 131, 170
Cavendish, Thomas, 181
Cawsand, 88
Cecil, Sir Robert (later 1st Earl of
  Salisbury), 151, 174
Cecil, Thomas (later 1st Earl of Exeter),
  151
Cecil, William see Burghley, Lord
Chancellor, Richard, 72
Chandos, Grey Brydges, 5th Baron,
  194
Charles, Archduke of Austria, 29, 37
Chapel Royal, 193
Charles the Bold, Duke of Burgundy,
  13–14
Charles I, of England, 112, 212
Charles II, 102n, 212

Charles V, Emperor, 14–15, 20, 45, 49
Charles IX, of France, 66
Charmouth, 144
Chartley, 111
Chaucer, Geoffrey, 122
Cheapside, 52, 208
Chelsea, 23, 206, 214
Chesapeake colony, 180, 184, 187
Cheshire, 153
Chichester, Sir Francis, 91n
Chesil Beach, 144
Chile, 16, 83, 181
Chilterns, the, 23
China (Cathay), 72–3, 181–2
Christopher (ship), 80
Church of England: Henry VIII and,
  16; Elizabeth declines title of Head
  of, 28; Elizabeth reforms, 27, 28;
  liturgy and forms of worship,
  28–30, 189–90, 195; see also Prayer
  Book, Anglican
Cimaroons, 75–6, 79–80, 84
Clare Island, 166
Clear, Cape, 166
cloth trade, 17–18, 60, 62, 95
coalmining, 60, 61
Colchester, 158
Columbus, Christopher, 13, 16
Condé, Louis, Prince of, 36
Condell, Henry, 195
Connaught, 166, 167, 168
Conquistadores, 13, 83, 85
Constantinople, 181
Cornhill, 209
Cornwall, 62, 128, 132, 136, 137, 180
Cortes, Hernando, 83
Corunna, 129, 130, 132, 164
Counter-Reformation, 20, 27, 30, 46,
  55, 61, 62, 66, 100, 113
Court of Tumults, 47
Covent Garden, 208
Coventry, 51, 63
Coverdale, Miles, 18
Cranmer, Thomas, Archbishop of
  Canterbury, 15, 19, 21, 23, 28–9, 189
Cromwell, Sir Oliver, 186
Cromwell, Thomas, 15–16
Crooked Billet tavern, 207
Crown tavern, 209

INDEX

Essex, Robert Devereux, 2nd Earl of, 171, 174, 196–7
Essex, Walter Devereux, 1st Earl of, 78
Euphrates, R., 72
Evelyn, John (grandfather), 62
Evelyn, John (diarist), 62, 208
Exeter, 184

Faerie Queene, 69, 175
Fair Isle, 164, 166
Falcon (ship), 78
Falmouth, 80
famine among urban poor, 175
Farnese, Alexander *see* Parma, Alexander Farnese, Duke of
Fens, the, 62
Fenton, Edward, 96, 153
Ferdinand (of Aragon), King of Spain, 13
Field of the Cloth of Gold (1519), 13
Finisterre, 129
Fish Street, 209
Fitch, Ralph, 72
Fitzherbert, John, *Book of Husbandry*, 61
Fitzwilliam, Sir William, 165, 167
Flanders *see* Netherlands
Fleet Bridge, 25
Fleming, Capt. Thomas, 135
Fletcher, Francis, 214–15
Flodden, Battle of (1513), 13
Florida, 16, 72
Floris Sea, 87
Flushing, 65, 106, 115, 122, 149–50, 153–4
Forth, Firth of, 32, 33, 97, 151, 157
Fotheringay Castle, 112
Foyle, Lough, 167
Foxe, John, *Book of Martyrs*, 61
France: Henry VIII's wars with, 13, 17; and Philip II, 21; threat to England, 24, 27; alliance with Scotland, 24, 30–34; peace treaty with Spain, 30; wars of religion, 35–6, 48, 62, 65, 66, 96, 104, 131, 170, 196; Elizabeth's policy towards, 68; colonization ventures, 71, 72; supports Don Antonio, 94, 96, 115; attitude to Armada, 131, 150;

Spanish and English intervention in, 170, 196. *See also* Catholic League
Francis I, of France, 13
Francis II, 31, 40
Friesland, 45, 65
Frobisher, Sir Martin: seeks 'north-west passage', 96, 181, 212; in Drake's 2nd expedition, 108; fights Armada, 126, 143, 145, 146, 152–3; in battle of Gravelines, 153; knighted, 153

Galicia, 130, 132
Galway Bay, 166
Gama, Vasco da, 16, 177
Garrick, David, 195
Gelt, battle of the (1570), 52
Geneva, 31, 32
Genoa, 16, 48, 67
Germany, 14, 17, 20, 34, 37, 61, 99, 155, 157
Gerona (galleass), 167
Ghent, 14, 104
Giant's Causeway, 167
Gibbons, Orlando, 175
Gift of God (ship), 187
Gilbert, Sir Humphrey, 78, 100, 181, 187; colonizing ventures, 176–8; death, 178
Gilbert, Ralegh, 187
Gladstone, W. E., 59
Glamorgan, 100
Glenconkein forest, 172
Globe theatre, London, 197
Gloucestershire, 62
Goa (India), 71–2
Golconda, 72
Golden Hind (Drake's ship; formerly *Pelican*): Drake's voyage in, 80, 82–4, 86–7, 90–91; decays at Deptford, 212
Golden Hind (pinnace), 135
Gonson, Benjamin, 97
Good Hope, Cape of, 16, 71, 88, 177, 181–2, 183*n*
Goodman's Field, 210
Gorges, Sir Ferdinando, 187, 188
Granada, 13

INDEX

licensed company of players, 194
Hudson, Henry, 181
Hudson Bay, 176
Huguenots, 35–6, 62, 65, 72, 76
Hungerford market, 208
Hunsdon, Henry Carey, 1st Baron:
defeats Dacre at battle of the Gelt,
52; defends Kent against Armada,
129, 158; takes 'dark lady of the
sonnets' under his protection, 158–9,
195; patronizes stage as Lord
Chamberlain, 195; death, 174
Hussites, 14
Hyde Park, 209

Incas, 13, 83
India, 71, 72–3, 176, 182, 183
Indian Ocean, 87, 182–3
Indonesia *see* East Indies
inflation, 17, 19, 56, 59
Inquisition, Holy: suppression of
heresy, 14, 79; in Netherlands, 47,
55; against English seamen, 50, 73,
80, 84, 90, 167, 209
Ipswich, 15
Ireland: state of, 171, 203; English
plantations, 78; Spain supports
risings in, 89, 169, 172; Armada and,
131, 165–8; Ulster revolt, 171, 174
Isabella (of Castile), Queen of Spain, 13
Italy, 15, 20, 34, 47, 60, 88, 99, 120,
125, 133, 166, 177
Ivan the Terrible, Tsar of Russia, 72

James I of England and VI of Scotland:
succeeds to Scottish throne, 42;
Elizabeth supports, 52, 54; and
pensions, 110–11, 113; on mother's
execution, 114n; on Armada, 157;
succeeds to English throne, 169;
Authorises Version of Bible, 175;
189, 191; hatred of Ralegh, 184;
ends war with Spain, 184; on
Virginia colony, 185; on Parliament,
211; patronises Shakespeare, 198, 212
James IV, of Scotland, 13
James V, 30
James, Isaac, 175
Jamestown, 184

Jane Seymour, 3rd Queen of
Henry VIII, 18
Japan, 183
Java, 87, 182–3
Jenkinson, Anthony, 72
Jesus, Society of (Jesuits): founded, 30;
in Ireland, 89; missionaries in
England, 101–2, 112; banned, 103
John (of Austria), Don, 78, 95
John of Gaunt, Duke of Lancaster, 114,
120
Johnson, Samuel, 59, 198
Judith (ship), 50, 73
Julius Caesar, 200
Justices of the Peace, 59

Kasbin, 72
Kemp, William, 195
Kenilworth, 38, 63
Kennebec River, 187
Kent, 62, 128, 129, 148, 158
Kerry, 166
King's Company of Players, 195
King's Head tavern, 209
Kinsale, 172
Knole, 175
Knollys, Sir Francis, 64, 174
Knox, John, 31–2
Kremlin, the, 72

Labourers, Statute of, 59
Labrador, 16
Lambeth, 213, 214
Lane, Ralph, 179
Langside, 42
Lanier, Emilia ('the dark lady of the
sonnets'), 159, 175, 195
La Rochelle, 36, 65, 131
Latimer, Hugh, Bishop of Worcester,
21
Laud, Archbishop, 188
Laughton, J. K., cited, 163n
Leadenhall, 208
League, the Catholic (France), 66, 104,
170
Leicester, Lettice, Countess of, 110
Leicester, Robert, Earl of: relations
with Elizabeth, 38–9, 65, 69; and
Mary Queen of Scots, 41, 65;

224

INDEX

Pacific voyage, 78, 80, 88, 90–91, 95; resorts to assassination, 101, 104; seizes Portuguese throne, 89, 114; 'Enterprise of England', 101, 111, 114, 124; seizes English shipping, 105, 108; faced by Elizabeth's intervention in Netherlands, 106; claims to English throne, 113–14, 124; plans Armada, 110, 115–17, 124–6, 128, 129–30, 139, 141, 144; directs Armada's strategy and movements, 133, 142, 147, 149–50; resigned to defeat, 168–9; intervenes in French religious wars, 170; death, 169

Philip III, of Spain, 169

Philippa of Lancaster, Queen of Portugal, 114

Philippines, 86–7

Pilgrimage of Grace, 16, 51

Pilgrims, the, 188

Pinkie, battle of (1542), 30

Pius V, pope, 102

Pizarro, Francisco, 83

plague, bubonic, 36, 81, 175, 195, 203, 206

Plate Fleet, 49, 73, 75, 77, 109, 170

Plymouth, 48, 49, 71, 73, 77, 80, 84, 88, 96, 97, 108, 117, 118, 120, 126, 127, 128, 130, 131, 132, 133, 135–42, 148, 159, 179, 180, 184, 187, 188

Poor Laws (and relief), 58–9

Pope, Thomas, 195

Popham, Sir John (Lord Chief Justice), 187

Portland, battle, of, 144–6

Portsmouth, 53, 147

Portugal: empire and trading monopoly, 16, 25, 48–9, 71–2, 89–90, 176, 182; and spice islands, 87, 89, 94, 182–3; and succession to Aviz dynasty, 89; annexed by Spain, 89–90, 94; coast blockaded by Drake, 120; reinforcement of Spanish Fleet, 105, 125, 127–8, 164

Prayer Book, Anglican, 19–20, 27, 28–30, 189–91

Preedy, Francis, 86–7

Protestantism: spread of, 14–15, 27, 31;

Bible translations, 18, 19; martyred under Mary, 21; Elizabeth and, 28; in Scotland, 31–3; in Netherlands, 46–8, 104; refugees in England, 62; *see also* Huguenots; Luther, Martin; Reformation

Purbeck, 146

Puritanism and Puritans, 27–8; and persecution abroad, 67; anti-Catholicism, 113; in N. America, 188; reject Anglican Prayer Book, 189; and stage, 193; on rustic pleasures, 210

Queenhithe, 208

Rainbow (ship), 153

Ralegh, Sir Walter: courts Elizabeth, 69; defends West Country against Armada, 128, 180; quoted on Armada invasion, 135; joins Fleet against Armada, 151; attempts colonization of Virginia, 163, 176, 178–80, 183; poems, 175; fall from favour, 181; Guiana expeditions, 183–4; imprisonment and execution, 184; literary achievement, 184, 191

Rape of Lucrece, 175, 193

Rastell, John, 177

Rata Encoranda, La (ship), 166

Rathlin, 166

Recalde, Don Juan Martinez de, 139–40, 142, 168

Recusants, 102

Reformation, 18, 27, 61, 97, 193

Requesens, Don Luis, 77

Revenge (ship), 98–9; in action against Armada, 143, 152; last fight, 180

Rhine, R., 59

Rhone, R., 59

Riccio, David, 41

Richard III, of England, 12

Richmond, 63, 177

Ridley, Nicholas, Bishop of London, 17, 20–21

Ridolfi, Roberto, 53–4, 65

Roanoke Island, 179–80

Robsart, Amy (wife of Robert Dudley), 38

INDEX

Rome, 102

Rowse, A. L., debt to, 9; on church liturgy, 29; on state of peace, 94n; on sea-power, 169n; on Elizabeth in later years, 173, 176n; cited, 35n, 39n, 56n, 72n, 86n, 106n, 108n, 118n, 127n, 159n, 172n, 174n, 180n, 182n, 183n, 185n

Royal Exchange, 57, 61, 209

Russia, 72

Rycote, 174n

Sagadahoc, 187

Sagres, 120

St Bartholomew's Day massacre (1572), 66, 68, 76, 112, 209

St Giles's Fields, 111–12

St Helena, 181–2

St Julian Bay, 81

St Lawrence Estuary, 72

St Mary Port, 157

St Nicholas Island, 88

St Paul's Cathedral (London), 205

St Quentin, battle of, 35, 47

St Stephen's Chapel, 212

Samarkand, 176

Sandridge, 181

San Juan (ship), 139, 168

San Juan de Ulloa, 48–50, 73, 76, 88

San Martin (flagship), 128, 140, 145–6, 152, 153, 154, 165, 168

San Salvador (ship), 140–41, 143

Santa Ana (ship), 147

Santa Cruz, Don Alvaro de Bazan, Marquis of: defeats French in Azores, 96, 115; Armada plans, 115–16, 124, 125–6; Drake's counter-Armada and blockade, 109, 120; death, 124

Santander, 168

Santiago, 108

Scheldt, R., 149, 154

Scillies, 129, 131, 132, 133

Scotland: Henry VIII's war with, 13, 17; alliance with France, 24, 30–34; religious dissension in, 31–3, 42; Elizabeth intervenes in, 32–4, 97, 105; Sussex enforces peace in, 52; Armada encircles, 156–7, 161,

164–5; see also Mary, Queen of Scots

Scott, Sir Walter, 197

'sea-beggars' see United Provinces

Selsey Bill, 147

Settlement, Act of, 18

Seville, Bank of, 109

Seymour, Edward see Somerset, Edward Seymour, Duke of

Seymour, Jane see Jane Seymour, Queen

Seymour, Lord Henry, 128, 131, 147, 151–3, 156, 165

Seymour, Lord Thomas, 19

Shakespeare, William: quoted on militia, 35, 35n; sees Elizabeth, 63; paraphrases Drake, 82; quoted on invasion, 115; and 'dark lady of the sonnets', 159, 175, 195; dedicates poems to Southampton, 175; literary and dramatic achievement, 189, 191–202, 204; life, 191–3, 195; first folio, 195; plays, 196–202; on Queen Elizabeth, 45, 201–2; retirement, 218; death, 201

Shannon, R., 165

Sheffield Castle, 1

Shetlands, 161, 165

Shoreditch, 194, 204

Shrewsbury, Elizabeth Talbot, Countess of ('Bess of Hardwick'), 175

Shrewsbury, George Talbot, 6th Earl of, 103

Siam, 72, 183

Sidney, Sir Philip, 121–2, 191

Sierra Leone, 88

Sixtus V, Pope, 121

Slave Trade, 49

Sligo Bay, 166

Slugs, 128, 130

Smith, Capt. John, 185, 187

Smith, Miles, Bishop of Gloucester, 191

Smithfield, 208; fires, 21, 27

Smythe, 'Customer', 183, 183n

Smythe, Sir Thomas, 183–5

Solent, 146

Solway Firth, 52

INDEX

Somerset, Edward Seymour, Duke of (Lord Protector), 18–19, 23, 38, 58
Soundings, the, 131
Southampton, Henry Wriothesley, 3rd Earl of: as Shakespeare's patron, 175, 192–3, 195–6; supports London Virginia Company, 186; and Essex, 196–7; imprisoned in Tower, 197; mother's marriage to Heneage, 198
Southwark, 210
Spain: power, 13, 24–5, 30, 89–90; empire and monopoly, 25, 48–9, 71, 93; as threat to Elizabeth, 27; peace treaty with France, 30; army, 34, 35, 100, 159; strained relations with England, 45, 50, and Netherlands, 45–6, 65–8, 72, 77, 95, 100; Catholicism, 46; ships harassed, 50, 72–3; plots intervention in England, 51–3; Elizabeth's diplomatic policy towards, 68, 77; treasure seized, 76–7, 88, 108; Drake and, 93; sends troops to Ireland, 89, 169, 172; annexes Portugal, 89–90, 94; naval power, 90, 94, 96, 169; plans Armada, 96, 115; war with, 107, 169–70; trading monopoly challenged, 107, 176, 178; credit reduced, 109; truce with United Provinces, 169–70; later armadas, 169; wealth, 172; cruelty to English prisoners, 176n, 209; intervenes in French religious wars, 196; end of war with, 184; see also Armada; Inquisition; Philip II
Spanish Main, 73, 74, 75, 77, 108
Spenser, Edmund, 69, 191, 203
Staffordshire, 51, 62, 111
Staines, 213
Star Chamber, Court of, 12
Stocks Market, 208
Stow, John, 205, 210–11
Strachey, Lytton, 201n
Strachey, William, 201
Strand, the, 208, 211–12
Strange, Lord see Derby, Ferdinando Stanley, 5th Earl of
Stratford-upon-Avon, 36, 63, 192, 195
Supremacy, Act of, 28; Oath of, 29

Surrey, Thomas Howard, Earl of and 2nd Duke of Norfolk, 13, 62
Susan Constant (ship), 184
Sussex, 62, 112, 148
Sussex, Henry Radcliffe, 4th Earl of, 194
Sussex, Thomas Radcliffe, 3rd Earl of, 52, 147
Swan (ship), 80
Sweden, 37
Swilly, Lough, 166, 167
Swiss mercenaries, 99
Syria, 72, 181
Tagus, R., 116, 118, 120, 123, 128, 130, 140
Tallis, Thomas, 175
Tarleton, Richard, 194
Tempest, The, 200–1
Temple Bar, 212
Terceira (Azores), 94, 96, 124, 141, 142
Ternate, Sultan of, 87, 90, 94, 96, 107
Terra Australis, 79, 83, 86
Teynham, 20th Baron, 183n
Thames Estuary, 45, 73, 117, 156, 210–11, 213–14
theatre, 175, 193–5; licensed companies, 194–5; and London life, 204–5; see also Shakespeare
Thirty-nine Articles, 28
Throgmorton, Francis, 101–3, 111, 112
Throgmorton, Sir Nicholas, 97, 101
Tiger (ship), 178
Tilbury, 158, 159, 160, 164, 174
Tobermory, 166
Tomkins, John, 175
Torbay, 142, 144, 182
Tower of London, 24, 38, 41, 54, 211
Traill, H. D., cited, 58n
Trent, Council of, 30, 46
Trimley, 181
Trinidad Valencera, La (ship), 167
Tripolis, 181
Triumph (ship), 145–6, 153
Troilus and Cressida, 198
Turks, 78, 79, 181
Tusser, Thomas, 61
Tutbury Castle, 51, 103, 111
Twelve Years' Truce (1609), 169
Tyndale, William, 18–19, 19n

INDEX

H. Gravelot delin.

Publish'd by John Pine.